Critical Pedagogy

Related Titles of Interest

For further information on these and other related titles, contact:
  College Division
  ALLYN AND BACON, INC.
  75 Arlington Street, Suite 300
  Boston, MA 02116
  www.ablongman.com

THIRD EDITION

Critical Pedagogy

Notes from the Real World

Joan Wink

California State University, Stanislaus

Boston ▪ New York ▪ San Francisco
Mexico City ▪ Montreal ▪ Toronto ▪ London ▪ Madrid ▪ Munich ▪ Paris
Hong Kong ▪ Singapore ▪ Tokyo ▪ Cape Town ▪ Sydney

Executive Editor and Publisher: *Stephen D. Dragin*
Senior Editorial Assistant: *Barbara Strickland*
Marketing Manager: *Tara Whorf*
Manufacturing Buyer: *Andrew Turso*
Composition and Prepress Buyer: *Linda Cox*
Cover Administrator: *Joel Gendron*
Editorial-Production Service: *Omegatype Typography, Inc.*
Electronic Composition: *Omegatype Typography, Inc.*

For related titles and support materials, visit our online catalog at www.ablongman.com.

Between the time Website information is gathered and then published, it is not unusual for some sites to have closed. Also, the transcription of URLs can result in typographical errors. The publisher would appreciate notification where these errors occur so that they may be corrected in subsequent editions.

Library of Congress Cataloging-in-Publication Data

Wink, Joan.
    Critical pedagogy : notes from the real world / Joan Wink.—3rd ed.
        p.   cm.
    Includes bibliographical references and index.
    ISBN 0-205-41818-X (alk. paper)
    1. Critical pedagogy—United States.   I. Title.

    LC196.5.U6W54   2005
    370.11′5—dc22

                                                                    2004057266

Printed in the United States of America
10 9 8 7 6 5 4 3 2   09 08 07 06 05

4 'Lil Ranchers: Austin, Wynn, Luke, and Wyatt

CONTENTS

PREFACE

I started teaching in 1966. After my first year of teaching, I assumed that I would never teach again: False Assumption #1. I have been teaching and learning since then, and this book tells what I have learned as I taught. Life and critical pedagogy often challenge our long-held assumptions.

The Purpose

My purpose is to think new thoughts that are applicable to critical teaching and learning for the twenty-first century. I do not teach the way I taught in 1966; I do not learn the way I learned in 1966; I do not believe the way I believed in 1966; I do not know in the way I knew in 1966. My ways of knowing come from my experiences with living, learning, and teaching since that time.

If I were to describe my ways of knowing, I suspect I would say they are holistic (I want to see the whole puzzle first), gender-based (being a wife, a mom, and a grammie has taught me more than I can yet understand), linguistic (I love languages), and pluralistic (the "other" anything fascinates me). There you have it—the mystery is gone. The professional and personal are so interwoven in my experiences that I no longer try to pretend they are separate. I did not think that way either in 1966.

In this book, we will see teaching and learning through the lens of critical pedagogy. When I began teaching, I saw schools through the lens of behaviorism. I no longer see that way. When you are finished with this book, I do not expect you to think, to know, and to see the way I do. I would hope that you have reflected critically on your own theory and practice and understand your own perspective better.

I do not want every page of this book to be affirming to all. I do want to prod and to poke a tad; I want you to think and to rethink and to unthink. I want you to relate your new thoughts to the context of your life and your experiences.

Organization

The organization of this third edition follows the same pattern as the first edition—Critical pedagogy: How in the world did I get into this? What in the world is it? Where in the world did it come from? How in the world do you do it? And why in the world does it matter?

What Has Changed Since the Previous Edition?

The world has changed. Pedagogy has changed. Language has changed. The world is more frightening, and the response has been controlled pedagogy and controlled language, all of which leads to controlled thought. In this edition, I will write critically and honestly of my perspective on some of the changes. Specifically, new passages have been added throughout the text on high-stakes testing, teacher accountability, mandatory curriculum, and bilingual education.

Ideology now trumps thought in many pockets of pedagogy. My goal is to pick these pockets apart. In spite of my deep concern for the path we are now walking, I will close this edition with another challenge from Freire as he called us to a "pedagogy of hope."

The first edition of this book triggered the following two questions more than any others: What is it? How do you do it? I am hoping that this third edition will more thoroughly address these two questions.

The Preface is shorter than that in the previous two editions. The previous Introduction is gone. The previous editions had five chapters; this edition has eight. Each chapter concludes with a new section, "Practicing Pedagogy Patiently," with suggestions for turning theory to practice. In addition, this edition will contain definitions: mine, others', and yours. Each time critical pedagogy is defined, it will be set off in bold type.

Chapter 1 tells of my real world. The Jonathan story of literacy used in the first two editions has been replaced with a new story that challenges assumptions—or at least it challenged mine.

Chapter 2 tells the story of students and teachers who taught me that much of critical pedagogy is discovered in that enlightened and often uncomfortable space of relearning and unlearning. This chapter includes stories of some of my own recent relearning and unlearning.

Chapter 3 deconstructs the language of critical pedagogy by demonstrating the language in real classroom experiences. My goal is to respond to a consistent request by readers: Show me what it means.

Chapter 4 is new. The goal is to respond to a consistent request by readers: Tell me what it means.

Chapter 5 traces the roots of critical pedagogy through Latin America, Europe, and North America. A new section is a transcription of Freire's own words in a presentation on teaching and learning.

Chapter 6 focuses on classroom activities. It begins with those activities, which are new to this edition. In the latter half of this chapter, I revisit some of the methods that were included previously; however, they have been greatly condensed.

Chapter 7 is new and focuses on critically engaging families in critical pedagogy.

Chapter 8 offers a glimpse of some of my own emerging answers and offers the readers the opportunity to discover critical pedagogy in the context of their own lives. This edition concludes in a new manner with a visual look at the way in which one secondary teacher turned critical pedagogy into action through her art.

A Word about Pronouns

Most of my life I always read *he* or *him* when an indefinite pronoun was used. Of course, I knew it meant me. Then I entered a time when I read *he* and *him,* and I delicately suggested that it didn't seem to include me. Of course it includes me, I was told. Another phase of my reading began, and I read *he* or *she* and *him* or *her*. Of course, it meant you and me, but it was so awkward. Now I am entering another pronoun phase of my life. My options are (a) *he* and *him*, or (b) *he* or *she* and *him* or *her*, or (c) alternating chapters using *he* and *him* and chapters using *she* and *her*. That, too, feels uncomfortable. Therefore, I have decided to do what feels right. The indefinite pronouns I have chosen for this edition are *she* and *her*. For me, it is a game of catch-up. Maybe in my life, we'll find the perfect pronoun, but until that day comes, of course I mean everyone.

No one has received more input on this book than I. I am well aware of what readers love and what readers don't love. I even have a pretty good understanding of who likes (and who doesn't like) which pages. And I know which pages are never mentioned. Here is my rule of thumb for writing the revision: If the pages sang to many readers, I left them in—even if it was a new song for some readers. If the pages did not sing, I cut them out.

The first edition provided me with many surprises, which are the continuing story of my learning-relearning-unlearning. In this third edition, my plan is to share some of these surprises.

Preface Notes

Having less Lev Vygotsky in Chapter **5** does not mean that I love him less than I did a few years ago. However, a more complete picture of Vygotsky is now available in *A Vision of Vygotsky*, which I wrote with LeAnn G. Putney, available at www.ablongman.com.

Acknowledgments

It is said that writing is a solitary process, and often it is. However, much of writing a book is collaborative and social. I very much appreciate all of you, who share so much with me, and I hope some of these pages reflect you. I can never repay your generous spirit; I can only pass it on to others. Thank you.

To the many educators, who live complex and demanding lives but still take time to enrich mine.

To the faculty, staff, and administrators of CSU, Stanislaus.

To my colleagues at the local county offices of education.

To my colleagues on the lively listservs.

To the Prairie People, particularly Mary-Kay.

You all bring new meaning to generosity.

The creation of a book is a fascinating process with a large team working together. At the helm is my refreshingly low-maintenance editor, Steve Dragin, in a seemingly high-maintenance world. Steve keeps us all moving forward at a brisk and focused pace with his subtle humor and quiet confidence that we will actually get a book into your hands to read. If you are reading this paragraph, you are indebted to Steve, but not as much as I am. Thank you, Steve: you are a terrific editor for me. I also appreciate all of the support that I received from Barbara Strickland, Tara Whorf, Robb Bates, Donna Simons, Mary Young, and Dawn McIlvain. In addition, the Allyn and Bacon reviewers responded quickly and critically. I appreciate the questions you raised, so that I could address them. Thank you to Lois McFadyen Christensen, University of Alabama at Birmingham; C. Lynne Hannah, Shepherd College; and Evangelina B. Jones, San Diego State University.

Denise, your research and technical expertise created this book, also. However, it is your humor and quiet support that I appreciate as much.

To my husband, Dean, and ever-growing family: You are the best!

It takes a ranch.

Critical Pedagogy

1 Welcome to My Real World

Kids, cows, and computers are central to my life. Family, friends, and fun fill my days. Pedagogy and passion sustain me as I continue to focus on power and problems in schools and society. Critical pedagogy has taught me that power and problems have one thing in common: There will always be enough for all of us. Think of it this way: Power and problems are not finite; they are not fixed; and they certainly are not like a piece of pie—If I give some away, there will be no less for me. Power is the process of collaborating with others as we seek varied solutions to complex problems, which are ever changing.

Critical pedagogy continues to teach me that critical pedagogy is also complex and evolving. It is not finite; it is not fixed; it is not easily defined and understood in a neat little package. However, initially, I think it is helpful to understand that *critical* does not only mean *criticize*. Critical also means to see deeply what is below the surface—think, critique, or analyze. *Pedagogy* does not only mean how a teacher teaches. It is about the visible and hidden human interactions between a teacher and a learner, whether they are in a classroom or in the larger community. Critical pedagogy looks for the *why* that leads to action.

*Pedagogy is to good interactive teaching and learning
in the classroom as critical pedagogy is to good interactive
teaching and learning in the classroom and in the real world.*[1]

The publication of the second edition of this book enriched my life with new ideas, friends, and surprises. One surprise continues to be a group of questions that I am asked: What is it like to write a book? Where do you write? When do you write? What do you do? This group of questions makes me realize that there are many people who want to write. I have chosen to begin this third edition with a peek into the context of the changes in my real world as it relates to writing and thinking. As I answer some of your questions, we will generate new ones as we seek multiple answers to complex problems. It is my wish that this interaction between us will encourage you to write. As we write, we think. As we think, we solve problems and find new answers. Critical pedagogy calls us to this action.

The first edition of this book was written in the midst of my real life as a professor at a state university. I was teaching full time, and most pages were written between 3:00 A.M. and 6:00 A.M. and on weekends. I longingly watched as other professors went away and wrote in peace during their sabbaticals. The second edition was written in the midst of my other real life on the prairies during a sabbatical. The anticipated peace of the prairies seemed elusive, as the compelling reality of ranch life often took priority over a paragraph. Lives are filled with change and contradictions, yet we are often surprised when we bump into this predictable life process. Schools, too, continue on a path of change and contradiction.

Now comes the third edition, and I am writing at the university and at the ranch as I juggle my two oh-so-real worlds. The fact that I am even writing a third edition takes me by surprise. The opportunity came at a moment when I was sure I could not find time for one more project. Classes and an ever-growing family made this seem impossible. My real world, if anything, is more real. How do I write? In the nooks and crannies of life and always somewhere precariously balanced between grit and grace.

Life is often filled with contradictions, ironies, and unforeseen joys. My life in schools has been much the same.[2] When I started teaching, I imagined that it would be predictable, controllable, and safe. I thought, "I will teach, and they will learn." As Edelsky (1991) writes, I was sure that I would be cool and detached; I was confident that every moment would be rational. My experiences in schools have taught me something different. Human relationships are at the heart of schooling (Cummins, 1996, p. 1). Indeed, it has been the passion and the personal interactions that have put the power in pedagogy for me. Although many of my experiences in schools and in life are not as I thought they would be, it is only the study of critical pedagogy that made me realize that the potential of pedagogy is all about people. I thought my life in schools would be about me, teaching. I now think that Paulo Freire was right: Education is radically about love (personal communication, N. Millich, November 3, 1998).[3]

I marvel at the outside influences on my life. I also marvel at the outside influences on teaching and learning. Critical pedagogy enables us to see those influences more clearly and to articulate them. Critical pedagogy also enables us to take action in our real world when necessary.

Even though my real world has changed little since the publication of the last two editions, the world has changed drastically. As I continue to marvel at the influences on my life, I now shudder at the outside influences on schools. My years of public school experiences do not prepare me for the reality of classrooms for teachers and students today. Never have diversity and democracy been more threatened by outside influences, which tend to come from those who have far less experience in schools than I. In this edition, I address those influences, specifically controlled curriculum, high-stakes testing, bilingual education, accountability, and the frightening links between corporate powers and the powers of the government.

Pearson (2003) expresses my feelings when he longs for the opportunity to write of his passions and not politics. It is a luxury those of us with experience and knowledge of teaching and learning cannot afford. If only I could write of languages, literacies, and cultures. If I have learned one thing in my years in schools it is that language and thought are the same thing. He who controls our language controls our thought. Language is now controlled via mandated curriculum. Pearson (2003) warns that if this continues, we will have a generation of teachers who revere controlled curriculum. I would add that controlled curriculum is controlled language is controlled thought.

> Followed to its logical conclusions, the politics we are currently implementing will lead us to a generation of teachers who pay homage to externally imposed standards rather than to the needs of children and their families as the primary criterion for determining what students do in their classrooms. To establish their curriculum, they will look over their shoulder rather than look their students squarely in the eye. (Pearson, 2003, pp. 14–15)

When language is controlled in schools, thought is controlled in the future. This is damaging to a democracy. Our work is now; we cannot fail. We are called by Paulo Freire **to name, to reflect critically, to act**—there it is: the best definition of critical pedagogy.

Now here is the point: Each of us has our own real world. It informs us; it enlightens us; it amuses us; it challenges us. And each of our worlds is a part of who we are. Each of our worlds contributes to and enriches us and others. Our own unique real world is the culture we know best; it is where we feel most at home; we speak the language; we know the perspective. No one's real world is the best; it is just what we know. No one's culture is the best; it is just what we know. No one's language is the best; it is just what we know. Critical pedagogy has enabled me to appreciate and celebrate others' ways of knowing even when I don't understand and might not have experienced them.

You might think that authors live and write in a world you will never know. Authors are people writing in their own worlds. All of our real worlds are unique, busy, and often exhausting.

It is the legacy of my real world that informs my perspective. As I reflect on my life on the prairies and my other life in schools and at the university, I draw these conclusions:

> Prairies: The greater the diversity, the healthier the environment.
>
> Perspectives: The greater the diversity, the broader the thought.
>
> People: The greater diversity, the better the democracy.

It is the legacy of critical pedagogy that gives me the courage to express my perspective. I am confident that critical pedagogy will encourage you to read and write your world.

Not only was I surprised that so many readers wrote to ask me questions about reading and writing in my world, but I was also surprised at the diverse reactions along gender lines. The irony is that one of my greatest fears with the publication of the first edition was that my feminist colleagues would feel that I had not been strong enough on our shared interests. Instead, the exact opposite has happened. My formal educational experiences have been in the world of languages, literacies, and cultures; however, I am limited in feminist pedagogical academic study. A reader of the first edition once wrote to me to say, "It feels like you are reading us while we are reading you." However, when it came to gender issues, many readers were reading me critically. I was writing the word, and the readers were reading the world.[4] Often, in the first two editions, I thought I was writing about dominant and nondominant cultural groups, and readers were reading men and women.

Some of What Was Not Said in Previous Editions

In what follows are two examples of what was not said in the first edition but apparently came out between the lines.

First, many years ago, when I was about thirty years old and lived in an evil state far, far away, I completed my units for a master's degree, wrote my thesis, and went to turn it in to my lead professor, who told me that I would receive his signature on my completed degree plan if I would sleep with him. I walked out the door and never looked back. I, like many graduate students and teachers, had a very demanding and complex life. Mine included a three-year-old, a six-year-old, a husband changing jobs, and a U-Haul truck sitting out in front of the house. I never mentioned my professor's proposition again—not to my family, not to anyone. This time period still remains blank on my resume. For years I worried that others would find out about my failure. My adult children will learn about it when they read this.

I Dropped Out

Mostly, I recall the shame I felt. It is now clear to me what was taken from me that day: Time, money, a master's degree, courage, and self-confidence are a few of the things that come to mind. Critical pedagogy has also enabled me to understand more fully what role I was playing in that process. I never should have walked away. I should have taken action to make sure that it was he who walked away from that university and carried the shame, not me. Critical pedagogy calls us to action.

Here is what happened the next few years: I stayed away from universities for fear that I would be found out. Eventually, I did a second M.A. in another state; I remember worrying that this university would wonder about those empty years on my resume. When I successfully completed that M.A., I was sure that it was just luck. So I did yet another M.A.—apparently to assure myself that I could. So let me count—I now have three M.A.'s: two for which I received diplomas and one that was left in that evil state far, far away. I was forty-five years old when I started my Ph.D. and began exploring critical pedagogy. The language was new to me—but not the ideas. In 1991, I was finally ready to take up my first tenure-track assistant professor position.

Coincidentally and simultaneously, the fall of 1991 was the time of the Anita Hill–Clarence Thomas hearings. I, like many, sat on the couch and watched. I was spellbound. After a few days of this, I said to my husband, "No one ever made a pass at me in the professional world. Listen to all of these stories. You would think this was rampant in the workplace." I stayed on the couch, turned back to the television, and suddenly burst into tears. It all came back. I might have conveniently arranged to forget it, but apparently I was still carrying it. The memories consumed me and shocked me. Shocked my husband, too.

Wolf (1993) wrote about the Anita Hill–Clarence Thomas hearings as a time of "genderquake" in the United States. I now recognize that the earth shook for me too.

> We may never know the truth or falsehood of what was alleged in the hearing room, but what is certain is that something critical to the sustenance of patriarchy died in the confrontation, and something new was born. The sight of a phalanx of white men . . . showing at best blank incomprehension, and at worst a cavalier, humiliating disregard for women's reality and testimony, was a revelation to the nation's women of the barrenness of democracy without female representation, as well as being an unmasking of male authority. (Wolf, 1993, p. 5)

Second, it was not long after this when I learned, over a cup of coffee with a male colleague, that my men friends with comparable professional experience were paid more than I at the university. I remember him saying, "Joan, I could never be you. I couldn't afford to support my family." For a brief second, I remember thinking that the issues of power that revolve around gender were not mine; I was more at home in the world of power as it relates to cultures and languages. The legacy of critical pedagogy flashed in front of me: to name, to reflect critically, to act. This time I did not walk away, and the yellow roses planted in my front yard are my personal and, until now, private celebration of the three-year battle it took for me to convince a large educational system that social justice does matter. Nieto (1996) says that critical pedagogy is an exploder of myths. It sure exploded a few for me.

Critical pedagogy has made me look back and rethink my life in schools. Maybe it wasn't as I first thought. Critical pedagogy helped me to unlearn, to unpack, and to rewrite my experiences. Critical pedagogy is about reading and writing our real world. Critical pedagogy gives us the courage to say what we have lived.

People consistently tell me that my book is personal. Yes, I know. I am writing about what I have personally experienced in life and learning. Critical pedagogy has enabled me to name, to reflect critically, and to act. Nieto (1996) says that this three-step process need not be linear and direct. That was true for me. It took a couple of kids, four grandkids, one husband, three and a half decades, and several states. Linear or not, I hope that critical pedagogy will be as powerful in your life.

Literacy: Jonathan to Wyatt

I learned to read by way of phonics in the first grade. First, I learned the individual letters and their sounds; from letters and sounds, I moved to individual words; from words I went on to sentences, to paragraphs, to pages, to stories. I learned to read by building up the parts—from bottom to top. Reading specialists would say that I was a parts-to-whole reader. Some would say that phonics gets the credit. I slowly and carefully put the puzzle together piece by piece. In school, I read every assignment, every chapter, every set of comprehension questions at the end of chapters, every spelling list, every grammar assignment. I read everything I was told to read; I got good grades and graduated at the top of my high school class.

One problem: I hated to read. I read only the exact number of pages assigned; I never took a book home to read for pleasure. I went to college and continued the same pattern. I spent every free moment in the library, got good grades, graduated with honors in literature, yet I still hated to read.

When my children were babies, I started to read to them. The baby books said that I should, so I did. With our first child, Dawn, something started to change: I loved the big black-and-white checkered book *The Real Mother Goose*. I thought *Winnie the Pooh* had been written just for me. By the time we got to *Charlotte's Web*, I was hooked on books. I used to secretly read *The Secret Garden* even when Dawn was asleep. With our son, Bo, I broadened my literary base. I probably have read *The Three Little Pigs* several thousand times, and I still huff and puff with vigor. *Pecos Bill* was the highlight of Bo's preschool years at home. From there, he moved on to BMX magazines, and we both became authorities on racing bikes. After BMX magazines, he moved on to motorcycle books. From there, he jumped right into Stephen King and left me in the dust. It was at this point in my life that I had to find my own books to read. I was probably about thirty years old.

When did Dawn and Bo learn to read? I have no idea, but it was before kindergarten. One day, Dawn came home from kindergarten crying because the librarian wouldn't let her check out *The Secret Garden*. The librarian said that it was too hard for kindergartners and only third graders could have it. The same librarian would let the students check out only one book at a time, a rule that Dawn hated. One day, she checked out her one allotted book, shoved three more inside her T-shirt, and headed for the exit. She had detention for a week. (This meant that we all had detention for a week, as we lived in the country an hour away from school.)

Dawn and Bo learned to read opposite the way that I did. Reading specialists would say that they were whole-to-part readers. They looked at the picture of the whole puzzle first and then put the pieces together. Do they love to read? Yes. Do they read for pleasure? Yes.

When I first started to notice all of this, it seemed like a contradiction. How could my kids possibly learn to read if they didn't do the same thing I had done? Didn't I need to teach them the sounds, the letters, the words first? However, it was clear to me that they were not interested in the parts. They wanted the whole story again and again and again. Since that time, I have been very interested in the various ways in which children learn to read and read to learn. This is what triggered my interest in holistic and critical teaching and learning. It seems that many kids who were read to as little children learn to read and love to read. Homes with books and ideas and love seem to produce children who love to read—except for Jonathan, who was a twelve-year-old contradiction in my educational space.

In the first two editions of this book, I shared the story of Jonathan, who had it all: a family, love, food, fun, and books, books, books. Everyone read and was read to. Jon went to school and got even more—more books, curriculum, teachers, and fun. Still he struggled with reading; his family continued to read great books with him; they talked through all of the content of the curriculum. Jon knew lots, and he knew it all in two languages. He carried his knowledge around in his head, and he had many other talents. In addition, he was a great citizen of the schools. Still, he did not decode reading until the fifth grade. When he learned to read, it was because of a program that was the antithesis of my best judgment. From Jonathan, I had to unlearn much of what I thought to be true. He taught me that one size does not fit all when it comes to reading, teaching, and learning. Yes, kids with books learn to read, but we must still be alert to the exceptions. We must also hear the whispering of the juxtaposition. Jonathan is the whispering of the juxtaposition for me. He is the voice of the other. Jonathan teaches me to keep learning from the opposites of my beliefs.

The Whispering Continues

Just when I thought the whispering of the juxtaposition had accomplished its task, it returns to sit on my shoulder with yet another lesson to unlearn about literacy and life. This time it is even closer to home: my grandson, Wyatt, age seven as I write.

Potter Pedagogy

Like Jonathan, Wyatt has it all—family, love, food, fun, and books. Recently, he and his little brother and sister have been consumed with the Harry Potter series. When I say "consumed," I mean that their mom (whom I have loved since the day I birthed her thirty-five years ago) read the entire series aloud twice in only a few short months. As she wrote to me in a letter,

> The kids and I have entered new worlds together, delighting in what we have found. Through the books we've discovered a new vocabulary, which now has become our familial code language in love. If one of them is having a rough day and needs love or just wants to express love to me, they will come to sit on my lap, reach up to grab my nose and say, "Got your conk." Peeves the poltergeist tortures the "wee student beasties" by doing this one evening in the halls of Hogwarts. This scene tickled our fancy to no end as we read curled up on Wyatt's bed that evening. It has become a part of our family rhythms of reaching out to the other. This saying has become synonymous with "I love you."
>
> Is there magic in these books? Certainly. Are there elements of good and evil? Yes. Of course, but I'd much rather discuss the relevance of bravery as opposed to wickedness within the confines of a story, to be discussed together, than have my children see people toting machine guns on the front page of the paper daily. Through story we gain context for reality, as we talk about truths that are too large for mere facts to fully encompass.

However, in spite of these months and years of books and love, Wyatt was a very reluctant reader in the first grade. Like Jonathan, he carried an amazing amount of knowledge in his head and could express it well with a vast expanse of oral language, but he did not decode, which has primacy in first grade. All my years of saying, "Just keeping reading with the kids," again was called into question. However, as anyone who has ever experienced a child not learning to read when he is supposed to knows, it is terrifying. Where on earth did we ever get the idea that all children need to learn to read at the same age, much less in the same way?

The Path to Pokémon

Somewhere between grit and grace, I took a deep breath and told Dawn, Wyatt's mom, "Just keep reading with the kids," as she agonized over his not reading in first grade. Her response to me follows:

> Hell has officially frozen over. This is what I muttered to myself as I stood in line about to purchase my first pack of Pokémon cards for Wyatt. Pokémon intuitively appalls me. Wyatt's peers have been collecting the cards for years, but I refused to buy any for Wyatt.
>
> "Mom, you and all the girls' moms are the only ones who don't allow Pokémon," Wyatt told me earnestly one day.
>
> I remained unmoved.
>
> Then one day one of Wyatt's friends came over to play. He brought his binder full of Pokémon cards to show Wyatt. I remember thinking, "Oh, no. How quickly can I get them away from those cards and onto the trampoline?"
>
> Except that Wyatt spent the next two hours reading those cards. He and his friend sat on the living room floor going over every letter and word in detail. As I dried dishes in the next room, I became aware of Wyatt's efforts to read all of those cards. Wyatt usually shies away from any attempt at individual reading. Now he sat poring over letters and words, trying to make meaning.
>
> "He's reading!" I thought to myself.
>
> The next day I purchased Pokémon cards and a collecting card binder. Wyatt has been reading those cards daily ever since. His literacy has grown considerably.
>
> Mom, just like you had to unlearn many of your assumptions when Jonathan learned to read, I'm currently in the midst of unlearning much of what I've assumed about what constitutes appropriate routes to literacy. Paulo Friere counseled us to follow what holds meaning for the students. No one path exists; only multiple, intertwining paths to literacy and learning. I'm in the midst of taking a leap of faith and following Freire's wisdom, even when the path involves Pokémon.

Captain Underpants to the Rescue

Critical pedagogy is a challenge to our assumptions. We are often resistant. The whispering of the other can be jarring. Dawn's words to me about Wyatt's literacy development challenged many of her cherished assumptions about "high-quality" literature. On the surface, this is a story of one boy as he learns to read, but it is also a story of one mom unlearning—never a pleasant experience. Dawn's words to me continue:

> Just when I thought I could sink no lower than reading *Pokémon* to the kids, *Captain Underpants* became a part of our lives. I have read the J.R.R. Tolkien and Redwall series. We've read the Harry Potter series, umpteen Norse, Celtic, and Southwestern myths and legends. The kids love the tales of adventures, and I love the exquisite use of language of the writers, and I am proud of the rich vocabulary these books gave me. However, what they didn't seem to do was to teach Wyatt to read.
>
> "Honey," you told me over the phone a month ago, "you've got to quit reading all that hard stuff to them. Those books are too intimidating for Wyatt to pick up and try to read himself."
>
> That is when the *Captain Underpants* series by Dav Pilkey began arriving in our mailbox. I must admit, had it been anybody other than you sending these, I would have immediately donated them to someone else. Wyatt was beside himself with glee. Finally, he too owned a *Captain Underpants* book, previously spoken of in only hushed and reverent tones when I was out of earshot.
>
> We sat down to read. I picked up the book gingerly between the tips of my thumb and index finger, much as one would pick up some foul vegetable that had been left in the fridge far too long. I probably even had the same expression on my face.
>
> "I cannot believe I'm reading this," I thought. I took a deep breath and repeated silently to myself, "Let go and let Grammie."
>
> And so we began. First, I read three pages for every forced paragraph that I could get Wyatt to read. Within days, Wyatt's reluctance to attempt to read lessened dramatically, and we were now taking turns: one paragraph read by him for every two pages I read. Within two weeks, we were taking turns every other page.
>
> "He's reading!" I thought to myself, "He's reading about some weird little dude saving the world in his BVDs, but he's actually reading!"
>
> I sat on the bed every night and tried to muffle my giddiness behind nonchalance, as Wyatt sniffs out performance expectations better than any Labrador—and then promptly shuts down.
>
> "Mom," I called you "it's the darndest thing I've ever seen. He's reading!"
>
> Last night when I walked into Wyatt's room, he greeted me holding up the Hercules book his brother had checked out from the library.
>
> "Mom, tonight I'm going to read to you."

"Great, Wyatt!" and I climbed up onto his bed, and he read this book to me that he'd never seen before in his life. Of course, I help him with words when he stumbles. He is definitely a sight word reader. Phonics and phonetic rules confuse him almost as much as they do his mother.

Apparently a twisted little, underwear-wearing superhero taught my son to read. He swooped into our lives at just the right moment. This was the month Wyatt learned to read. Who would've thought being able to read "poo poo" was the key to literacy?

Now, if you'll excuse me, *Captain Underpants* is about to save the world from the attack of the talking toilets. Wyatt has promised not to keep me in suspense any longer and read it to me.

"Tra-la-la," which is what *Captain Underpants* says when he goes off on his adventure to rid the world of evil and talking toilets.

Jonathan and Wyatt teach us that there is no one perfect way to literacy. Families and teachers need to do whatever is necessary to lead kids to books. And the power of literacy will open the door to the great diversity of thought.

Contradictions and Change

Now why in the world am I beginning a book on critical pedagogy with a story about Jonathan's and Wyatt's reading? Critical pedagogy is to literacy as theory is to practice; they are inseparable partners in schools.

Reading the word and the world (Freire & Macedo, 1987) is the bottom line for critical pedagogy. Critical pedagogy begins and ends with literacy, whatever the context is. As I read the word and the world, I see that this is a more difficult sociocultural political context than it was when the second edition was written. I believe that public education is under greater threat than it was previously. Simple answers to complex questions are more appealing to more people. Critical perspectives are more criticized.

Because I am a holistic teacher and learner, Jon's and Wyatt's inability to read at the prescribed time was an affront to my beliefs. It slowly began to dawn on me that Jonathan and I were living what all those critical pedagogy books called "the other." In addition, critical pedagogy often feels like the other for many.

What is the other? It is all I haven't experienced. It is what I don't know and understand. It is the upside-down to my right-side-up. For each of us, the other is unique. My other need not be yours. However, many of us are often uncomfortable with the other. The antithesis does not affirm. The other asks us questions, and our answers don't fit. This text is filled with stories of the other and how students and teachers have reacted to it. I wanted you to see how I reacted when it happened to me.

When Jonathan's parents asked me why he wasn't reading, I tried to explain it away on the basis of my own ways of knowing. Finally, Jon's parents found pieces of the answer in the other. Dawn found the answer in the other.

In my preparation to be a teacher, no one ever told me about contradictions in education. No one ever told me about change in education. However, critical pedagogy has taught me that education is rife with complexities, contradictions, multiple realities, and change. Reading books about critical pedagogy forced me to see the contradictions and changes in education even when I didn't want to see them.

Jonathan's literacy was a contradiction in my educational space. Wyatt's literacy was a contradiction in his mom's educational space. My observations and reflections of Jon and Wyatt teach me the following:

I must continually challenge my long-held assumptions.
I must let practice inform my theory.
I must continually build theory that informs my practice.
I must find new answers for new questions.
I must grapple with multiple ways of knowing.
I must listen, learn, reflect, and act.

It is humbling to write about Paulo Freire, but from his legacy, I have learned that we all experience contradictions and change that challenge our assumptions. No one ever said that teaching and learning would be like this. You can imagine my surprise.

Probably, the most important legacy that I have received from my study of critical pedagogy is that all of us need to reflect critically on our own experiences and those of others; then we need to connect these new thoughts to our own lives in new ways. We do not come from a tradition in schools that encourages critical reflection. We, in schools, are often so busy doing that we fail to take time for thinking. Thinking about important ideas needs some nurturing in our classes. It takes time. The outcomes are not immediately visible and are difficult to quantify initially. And it looks like we're not doing anything.

Many of the contradictions and changes in education cause conflict within each of us. Critical pedagogy has helped me to understand that this is all a natural part of learning. Let's think about it: How can learning possibly be static? It is inherently grounded in change. I find that when I take time to reflect on the many contradictions and changes, I am more comfortable moving through conflicting feelings and complex understandings. I used to resist; I used to deny; I used to be very uncomfortable whenever I entered this awkward, itchy space of not knowing. Now I understand more fully that the many paradoxes of education are not as painful when we can articulate all of the change that is swirling around us. In fact, it can even be fun.

"I hate ambiguity," a grad student said to me and her classmates.

"No," I responded, "we must welcome ambiguity; we must relish ambiguity; we must frolic and play in ambiguity because then we know we are moving along the learning curve." Since that time, the class and I have had a lot of fun laughing about how much we love and hate this space of ambiguity. The class now recognizes every time we enter its slippery surface.

For me, these contradictions have become the whispering of the juxtaposition. In my educational space, when I bump into a contradiction, I try to imagine the juxtaposition that sits quietly on my shoulder and whispers in my ear to listen and to learn.

The shimmering differences are what we feel as we continue to walk down our unique learning path; they cause the dissonance we feel when we are at the crossroads of contradiction. In this enlightened—and often uncomfortable—educational space, relearning and unlearning begin.

Looking Ahead for Elusive Answers

I, like you, am constantly searching for those very elusive answers. Of course, what I usually discover is just new questions. My intention is to share some of the milestones along my path as I have searched for answers. I don't believe that my answers need to be your answers, but I am confident that if I share my searching, something that I say may trigger another thought for you in the context of your life and your learning. Throughout the text, readers are invited to read and write their search for answers with me. The answers we have today are often fleeting because the social, cultural, political, and historical context of our lives will change, and tomorrow will be different.

What questions are the most important to you in the context of your life and learning right now?

```
```

What are some of your elusive answers?

```
```

Practicing Pedagogy Patiently:
Home Run Reading

Wyatt hit a home run with his reading when *Pokémon* and *Captain Underpants* began to arrive in his mailbox. His mother, my daughter, hit her home run with her reading when she discovered *The Secret Garden*. Wyatt's uncle, my son, hit his home run when he found BMX magazines. In spite of the various ideological battles swirling around literacy, here is one thing we can agree on: Reading is good, and free voluntary reading is even better.

Von Sprecken, Kim, and Krashen (2000), Trelease (2001), Fadiman (1947), and Elley (1992), found that, contrary to public opinion, the majority (84 percent) of children do like to read. Most (75 percent) had a home run book experience that hooked them on books. This is great news, because reading is its own reward. Reluctant readers are simply waiting to find their own home run book.

As we practice pedagogy patiently, we are called to get books and kids together. Play ball.

NOTES

1. For this comment, I am indebted to two Arizona graduate students and teachers, Marta and Consuelo, who shared it during an activity we did in a class. On the chalkboard, I had written: Pedagogy is to _____ , as critical pedagogy is to _____ . The class and I both thought their idea captured much about critical pedagogy.

2. I am indebted to the first edition of *Life in Schools: An Introduction to Critical Pedagogy in the Foundations of Education* (1989) by Peter McLaren for opening the door to critical pedagogy for me. It is often said that when one is ready to learn, a teacher will emerge. This book was my teacher. It affirmed what middle and high school students in Arizona had previously taught me. Though McLaren was writing about students in Canada, every time I pick up that book, I still see the faces of students from the desert Southwest. My hope is that you are envisioning students who have taught you.

3. Nico Millich, a friend and colleague, and I were brought together by our mutual interest in Paulo Freire and critical pedagogy. He has shared various stories with me of his time in El Salvador with Freire, where Millich was when he first heard Freire make this comment. Millich continues to follow his interests via liberation theology.

4. This is a reference to my favorite book by Paulo Freire and Donaldo Macedo: *Literacy: Reading the Word and the World* (1987). I have met many people who say that *Pedagogy of the Oppressed* (1974) by Freire is their favorite. I also encourage you to read the update of *Pedagogy of the Oppressed,* which is entitled, *Pedagogy of Hope: Reliving Pedagogy of the Oppressed* (1994).

CHAPTER

2

How in the World Did I Get into This?

Critical pedagogy has pushed me to reflect on my past and my future. What I have learned from these musings has caused me to see and to know in new ways. The contradictions and the changes have made me stop and rethink what I used to know about teaching and learning.

The Benson Kids: Teaching Is Learning

The truth is that much of what I know about teaching and learning, I learned when I was teaching Spanish and English to junior and senior high school students in Benson, Arizona, a rural community in the desert Southwest. Initially, I thought, "I will teach, and they will learn." Gradually and painfully, I began to recognize that my assumptions were wrong. In fact, much of the teaching methodology that I had learned previously just didn't seem to work.

Within the first twenty-four hours, the students started teaching, and I started learning. I learned all twenty-eight eighth graders' names and faces only to discover that they had—yes—told me the wrong names. I had other classes, but this group was my homeroom class, and I would be spending the majority of my day with them. My new colleagues were quick to warn me about all the "problems" that I had received. The students had many labels, which I have since learned to hate: *at risk, troublemaker, problem child, minority, limited English proficient*, and so on. Many of the families lived in areas that we would today call low-socioeconomic communities. It seemed to me that they were just families that were working as hard as they could, doing the best they could, and trying to enjoy their life a little.

I was hired to teach language arts. When they asked me whether I could teach language arts, I thought, "Sure, what could be so difficult? I know about languages and literature, so I certainly must know about language arts." When I walked into the classroom the first day, I soon learned what could be so difficult. There, lined up on a shelf that ran the length of one wall, were all the texts: twenty-eight light-blue spelling books, twenty-eight royal blue basal readers, twenty-eight tan penmanship books, twenty-eight large burgundy grammar books (at last, something I recognized—in fact, I had used that book when I was their age), and twenty-eight yellow language arts workbooks. Let's see: $5 \times 28 = 140$ texts for my eighth graders,

14

and I would have other books for my sixth and seventh graders. I knew that I would never be able to keep track of all these books, so my first decision was one of the best I ever made: Toss the texts. At that time, I did it out of desperation, but doing so taught me more than several teacher education courses had ever done. The truth is that we didn't really toss the texts; we just left them in nice visible stacks on the shelf in case anyone ever wanted to use them (or see us using them).

On the second day, one of the boys who was considered by his peers to be among the biggest and baddest asked a really good question: "If we aren't going to use them books, what are we going to do until June?" Danny, spokesperson of the eighth graders, asked with a hint of challenge in his voice.

"Let's just read and write," I responded.

"Read and write?" they said in unison. "What?"

"Whatever we want," my mouth answered. I can assure you that no one in the room was more surprised than I by my response. But you must remember that I was just trying to get through the day.

"Anything?" they pushed.

"Anything," I innocently answered.

That day after school, I drove to Tucson to explore the used book stores. There, on the floor in the back of one store by the gardening books, I found a little worn paperback entitled *Hooked on Books,* by D. N. Fader and E. B. McNeil, which was published in 1966. I had never heard of Fader, or McNeil, or this book, but it seemed right for the moment. I took the book home and read it from cover to cover.

Fader and McNeil had some unusual ideas for the time. They said that students should read and then write about their reading in journals. They said that teachers should not correct errors but that I should respond meaningfully to what the students wrote. Not correct grammar and spelling errors? Heresy! Fader and McNeil also said that students could write anything they wanted, and I was to assign only a specific number of pages, which would increase with each passing week. Quantity over quality, I thought. But, remember, I was desperate. I had twenty-eight students to face the next day, and they were probably expecting me to have some answers.

On the third day with my students, I told them what I had found, and we discussed their ideas. They agreed to go along with me. During this discussion, I also mentioned to the class that I had just read a journal article that said it really didn't matter if I corrected all their errors. The article said that they wouldn't learn from my corrections. I vividly recall Albert, who already had a reputation for his behavior, mumbling for me to hear, "I could have told you that." These were disturbing ideas for me because all I could think about was the enormous amount of time I had wasted correcting students' papers with the mighty red pen.

In those days, we had no idea what a journal was, so we just used the school-supplied lined paper, which we placed inside school-supplied construction paper. The first week, I assigned five full pages, both sides, every line filled. The students were shocked and sure that they couldn't do it.

My actions in the classroom now ran counter to anything I had ever been taught, but I had gone too far to turn back. The students slowly began to find materials to read; even more slowly, they began to write. Danny, of course, was the first to issue a challenge. I noticed the magazine, which in those days we called a girly magazine, and knew that every eye in the class was watching. However, my parenting had prepared me for this, and I shot him the old "Mom eye." Today, I would not be so gentle. Today I would grab the magazine and use it for curriculum to demonstrate how little girls and little boys are socialized in different ways in our culture. Danny was lucky; he knew me before I knew about gender biasing.

José was the next to issue a quiet, but direct, challenge. The entire class was busily reading and writing. I was quietly walking among the desks and responding to students. When I came to José, I noticed that he was writing rapidly. He had a large book, the Tucson phone book, and he was copying names. Long lists of names filled his blank papers. *Hooked on Books* had prepared me for this. Fader and McNeil told me that this would happen. They told me that the student would soon tire of this and would want to move to something that interested him.

"What are you writing, José?" I asked.

"I'm copying the phone book," he replied.

"Where are you in the alphabet?" I asked.

"I'm still on the A's," he answered.

"Okay," I said and moved on to the next student.

José never made it to the B's. From the Tucson phone book, he went right to reading about geography and writing about places he found in the almanac. José eventually graduated with honors in English and in Spanish and is now a pilot in the U.S. military. He has visited most of those places he used to write about.

Each Monday, I assigned more pages. Each Friday, I went home with a huge stack of messy, dirty construction paper journals, each filled with treasures and literacy. The next Monday, the students got their journals back with my comments, thoughts, questions, and stickers. I remember the absolute joy and delight I saw on the faces of those "problems" when they read my responses on Monday. I finally quit adding more pages when we hit thirty per week simply because I couldn't carry everything. I knew that Fader and McNeil were onto something powerful when the kids groaned and complained when our free reading and writing time was over.

Remember the blue basals that had been left on the shelf with the other texts? Eventually, they were used by one boy, Gilbert, who read every single story in the blue basal. He not only read every story; he thoroughly enjoyed them. Gilbert had been considered a nonreader who had resisted every basal to date. During the spring months, he continued to explore the texts stacked on the shelf and shared his discoveries with me. I think he thought I should have this information. On reflection, I think I was not fooling Gilbert; he knew that I needed all the help I could get. In late spring, the students took the annual achievement test. As with several other students, Gilbert's reading scores jumped three grade levels.

"What did you do for Gilbert?" the principal asked me.

"What did I do? What did Gilbert do for himself and for me!" I thought to myself.

The other twenty-seven students and I completely enjoyed the freedom of reading and writing. As the students took control of their own learning, their reading and language scores soared. Gilbert read his texts; the other students read science fiction, history, novels, texts from other classes, and even poetry. I read educational journals. I didn't understand it then, but I do now. From these students, I learned the following:

- Reading improves writing.
- Choice matters.
- We get smarter when we write.
- We love it when someone responds to our writing.
- Flexibility and a sense of humor help.

All my teaching and learning since those years has been directly related to my experiences teaching and learning with the Benson kids. We discovered by reading, talking, writing, hearing, experiencing, risking, and musing, and we learned together. We learned that it all takes time—the great enemy of public education! Every time I read books about critical pedagogy, I see their faces, I hear their questions, and I remember their laughter and tears.

What can be learned from this today? The Benson kids gave me the pedagogical principles, or "Benson basics," that have sustained me through three decades of teaching. I was lucky enough to come of age in teaching when we were expected to teach children and not just the curriculum and the standards. The following words resonate with me: "In my 35 years of teaching and my 6 decades of living, I have never met a *standard* child" (J. Yatvin, personal communication, September 5, 2002).

Teachers tell me that today, real reading, writing, and responding have too often been replaced with one-word-right-or-wrong blanks to fill in. Choice is vanishing; flexibility has been transformed into rigidity; and even the thought of a sense of humor is no longer funny.

Teachers tell me that cynicism and silence are pervasive in schools today. It is painfully clear that the real world of teaching and learning today is vastly different from when I learned my Benson basics. Could I make it today if I were just starting my career? I do not know, but I am sure that I could not make it without critical pedagogy: to name, to reflect critically, to act.

The most challenging question I am asked today is "How can teachers survive during this era of prescribed pedagogy?" We begin the search for that answer together; critical pedagogy will guide us. First, we *name* as we experience it, and I am doing that right now. Second, we will *reflect critically* together throughout the pages of this book. Third, we *act*. The answers do not lie in cynicism or in silence.

Learn, Relearn, and Unlearn Your Way to Critical Pedagogy

A group of those Benson kids were in my classes in the seventh, eighth, ninth, tenth, eleventh, and twelfth grades as their classes and my teaching assignments changed.

In those years, the only thing I knew about accountability was the students' success, and succeed they did. I watched them go from being isolated, marginalized "problem kids" to student leaders during their high school years. In those years, I didn't know about collecting data. I knew only that when those students graduated with two honors' cords (one in Spanish and one in English), the proud tears of their families were data enough for me. Teaching and learning with this group of students for six years gave me the courage and patience to learn, to relearn, and to unlearn, which eventually led me to a study of critical pedagogy.

To Learn: Difficult Learning Experiences

The Benson kids taught me that we learn by reading, talking, writing, listening, experiencing, engaging, interacting, solving problems, posing problems, and taking risks. And we do it better if we are in a safe and secure environment with an adult who cares about us. Learners choose what to learn. If it doesn't matter to learners, it doesn't matter.

In my own experience, I can remember several learning experiences that were not wonderful. My doctoral course on statistics, for instance—now there is something that was not fun to learn. However, there was one great surprise: As promised by his former students, the professor really did eat a piece of chalk in the middle of his lecture on multiple regression. In a class of fifty adult graduate students, I think I was one of two or three who noticed. However, I had been waiting and watching with eager anticipation all semester. If I had to learn stats, at least I was going to get to see the famous professor eat chalk.

Now that I am no longer teaching and learning with the Benson kids, I want you to know who my current students are. I am teaching in a state university. When I speak of the graduate students, I am talking about people who have been up since 6:00 A.M., washed a load of clothes, got their kids off to school, taught all day, went to an after-school meeting, and arrived at the university for a night class. Yes, I teach tired teachers. Even though the graduate students seem to be very hardy souls, sometimes I can see that learning isn't always wonderful for them either; for instance, sometimes when students read a new idea or hear a new thought, resistance and denial precede learning. We have all done this and probably will again.

To Relearn: Difficult Relearning Experiences

Learning can be very challenging, but the problem is that it always leads to relearning, which is more challenging. I think that relearning often involves a shift in methodology. When I walked into that Benson class, I had to shift my methodology from what I had learned previously to what I needed to learn from the students. Relearning takes places when students teach us all those things we didn't learn in teacher education.

Sometimes the adult students in the graduate classes are far enough along the relearning curve to understand that the ideas we generate in class are not for class only; rather, these ideas are to be applied to their own worlds. For example, María wrote:

> As I start off each new year in teaching, I have to *relearn* because each class is so unique that I can't use the same type of teaching methods or discipline. I never could understand how teachers could come into the first faculty meeting of September and have their lesson plans done for the entire year. Don't we have to base our teaching on the needs of our students?

It's reassuring that in our own struggle with relearning, we are in good company. Paulo Freire criticizes his followers for just being content with his first texts and not reading the critiques he has made of his own work, which show that learning and relearning never end (cited in Gadotti, 1994, p. 88).

My relearning has continued since the publication of the previous edition, in which I used the word *rigor* in a Freirian sense of academically challenging work. However, the word *rigor* seems to have been semantically altered, and today its use in schools often connotes mastery, inflexibility, stiffness, harshness, severity, and even cruelty. Teachers have told me that the construct of rigor is now akin to child cruelty as schools vainly attempt to bring all kids to "proficiency" in reading, math, and science, as required by the No Child Left Behind Act. Rigor is applauded by some and derided by others who wonder how we can possibly have all children above average. Rigor is particularly cruel for some children. For example, imagine being a child with a specific learning problem who is expected to demonstrate proficiency in reading, math, and science by 2014, when all children will be required to be at 100 percent of proficiency. To understand rigor in schools today, Koehler (2003) says, think rigor mortis. He calls for more vigor and less rigor. For Freire, rigor in schools was always balanced with the joy of learning. Frankly, I am struggling with my relearning of rigor. Critical pedagogy calls us back to the joy of rigor.

Authentic is another word I am struggling to relearn. For me, *authentic*, as in *authentic teaching and learning*, was at the very heart of real teaching and learning. In education, we strive for authentic learning as opposed to simulated learning experiences. However, I noticed that a colleague in the world of English composition and rhetoric had a tendency to wince when I said *authentic*.[1] "When terms like *authentic* are used, institutional power and class bias are erased from the picture. The actions of literacy instruction are portrayed as entirely benign and self-evidently beneficial to the students" (Newkirk, 1997, p. 90).

Relearning is tough. Mine continues.

To Unlearn: Difficult Unlearning Experiences

Learning and relearning prepare us for unlearning, which is the most challenging. Unlearning involves a shift in philosophy, beliefs, and assumptions. Unlearning is unpacking some old baggage.

When I was a little girl, I learned from my Grandma Grace that the melting pot was a symbol of all that was good. Eventually, I had to unlearn that idea because the melting pot was not so wonderful for everyone; some got burned on the bottom. This experience with unlearning was very uncomfortable because it challenged all my previously held assumptions.

The Lakota Sioux Indians who lived on the reservation two miles away tried to jump into that pot for the sake of being "good Americans." They tried to talk like Grandma, be like Grandma, think like Grandma, and act like Grandma, but no matter what they did, they could not look like Grandma. By doing what they had been taught was right and good, they gave up their language, their traditions, their beliefs, and, in many cases, their very souls. When they leaped into that hot pot, far too much was boiled away. I finally came to learn that the pot is really about power. The melting pot worked for my Grandma but not for her neighbors.

As a European American feminist from a prestigious West Coast university recently told me: "I have long considered myself to be an enlightened feminist. However, my comfortable framework was ripped out from underneath me when I met Pam, an African American feminist who consistently points out the multiple ways in which the feminist movement is Eurocentric."

My unlearning continues. In the second edition of this book, I wrote of *the rule of thumb* in the sense of one's own internal compass. Suddenly, I began to receive numerous e-mails from readers telling me that the expression, *rule of thumb*, had its semantic and linguistic roots firmly planted in an old English law which states that it was a man's duty to beat his wife with a rod the width of his thumb. I assure you that my unlearning felt jarring and jolting. I made several changes throughout the manuscript—wherever I found any reference to the phrase *rule of thumb*.

My unlearning continues. Later, the attention to detail of my production editor at Omegatype Typography called my attention to www.debunker.com/texts/ruleofthumb.html where I learned the *rule of thumb* does not refer to such a dreadful old law. Rather, the belief that it does, lies somewhere between revisionist history and urban legend. I invite you to read the research on the website.[2]

Sometimes, unlearning takes time and feels like a long leap across the great paradigm divide. For example, when I moved from behaviorism to transformational teaching and learning, it took decades, and not every moment was wonderful.

Summarizing relearning and unlearning, Karie, a teacher, said to her colleagues, "Relearning asks us to add new knowledge, and unlearning asks us to let go of the known." Unlearning is more difficult than relearning because it requires that we part with previous knowledge, schema, and theory that are known and comfortable. Unlearning is central to critical pedagogy, and it often feels terrible. This is good. Does it feel as though everything you ever learned, you now need to relearn and unlearn? This is good. At least for me, it often seems that all I ever held to be true about teaching and learning has been called into question. Many of my long-held assumptions have not stood the test of time.

Looking Ahead for Your Stories of Relearning and Unlearning

As critical pedagogy forces us to shift from passive to active learning, I invite you to reflect, read, and write with me. What have been some of your most difficult relearning and unlearning experiences?

Practicing Pedagogy Patiently: Tanesha Hits a Home Run

Tanesha was a reluctant sixth grade reader when she started a summer project that provided books, magazines, and lots of time for 200 urban middle school kids to read for six weeks. Tanesha, like most of the other students in this program, had previously had little access to books. However, in this project, Tanesha and her friends were surrounded by adolescent high-interest reading materials, amounting to twenty-five books per student. The students could read for pleasure for two hours per day. Children could read whatever they selected, and accountability was minimal: Students only had to fill out a simple form for each book they read with the name and title of the book.

Shin (2004) found that she had to practice her pedagogy patiently, as not only did she bring kids and books together, she also wanted to add direct encouragement to her study. Tanesha initially wanted no encouragement, much less direct encouragement. Shin was patient and continued to encourage, until Tanesha eventually hit a home run with a Goosebumps book. Once Tanesha found her home run book, she continued to read and eventually moved on to much more difficult reading. By the end of the six weeks, this reluctant reader had finished reading forty books.

NOTES

1. This discussion has been informed by my ongoing dialogue with Dr. Steph Paterson.
2. This discussion has been informed by Paul J. Felton, a student in the class of Dr. Anne-Louise Brooks of the University of Prince Edward Island in Charlottetown, PEI, Canada, and Dawn McIlvain, my production editor at Omegatype Typography.

3 What in the World Do You Think It Is?

"The whole is greater than the sum of its parts, but it's the parts that make all the difference," the student said to me when we were discussing the language and definitions inherent within critical pedagogy. The first objective of this chapter is to look at some of those parts while always keeping the whole in our vision. For example, it is often said that a definition of critical pedagogy is **to name, to reflect critically, to act.** However, if *to name* is strange and unfamiliar language, a part of the whole is lost. I am hoping to make the strange familiar and the familiar strange (McLaren, 1989, p. 167) as the parts are integrated into the whole.

Furthermore, even if the parts and whole are integrated, unless the theory and practice are united, we fail to bring critical pedagogy to life. Therefore, a secondary objective of this chapter is to unify the theoretical constructs with classroom practice. This is a lofty goal indeed, integrating not only the parts into the whole, but also theory into practice.

This chapter will challenge readers to generate their own understandings based on their own lived experiences. The narratives provided here serve as scaffolds for each reader to build her own schema of semantics for defining the language of critical pedagogy. Unlike in previous editions, my definitions and those of others will follow. I begin.

A Word about Language

Edelsky (1991) notes that traditionally, we have been taught to keep our academic discourse cool and detached. We come from a tradition of thought that teaches that advocacy and passion are irrational and detachment equals rationality. Passionate language conjures up unruliness and disorder (Peller, 1987). Passion combined with an oppositional position evokes fears of dethroning, of revolution. However, as Edelsky notes (p. xxi), it is really style they object to.

I have lived to see Edelsky's thoughts on language and style come true. My style of writing today is the very opposite of how I was taught, or schooled, to write years ago. My style is not cool or detached, and I hope passion is on each page. I have left the rational, five-paragraph essay behind, and certainly I must be a bit of a disappointment to my marvelous former writing teachers, many of whom were men. It took me many decades to understand that writing is also gender-centric. I'm sure many of you understood that sooner than I did.

However, having said that, I know that I am personally indebted to the esoteric and abstract language of critical theorists. Indeed, it was the very rigor of the language that enabled me to break through several self-imposed intellectual and even emotional barriers. Nevertheless, I am deeply aware that it was only during a very privileged time of my life that I was able to sit alone in a university library month after month and struggle with the language (and thought) of critical pedagogy. I am also mindful of the fact that most of the teachers and students I admire so much will never have this incredible opportunity.

Therefore, I choose to break with the academic norms; I choose to deconstruct the deconstructionist language so that students and teachers with incredibly challenging and complex lives and responsibilities will have access to critical pedagogy. I know that readers will bring the context of their own experiences and will construct their own meaning. My wish is that the readers of this book will eventually toss it and move on to others, to whom I am so deeply indebted.[1]

Dawn Does Critical Pedagogy

> *"All the toys are old, broken, and dirty," she said as she burst through the door. Dawn had just returned from her first day of teaching bilingual kindergarten in a district that had never had a bilingual program, although the majority of their students historically came from migrant families who spoke Spanish.*
>
> *"The last teacher left boxes and boxes for my kindergarten students. It's just junk. I snuck out to the garbage and threw it away. There were even teaching materials from the 1950s," she groaned.*
>
> *Dawn was born in 1968. I know—she is my daughter.*

Critical pedagogy teaches us **to name, to reflect critically, and to act.** In this case, Dawn named it: junk. She critically reflected, probably as she snuck outside to find the garbage. And she acted: She tossed it. Critical pedagogy helped Dawn to understand that forty-year-old teaching materials in English would not meet the needs of her Spanish-dominant kindergarten students.

Pedagogy is the meaningful interaction between teaching and learning. In addition, critical pedagogy seeks to take action to improve teaching and learning in schools and in life. Suzette began teaching after a successful fourteen-year career in business. Pedagogy and critical pedagogy meant very little to her until her third year of teaching, when her pedagogy kicked in the day she realized that the students were not achieving because of her mandated teacher-centered teaching and the complete irrelevance of the materials she was assigned to use.

"Thank God, I realized that it was not the students; it never was the students. If I were to help these students be successful, I needed to do whatever was needed," Suzette said. "When I started teaching, I thought I knew a lot about teaching. Now the students were teaching me to relearn."

Further reflection led to action. "First, I had to *name it:* The materials were irrelevant for the students. Second, I had to *reflect critically:* This was the relearning and unlearning, and it was painful. Third, I had to *act:* Now we focus on meaningful language activities across the curriculum. The amount of curriculum coverage no longer matters as much as the quality of curriculum coverage."

When Suzette's pedagogy kicked in, the pedagogy of the classroom was transformed into critical pedagogy.

Definitions

One way to begin this chapter would be for me to list several definitions of critical pedagogy right now. I am resistant to doing that because readers might be tempted to memorize any one of them as if it were the one true definition. Even if you memorize a definition, you will soon forget it unless you own it and it matters to you.

"It should be stressed that there is no one critical pedagogy" (McLaren, 1998a, p. 227); therefore, I prefer that we move together through these pages until you create a definition that matters to you. I know—It takes longer this way. It is more difficult this way. But once you have created some meaning for critical pedagogy for yourself, you will never forget it, and you will be able to enrich your meaning as you learn and experience more. So if you are groaning now, I understand. The grad students in my classes understand. They all periodically love and/or hate to learn in this mode of critical pedagogy; it was so much easier when we could just sit passively and repeat what was transmitted. In using this text, you need to engage actively. If you find an idea you love or one you hate or one you don't understand, call a friend and discuss it until you create some meaning. In reading this chapter, the words of Wheatley (1992) might ring true:

> They were eager to create a model or framework into which they could slot information. I was intent on letting information do its things. They wanted to get organized at the start; I wanted them to move into confusion. I urged them to create more information than they could possibly handle. I guaranteed them that at some point the information would self-organize in them, crystallizing into interesting forms and ideas. (p. 150)

Many people (including teachers and students) say that they just can't write, but they talk very well. Writing is just talking on paper or a computer monitor. If you have trouble writing, just talk with someone or talk with yourself, then capture what you just said on a napkin or scrap of paper or in a journal. Or go to your computer and start "talking at the blank screen" (some call this writing) until you make some sense of your own thoughts. I used to think that I wrote for a grade, for an assignment, or for someone else. I have finally figured out that I write (a) so that someone will respond to my thoughts, and/or (b) so that I can further develop my thoughts. Critical pedagogy has helped me to understand that when I write, I am clarifying my own thinking.

Generative Definitions

Generative literacies and generative knowledges are the focus of critical teaching and learning. As an example of each, let us begin with what we will call generative definitions. Define each of the following three words on the basis of your own experiences.

Critical:

Critical is a prodding, probing type of word. It is like an advanced search on a Web search engine, which goes in and looks around, then doubles back and looks again. Our critical perspectives find new ways of seeing and knowing. Within this book, *critical* does not mean bad; it does not mean "to criticize." Rather, it means "seeing beyond." It means looking within and without and seeing more deeply the complexities of teaching and learning.

Pedagogy:

Many years ago, I thought that pedagogy was about me, teaching. I might have even thought that it was the science of me teaching. Now I think it is far more than that. I think pedagogy is the interaction between teaching and learning. Good pedagogies give us that electricity we feel when we are totally focused on the unified process of teaching and learning. Bad pedagogies are at best boring and at worst painful.

Critical Pedagogy:

Critical pedagogy is a way of thinking about, negotiating, and transforming the relationship among classroom teaching, the production of knowledge, the institutional structures of the school, and the social and material relationships of the wider community, society, and nation state (McLaren, 1998b, p. 45). This definition was added to the second edition in direct response to the many requests I received for a "real" definition. My definitions continue to be woven into the context of theory and practice. In this third edition, I offer yet another definition, based on the influence of Greene (2003), who also struggles to define critical pedagogy. To find her answers, she turns to poetry, and one of her citations, from Rukeyser (1973, p. 374), rings true for me, as it asks us to tell the truth about our experiences:

> What would happen if one woman told the truth about her life?
> The world would split open.

Critical pedagogy is a prism that reflects the complexities of the interactions between teaching and learning. It highlights some of the hidden subtleties that might have escaped our view previously. It enables us to see more widely and more deeply. This prism has a tendency to focus on shades of social, cultural, political, and even economic conditions, and it does all of this under the broad view of history. After we look through the prism of critical pedagogy, it seems clear that the basics are not as basic as they used to be—or at least as basic as we used to think they were.

Now that you have mused and written your definitions, let me share with you some definitions that came from students who have finished their undergraduate work and are ready to begin a teaching credential program. This was a highly diverse group that had not previously studied critical pedagogy. Together they had discussed and read about the idea for only a couple of days. Their definitions of *critical pedagogy* follow:

> A state of mind, a place of reference
> A framework from which to build
> A questioning frame of mind
> It makes us double-check our action and the action of others
> It makes me do the best I can

It empowers with a perspective needed to ask good questions
It makes me actively commit to do something
It makes me see beyond what was taught yesterday

Now that you know how I feel about definitions, you will appreciate my trepidation in defining *critical pedagogy*. I am fearful to give a definition, but I know very well that my readers want one. In an earlier draft of this document, I attempted to solve this problem by hiding the definitions within paragraphs about teachers and learners. At least, I thought I was hiding the definitions.

I was walking through the computer lab and happened to glance down at a paper that a student had beside her computer. I noticed that it was the earlier draft of this document. I slowed my pace and looked more carefully at the hard copy to the side of the computer. I noticed with glee and dismay (oh, those darned contradictions of education) that she had found and highlighted in bright yellow all of the definitions of *critical pedagogy* I had placed in various paragraphs.

"If I understand this correctly, you don't want to define it for us; rather, you want us to find meaning for it based on our lived experiences," she said.

"Yes, that is exactly what I mean," I responded. "But I noticed that you have found all the definitions I thought I had so cleverly hidden throughout the document. You have highlighted them, even though I thought I had woven them within the context so that each reader would eventually discover and generate her own understandings of this somewhat abstract concept."

"Yes, I could tell you didn't want us to memorize your definitions. I could tell you were trying to hide them, but my understanding is that critical pedagogy means we have to look back at our own histories and generate new questions in order to find new answers based on our knowledges and literacies and cultures, right?"

"Right," I replied.

Karie, a teacher, said that at first she did not like the fact that I just didn't give her the definitions. "I'm used to getting my information in a linear, direct, transmission model of pedagogy, and I did not like having to think and generate my own definitions," she continued. Often, we have the definitions within us because of our experiences; we only need to struggle to find the language to define and articulate that which we already know. In this chapter, we are doing just that, as are the students who follow.

Phony from the True

The group was busily solving problems in the third grade class. The teacher had written on the board:

Estimation	Actual	Difference

First, the teacher asked the students to estimate how many rocks were in the piles on the table.

"Lots."

"37."

"83."

The children began to guess noisily and happily. When each group decided on their guess, they recorded their numbers on their individual papers and on a chart under the word estimation *on the chalkboard.*

Second, the teacher asked each group to count the actual number of rocks. They began counting each little rock and again recorded their numbers on their papers and on the chart under the word actual. *Many squeals of glee could be heard as the students discovered how many rocks were actually in the pile. The problem of the day was to discover the difference. I noticed that the teacher did not use the word* subtract; *she only talked about finding the difference.*

The students began to talk and think. They soon discovered that talking and thinking were more difficult than guessing and counting. One particular group of four students was noticeably struggling. They debated counting and guessing and adding while all the time shoving their little pile of rocks around the table. However, no matter what they tried, they could not agree on the difference or even on how to find it. It seemed that the word difference, *not the process of subtraction, was the stumbling block. It appeared to me that they knew the concept of subtraction, but the word* difference *stumped them. Eventually, they returned to a discussion of* estimation *and* actual, *concepts that they knew that they knew.*

Suddenly, a little boy in this group shouted, "I get it! I get it! Let's just take the phony from the true, and we will have it."

His teammates immediately understood and successfully solved the problem through subtraction.

In this particular situation, the students knew the concept, but it was the language that was denying them access to the answer. To *subtract*, a concept they already knew, they had to find language that they understood. In addition, when they returned to their discussion of *estimation* and *actual* in order to find the *difference,* they were looking for some previous knowledge to connect with the new knowledge.

The same can be said for the language of critical pedagogy. Sometimes, when we bump into new language, it feels as though we are being denied access to the concepts. That is how I felt when I first started reading the language of critical pedagogy. Many teachers and learners have lived the concepts of critical pedagogy, and they know what it is; they just don't know that they know.

We often would like to take the phony from the true, as the third grader put it. But is there ever one truth? One answer? One way of knowing? One right way? I doubt it. Certainly not in critical pedagogy. In this chapter, I will share the truth of critical pedagogy as I have experienced it. I hope that my truth is an authentic story that reflects my life in schools. I encourage you to reflect on my experiences, to muse on my musings, to think about my thoughts. However, my intention is not to transmit my knowledge as if it were the one true knowledge. Together, we will visit and revisit the concepts and language through the filter of real teachers and real students in real classrooms. The theory will be grounded in daily classroom practices so that you, the reader, can discover, generate, create, and internalize your own definitions.

Language of Possibility, Language of Critique

It is a common experience for educators initially to become aware of critical pedagogy through the unique language that surrounds it. This language is disquieting; we don't feel at home with new language. When we don't understand language, we are denied access to ideas, to concepts, to thoughts, to people. Where in the world did the language of critical pedagogy come from?

The term *critical pedagogy* was first used in 1983 by Henry Giroux in *Theory and Resistance* (Darder, Baltodano, & Torres, 2003), and it was a pivotal book in my own professional development. When that book found its way to me, I had no idea who Henry Giroux was, but I vividly recall the experience of reading it. The lasting memory is that the words on the pages were vibrating as I read. Giroux set a high threshold for language; it is a language that, although esoteric and abstract, takes us to deep places we already know and have been afraid of acknowledging. Giroux's language of possibility and language of critique demands that we take off our blinders. The problem is that exhausted teachers often accuse those in critical pedagogy of speaking in academese.

It's true, critical pedagogues talk funny—or at least, some do, sometimes, in buzzwords and jargon. We in education are often accused of this. I am personally not attracted to jargon, even though I have been accused of using it. Ouch. I remember a powerful voice (J. Stansell, personal communication, March 20, 1991) saying, "Joan, say what you mean, and mean what you say." That is my goal in this book. I am fully aware of the dangers I face in fulfilling my goal. In trying to simplify, I cannot slip into being simplistic. I want to clarify, not trivialize. I want to expand the language, not reduce it. What do all of those words mean? When I started reading about critical pedagogy, I felt that others knew and I didn't. I felt as if I had less value, less status, and less knowledge.

The irony is that this new language helped me to break out of previous ways of knowing. Another contradiction! The thing I thought was the barrier (language) was the very thing that helped me to break through the barrier. The language of critical pedagogy made me quite crazy at first and, ironically, finally opened the door to more complex understandings for me. The language of impossibility became the language of possibility for me. The gate became the drawbridge. It helped me to approach the other on the other's terms and not on my presupposed image of the other or what I wanted the other to be. My wish is that when you have finished this book, you will feel at home with the language and ideas of critical pedagogy. Recently, Kitty, a teacher, expressed it this way: "Now that I am studying more and more, I have words that describe my beliefs. Before, I thought they were only mine. Now, I am finding that my beliefs are written about in books."

Vygotsky: Reaching Back to Move Forward

In the process of teaching and learning, I, like all of you, encountered many new ideas. Sometimes these ideas fit with what we have long intuitively felt but never had the language or courage to express. I struggled to consume this new knowledge. The more I learned and the more I read, the more questions I had. It was a constant process that challenged all of my previously held assumptions of unlearning.

Finally, in desperation, I decided to try what I had always taught my students: Hook it onto prior knowledge. Construct meaning based on your own knowledge and experiences. My internal dialogue went something like this:

"What do I know?" I asked myself.

"Well, I know a little about language. Okay, that is a good starting point. Now, what language person, in particular, might be helpful?"

"Oh, yes, my old friend Vygotsky," I answered myself.

I sat down with my worn and tattered *Thought and Language* (Vygotsky, 1962). I started to read and reread. I tried to connect thought with language, ideas with words. Vygotsky taught me again that if I had one little thought and one word, I could begin to generate meaning between the two. The words would multiply, and the thoughts would grow. The dynamic relationship between the two would continue to create new meanings.

Word by Word

This is exactly what I did in the early stages of my studying critical pedagogy. First, I grabbed any word of critical pedagogy—just one word. "Anyone can learn one word," I told myself. And as the words grew, so did the thoughts, just as Vygotsky said they would (Wink & Putney, 2002).

In this case, language was the tool to help me understand, but it did not feel as though I was using a tool; rather, it felt like a process that enabled me to think more deeply and critically. A Polish friend told me about an English language class he had taken. He said, "They gave me this list of words but didn't tell me what to do with them." Vygotsky helped me understand what to do with these new words of critical pedagogy: I had to hook them to thoughts.

The ideas of Vygotsky empowered my learning of the language and the thoughts of critical pedagogy. As I learned each new word or thought, new linkages would grow with my prior knowledge and existing experiential base. The most important lesson I learned from Vygotsky was that I had the ability to create new knowledge by using the relationship between thought and language.

Initially, I didn't even know the vocabulary, but I knew that I knew the ideas. Kids in schools had long ago taught me these same concepts. My experiences had brought me to the same place. I just didn't have the language to express what I was thinking. So to even start, I had to learn the words. As I learned the words (in context) and played with the words, they gradually became mine. The words were sinking into the region of thought. Language finally began moving toward thought. Initially, these words were symbols without meaning; I had to play with them, read them, write them, and talk about them before meaning gradually started to develop. The relationship between the words and the thought, however, is never static; as words develop, thought develops; and as thought gradually develops, the words change with the emerging ideas.

In my particular case, the language of critical pedagogy, which at first had alienated, infuriated, and exasperated me, finally empowered me. From Vygotsky, I have learned that our words matter. Our words are not just neutral squiggles on paper. They are not just neutral symbols. It seems that even the mainstream pop culture is coming to understand the significance of words, as I heard a popular talk show psychologist (OK, it was Dr. Phil) say, "These words really are a big deal."

Our language joins with our thoughts to generate meaning. As we increase our use of words, our thoughts deepen. The language that we use matters. The language of critical pedagogy challenges us to see and understand deeply the school experiences of marginalized groups. Sometimes language hurts one group of kids, and sometimes it helps another group.

Critical pedagogy forces educators to look again at the fundamental issues of power and its relationship to the greater societal forces that affect schools. This comes dangerously close to being a definition! Critical pedagogy has made me look again at the fundamental issues of power that are involved in the creation of a "trash" track. Critical pedagogy is forcing me to think and rethink my lived experiences as compared with those of my African American colleagues. "Critical pedagogy asks how and why knowledge gets constructed the way it does, and how and why some constructions of reality are legitimated and celebrated by the dominant culture while others clearly are not" (McLaren, 1989, p. 169). For me, critical pedagogy is a new lens that enables me to see more clearly my past, my present, and my future.

One of the frustrating aspects of the study of critical pedagogy is our tendency to want others to transmit their knowledge of what it means to us: "Just tell us what it means!" During my initial encounters with these concepts, I was exactly like this. I felt angry, alienated, and excluded from this new knowledge. Repeatedly, I went to my professors to implore them to "just explain it." They repeatedly handed me another book. Each book triggered more questions.

Eventually, I came to the realization that I would have to find meaning for myself based on my own lived experiences. I do not believe that I can transmit my generated knowledge to you; however, I can share my story, and in the process, you can make your own connections based on your knowledge and experiences. This is not the "Cliff Notes of Critical Pedagogy," but it is a collection of understandings about the language of critical pedagogy.

As we begin, I suggest that we follow the guidance of Lamott (1994), who recalls her father giving advice to her brother when he was overwhelmed with a late school assignment in which he was to write a report on birds. The father sat down, put his arms around his son, and simply said, "Bird by bird, buddy. Just take it bird by bird."

Banking Model of Education

Freire (1994) articulated the banking model of education, in which the teacher has the knowledge and deposits it in the empty heads of the learners, who then have to give it back to her during testing. The knowledge is assumed to be correct and politically neutral. Critical pedagogy questions not only the knowledge, but also the method of delivery. As I write this, the No Child Left Behind Act is a classic example of the banking model of education.

Conscientization

The truth is that I can barely pronounce the word *conscientization*—not in English, not in Spanish, not in Portuguese. I understand it. I know when I didn't have it. (When I was in Benson, I had *Hooked on Books;* I did not have conscientization.) I know when I began to develop it. (After teaching and learning with those Benson kids for a decade.) I know when teachers and learners have it. I know when students don't have it. I recognize it when it is emerging in learners. I respect it. I understand its power. I love it. I just can't pronounce it very well. It can be a challenging concept. Patience is fundamental to our learning. Courage is fundamental to our learning. Just keep reading, reflecting, talking, and writing; soon you will come to understand its meaning on the basis of your experiences.

Conscientization moves us from the passivity of "Yeah, but we can't do that" to the power of "We gotta do the best we can where we are with what we've got." For example, I see teachers as powerful humans who can make a difference in the lives of students. However, they often feel weak because they see themselves as victims of a system that renders them passive. Conscientization enables students and teachers to have confidence in their own knowledge, ability, and experiences. Often people will say that conscientization is a power we have when we recognize we *know* that we know.

In schools and communities, conscientization is knowing that we know, and it is more. It means that we have voice and the courage to question ourselves and the role we are playing in maintaining educational processes that we do not value. Recently, at a faculty retreat, I watched a colleague explain that she was teaching a concept that she knows has been discredited by further research. We asked her why she continued to maintain a process she cannot support. She needs to know that she knows; she needs conscientization; she needs courage to stop maintaining processes she knows do not work. Later, at the same retreat, another colleague spoke about a test he gives his students every semester. I know him, and I know this test. It is everything he doesn't believe in. I asked him why. Why does he continue to give this test if it flies in the face of his considerable knowledge and experience? Later, when he was presenting to the entire faculty, he mentioned the test and said he had just realized he didn't know why he was giving it. I predict he won't give it next semester. Conscientization is emerging. He is coming to know that he knows. He is finding the power of his own voice, his own knowledge, his own experiences.

When I think of conscientization, I never think of a definition. I always think of people. Let me tell you a story of two teachers: One has conscientization, and the other doesn't—well, didn't.

Carmen Has It

I first met Carmen when she came to teach at a very low-status bilingual school in the South. I never could figure out why the district called this school the bilingual school; there was nothing bilingual about it. The teachers spoke English; the kids spoke Spanish. The teachers used English curriculum; the kids understood Spanish curriculum. I guess it was called the bilingual program because the Latino children went to school there. Until I met Carmen.

Carmen looked like a teacher who would be found in a Norman Rockwell painting. She had moved beyond the middle of life and had long salt-and-pepper hair pulled loosely into a topknot; small tendrils fell around her face. She had a slight build, but there was an air of strength and health about her. She looked very much like a woman who for many years had worked long hours and had eaten sparingly. Her clothes were a no-nonsense cotton that served her well in the classroom; her shoes were sturdy, as was her character. More than anything, one immediately noticed a sense of peace and purpose. She was courageous and patient. This was a woman who had known many teachers, many students, and many parents; together, they had been reading the world, reading the word (Freire & Macedo, 1987).

Eventually, I came to learn many things about Carmen—and from Carmen. Carmen understood about learning, teaching, languages, literacies, cultures, and knowledges. She had complex understandings and multiple perspectives. She thought that kids needed to learn, so she taught in a language that they understood: Spanish. In her class, the students were continually generating language and ideas, language and ideas, language and ideas. I suspect that she had read Vygotsky, too.

Carmen did not use the district-prescribed curriculum. She used the entire context of her students' lives for her curriculum. The state-mandated basals and materials served as just another resource to be used when needed. There were times when a certain activity viewed in isolation would appear to be much less than it actually was. Only the interaction of the entire context of her teaching could give full meaning to any activity.

For example, one day I walked into her class and noticed that Gilberto was again the center of attention. He was particularly adept at this, and I had come to think of him as "Gilberto, the most frequent office visitor." Gilberto had recently gotten a new, very short haircut. In true Gilberto style, he had arranged all day for his peers to be more interested in his new haircut than in the lessons the teachers had planned. Already that morning, I had heard a lot of grumbling from other teachers about him. However, there was something different about the kind of attention he was receiving in this class. Carmen and Gilberto were walking hand in hand behind each student's chair so that each had an opportunity to touch Gilberto's head. As they walked, Carmen was teaching the words and ideas: brush, comb, shampoo, rinse, hot water, warm water, cool water. Gilberto sat down, and Carmen wrote their language on the board. Together they created new thoughts and sentences with their generated language. Carmen wrote everything on the board. Teodoro mentioned that his hair felt ticklish. Carmen wrote "ticklish" on the board, and the students read the word and giggled. Soon all the children had their own journals on their desks and were busy using their language to write new sentences. Carmen knew the importance of including the children and their world in her lessons. After this particular lesson, Carmen walked across the hall to Rainey's classroom.

Carmen knew the power of Gilberto and his new haircut, and she knew that she knew: conscientization. She also knew that Rainey, a beginning teacher who worked with the same group of children for their English language development and their math and science, would need a little push in this direction or she would have continued with her prescribed lesson on the colors in English. The children would have memorized those lists of words, but they wouldn't have known what to do with them. Carmen knew how to make those words and ideas work for her students. Carmen soon had Rainey and the students busily involved with funny new words in English, words such as *ticklish, prickly, spike,* and *flattop,* words that never would have been on the English as an Additional Language list for memorizing.

Carmen and Gilberto had created an activity that mattered to the kids. Every minute was used for the learning and teaching process. In this classroom, Freire (cited in McLaren, 1989) would not find a "culture of silence." The children were not silent because they felt less or were afraid; they were silent only when it was meaningful in their learning. At the end of the day, each child had written a story using all of their new words and ideas about funny new haircuts.

Carmen, more than any other teacher, taught me the power of conscientization in the practice of her class. She knew her beliefs from years of experiences, books, ideas, and people. She turned her beliefs into behaviors in every moment of her life. Her students grew to love themselves; their teachers grew to love the students; the students grew into their own biliteracy; and, the power of this pulled the community into the process. The peace and purpose that was Carmen transformed the students, her colleagues, and their students. As you read this book, please do not memorize a definition; just remember Carmen. In addition, reflect on someone you know who has conscientization, and please reflect on your own.

> **Conscientization is . . .**

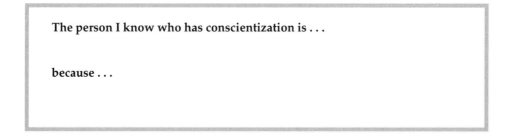

> **The person I know who has conscientization is . . .**
>
> **because . . .**

> **In my own personal development of conscientization,
> I would say that I . . .**

Rainey Doesn't—Well, Didn't

Rainey was as vivacious as Carmen was private. Rainey taught in English; Carmen taught in Spanish. Rainey had never been around Mexican kids; she continually complained to me about them and their behavior. Carmen had always been around Mexican kids; she continually told me how smart and loving they were. Rainey was new to teaching; Carmen was not. The first time I met Rainey in school, she desperately implored, "Okay, I've taught the weather in English. Now what do I do?" The first time I met Carmen, she matter-of-factly told me that I would need to get her some more books in a language the students could understand. It would be safe to say that Rainey did not have conscientization. Carmen did.

Rainey: BC.   Let me describe some of Rainey's behaviors *before conscientization* and *before Carmen*. The following is a list of things she said about her students at the beginning of the year:

> *Ollie:* One of the worst
> *Gilberto:* A terrible problem
> *Carlos:* Ugh
> *María and Irma:* Pitiful sisters
> *Cristina:* Doesn't know anything

Meetings with the families provided multiple opportunities to observe her behaviors, which told me much about her beliefs. Rainey would enter the school auditorium with a smile on her face, walk to the front row without speaking to any of the families, bury herself in the middle of the first row, where she was safely surrounded by the other teachers, and cross her arms. Several empty rows of auditorium seats always provided a safe buffer between the parents and the teachers. Rainey and many of her colleagues came from a tradition of family involvement that assumed that teachers would talk and families would listen. The purpose of this approach to family involvement is to change the families. Rainey subscribed to this thinking. But that was BC.

Rainey: AC.   Within a few short months, the power of Carmen began to work its magic. Rainey changed *after Carmen.* Rainey changed *after conscientization.* When she came to the family meetings, Rainey would arrive with a smile on her face and walk up to all the families and use her limited Spanish. They warmed to her approach and were more than willing to teach her more. Her use of their language grew. Soon she was visiting with so many family members as she entered the meetings that she could never make it to the safe front row of the auditorium. I began to find her in the middle of the parents wherever they were sitting. Rainey came to appreciate a new approach to family involvement. Instead of doing something to them, she came to understand why she should do things *with* them. Instead of trying to change the parents, she was soon trying to change the school.

Once, Rainey and Carmen were discussing family involvement and what the families needed. Rainey suggested that she could go to the university library and do a computer search to find out. Carmen nodded and added, "Or we could ask the families." At the next family meeting, the teachers asked, and the families told them their needs.

> *The Families' Needs*
> More family meetings
> A written copy of the teacher's schedule
> An understanding of the assigned homework
> More time with their children
> Less time with TV

Rainey and Carmen chuckled during the meeting as they thought about Rainey going to the library instead of just asking the parents.

Another example of Rainey: AC happened about the same time. The results of initiating and implementing a parent advisory committee are not often visible immediately, but they are worth the wait. Carmen always went to visit in the homes of her students. This was a very frightening thought for Rainey, and she resisted for months. Finally, she went to visit in the home of Carlos, one of her students who previously had almost convinced her to leave the teaching profession because of his behavior.

One day I was walking down a corridor in this school and realized that I was looking at Rainey and Carlos as they leaned on their elbows and stared out the window toward the playground; their bodies made dark silhouettes against the sunlight. Their heads were about an inch apart, and both were facing the playground. By the slow movement of their heads, I could see that they were quietly talking. I slipped back down the hall so as not to disturb them.

Rainey: BC thought that Carlos was the worst; she grimaced every time his name was mentioned. She and other teachers used to talk about him in the faculty lounge. I used to try to imagine how terrible it would be to be in the first grade when all of those in authority were against me.

As I watched Rainey and Carlos talk quietly and stare out of the window, I remembered how she used to talk about him; now she was talking *with* him. Rainey thought that Carlos had changed. I think that Rainey has changed.

I remember Rainey telling me about the home visit. She was astounded to discover that Carlos had a good home environment, with a loving and supportive family. His brothers and sisters were successful in school, and Rainey was relieved to learn that Carlos's mother shared her concern about Carlos. The mother could not understand why Carlos wasn't learning at the same pace as his brothers and sisters were, but she was too uncomfortable and alienated to come to the school and discuss her concerns.

Rainey told me that before the visit, she assumed that Carlos's behavior was a result of his home. She assumed that the child, the child's family, and the child's culture were the principal causes of his failure. After the home visit, she began to work with his mother to understand his behaviors, and his behavior immediately improved. Carlos is a different person when he is with Rainey.

However, Rainey still has a critical step to take. She still thinks that Carlos has changed. She needs to critically examine herself and her environment and come to the realization that she is a part of the process of transformation. In Carlos's search for knowledge and literacy, Rainey is a significant variable. I like to think that if Paulo Freire had been with me in that hall, he would have told me that this was conscientization: a transformation of the learner and teacher as a result of interaction between the two of them.

However, I'm not worried about Rainey. If she can move this far toward an intercultural orientation in the time that I have known her, soon she will know that she knows, and she will go on to help others read the world and read the word (Freire & Macedo, 1987).

Rainey: BC
- Before Carmen
- Before conscientization
- Before Carlos

Rainey: AC
- After Carmen
- After conscientization
- After Carlos

Codification

Codification is the concept, captured on paper, in the dirt, on the chalkboard, on the wall. It is the thought, painted. It is the symbol, symbolized. I have known teachers to codify thoughts in pictures, in action, in clay, in paint. Before Paulo Freire was banished from Brazil for developing literacy among the native peoples, I always visualize him standing in the shade of a tree codifying with a stick in the dirt the powerful ideas of rage and oppression that the workers were expressing. I have no idea whether he stood in the shade, and I have no idea whether he ever used a stick to draw in the dirt, but this is the image I carry with me to make meaning of codification. I have to tell you that I think Freire was onto something with this idea of codification. It captures the best of many powerful approaches to teaching and learning. It brings in the students' world and builds knowledges and literacies based on their own unique experiences. It puts the power back into teaching and learning. And it integrates the never-ending debate between *doing* and *living* critical pedagogy.

> Codes (or "codifications," in Freire's terms) are concrete physical expressions that combine all the elements of the theme into one representation. They can take many forms: photographs, drawings, collages, stories, written dialogues, movies, songs. Codes are more than visual aids for teaching. They are at the heart of the educational process because they initiate critical thinking.
>
> No matter what the form, code is a projective device that is emotionally laden and identifiable to students. . . . In essence, a code sums up or "codifies" into one statement a problem (or contradiction) that people recognize in their lives: need for English vs. loss of native culture, stress at work vs. need for work, disappointment vs. hope from expectations in the US. Each problem is complex without narrowly defined good and bad sides.
>
> After a problem or contradiction has been coded, we can begin to "decode" it— we can begin to unravel it or find workable solutions. (Wallerstein, 1983, pp. 19–20)

Critical pedagogy forces us to see the broad social, historical, cultural, and political context of teaching and learning. Critical pedagogy gives us the courage to say what we see. Critical pedagogy is grounded in justice, equity, and moral mandates. Critical pedagogy makes us ask fundamental questions such as "What is the right thing to do today in my teaching and learning in this particular context?" It is as broad as the world and as deep as our own individual lives. Critical pedagogy makes us look at the world, and it makes us look at our individual role in the world, the community, the classroom. Critical pedagogy is like a lens that enables us to see more clearly, more critically, more keenly.

Culture

Culture, like literacy, is far larger that we might have previously thought. First, language, culture, and thought (Vygotsky, 1986) are so intertwined that we cannot take one from the other. Thus, when we take language from someone, we indeed are doing untold harm, which will haunt us and hurt us in the future. Second, culture is not fixed, and it is not about food and fluff. Third, culture is not singular; actually, it is extremely multiple. Therefore, culture is multicultural. Unfortunately, many people see culture as only "my" culture. "All theories developed in Western behavioral science are based on tacit premises of Western Culture, usually the middle-class version most typical of professionals" (Spradley, 1980, p. 14.) Thus, many assume that "Cultural deprivation is merely a way of saying that people are deprived of 'my culture'" (Spradley, 1980, p. 14).

Each of us is a part of learning a culture, transmitting a culture, and generating a culture in the multiple facets of our daily lives. A Persian expression captures this well: "It is difficult for the fish to see the stream" (Campbell, 2004). Culture is dynamic, continuous, and cumulative, learned and shared, and is constantly at work in our lives (Campbell, 2004).

School cultures affect all aspects of teaching and learning on both micro and macro levels. For example, Dresser (1996) tells of a teacher who was using red ink to correct a paper and she wrote the name of the student in red in her comments. The parents of the student and the student were horrified because in their culture, writing a name in red is done only when a person dies or on the anniversary of the person's death. A second example of the effects of school cultures is the advent of high-stakes testing, which is drastically altering the entire culture of public schools in the United States. Testing now takes as much as 30 percent of time in school (England, 2003); that is 30 percent less time for teaching and learning. Much of the remainder of the 70 percent for teaching is spent teaching to the test. The "500-pound gorilla" (Kohn, 2002) has transformed the joy of learning into the terror of testing for students, teachers, administrators, and families. Critical pedagogy calls us to take back our schools.

Cultural Capital

Dawn worried that other teachers made disparaging remarks because her kindergarten students would not stand in a straight line. Although she was intuitively opposed to five-year-olds standing in a straight line, she could see that their failure to do so was having a negative effect on her students. When she said "forménse," they would gather in a circle around her, arms around each other, look at her, and smile. She thought that it looked like a group hug. The other teachers thought that it looked like unruly, poorly behaved Mexican kids.

She decided to teach them to stand in line so that they could have cultural capital. She told them to get in line and put their hands on the shoulders of the person in front of each of them. They dissolved into giggles as they tried to choke and tickle each other. Dawn took them to the basketball court and told them to walk on the line, where they tiptoed as if on a high wire. In the classroom they lined up sticks, rocks, blocks, pencils, and papers. Finally, they went outside to wait for the buses. "Forménse," she said. They immediately formed the best straight line. The other teachers began to smile approvingly.

When Dawn was in kindergarten, she had lots of cultural capital. She knew what was socially and culturally expected in the environment of school. She knew how to get into line, to keep her hands to herself, and to be quiet at certain times. She didn't always do it, but she knew. As a teacher, Dawn discovered that her students had little cultural capital, and they were blamed for it.

Dawn still struggles with this because she prefers the group hug.

Cultural capital is a process of powerful practices: ways of behaving, talking, acting, thinking, moving, and so on. These practices are determined unconsciously by the dominant culture and are used to promote success for specific groups in our society.

For example, in North American businesses and educational institutions, it is believed that we must speak in a very direct and concise manner to succeed. This manner of speaking is gender-specific and culturally laden; European American men like to speak this way, and they like others to speak this way. These high-status speech patterns carry value and carry men to the top. This linear-speak is valued by the power structures in North America, but this is not true in much of the world. Many cultural groups find that linear-speak provides a limited context, and they prefer to speak in a more enriched contextual frame. Much of the world (including some North American women) prefer to tell stories to make a point; they prefer to provide many perspectives and variables because they believe that listeners (readers) will generate meaning on the basis of their own lived experiences.

Often the nondominant culture buys into the dominant culture's way of thinking, supporting and encouraging it. For example, sometimes women and/or cultural minority groups still support more subtle forms of cultural capital. Their linear-speak is still bouncing around the offices. I recently had a very bright young businesswoman tell me that "you have to talk like men in order to get ahead." I am confident that there are many powerful and effective ways of speaking. The dominant society uses cultural capital to lure the nondominant groups into being like them. Nondominant people often are recruited for diversity, and then powerful dominant forces try to change their ways of knowing and being.

Sometimes cultural capital varies from region to region. It changes in various parts of the country. I remember an 80-plus-year-old man, Mr. Tom, talking to me about his brother. Mr. Tom lived on a ranch on the prairies and placed much value on all that ranchers know about cattle. His brother had recently retired from a brilliant career as a Boeing engineer, but Mr. Tom dismissed his brother's knowledge with one concise statement: "He doesn't know a damn thing about cows."

Critical teachers and learners struggle with ways of developing cultural capital with all. The work of August and Hakuta (1997); Garcia (1993); and Miramontes, Nadeau, Garcia, and Commins (1997) offer multiple ways of sharing cultural capital with all groups. After analyzing the data from thirty-three case studies, August and Hakuta (1997) identified the following factors as supporting cultural capital development:

A supportive school-wide climate, school leadership, a customized learning environment, articulation and coordination within and between schools, use of native language and culture in instruction, a balanced curriculum that includes both basic and higher-order skills, explicit skills instruction, opportunities for student-directed instruction, use of instructional strategies that enhance understanding, opportunities for practice, systematic student assessment, staff development, and home and parent involvement. (p. 171)

Dialectic

A *dialectic* is the tension between opposing thoughts, ideas, values, and beliefs. A dialectic is occurring as I write this chapter on definitions. I know that readers feel "Just tell me what it means," and I am feeling "Just discover what it means." This is a dialectic. I know that definitions can be very helpful along the unlearning curve, but I am terrified that someone will take them and memorize them. Please, please, please don't memorize these definitions. Please, please, please don't fall into the jargon pit. Definitions have value only if the reader sits, reads, reflects, connects, and muses on them.

Let me share with you another dialectic, which I live daily. I have many wonderful books. My books are my treasures and are personalized with family pictures, beautiful cards, pictures of authors, and cartoons which relate to the text. If you send me a card, I will tape it to the front of a book with a wide piece of transparent tape, and I will always think of you when I grab that book. The truth is that my books are really quite spectacular. I love them, and the students love them. I love to share them, and I hate to share them. Therefore I am in a constant dialectic—with myself. Every time I go to class, I try not to carry my books and tell about authors and ideas, but I am really quite helpless. I love my books so much that I can't help myself. I know that if I tell students about the books and ideas and authors, they will want to read my books. This is what I want and don't want. I want to share the books, and I hate to share the books. I don't want my books on my shelves, and I want my books on my shelves. Because so many grad students have families and major financial responsibilities, I try not to require texts, only to recommend. They can read my books. Of course, I do more damage than good, because they borrow and end up loving books too and eventually buy more books than I would ever require. Every year I am short a few books, which I don't really mind, because I feel that they probably have a good home and are being loved by someone else.

Paulo Freire talks about the dialectic of being "patiently impatient" (cited in Gadotti, 1994, p. 47). A dialectic involves seeing and articulating contradictions; it is the process of learning from the oppositional view. A dialectic brings to light a more comprehensive understanding of the multiple facets of the opposite. As we learn while teaching and teach while learning, we are in a dialectical process.

Dialogue

Dialogue is change-agent chatter. Dialogue is talk that changes us or our context. Dialogue is profound, wise, insightful conversation. Dialogue is two-way, interactive visiting. Dialogue involves periods of lots of noise as people share and lots of silence as people muse. Dialogue is communication that creates and recreates multiple understandings. It moves its participants along the learning curve to that uncomfortable place of relearning and unlearning. It can move people to wonderful new levels of knowledge; it can transform relations; it can change things.

"Dialogue is one of the most overlooked and undervalued educational tools we have at our disposal" (Ada & Campoy, 2003, p. 41). The work of Ada and Campoy demonstrates that dialogue is how we build on the strength of the students; it provides access to higher-order thinking skills; dialogue is the springboard to creative writing; and dialogue take the passivity away from reading and transforms it to engagement and inquiry.

Theresa worked with a student teacher in a high school classroom. Theresa was assisting the student teacher with a lesson, which included student dialogue. The homeroom or master teacher listened to this conversation and replied, "Well, I never thought of having the students talk about it."

Ada and Campoy (2003) use dialogue as a framework of teaching and learning with the creative dialogue, which grew from the creative reading method of Ada (1988a, 1988b, 1991). It has been my experience that any teacher in any context can draw on this framework to enhance critical teaching and learning. It very much is the hidden treasure that is always sitting on my shoulder as I teach.

The creative dialogue has four phases, which often proceed in the following manner but can take place in any order.

1. In the *descriptive phase,* the learners, be they readers or listeners, approach the text or dialogue and begin to understand the content, characters, setting, and plot and the author's intent. This is the phase, often the first, when the reader or listener begins to "get" the idea of the text. It is you sitting and reading this book for the first time. I hope that this will be only your initial understandings of critical pedagogy and that you will do more with it.

2. The *personal interpretive phase* takes place when the reader or listener brings her world to the text. When the reader and the words on the page join together on the basis of the personal experience of the reader, reactions can range from joy to anger, from affirmation to rejection. The personal interpretive phase takes place as you fit critical pedagogy into your experiential knowledge of teaching and learning. The reactions will vary.

3. The *critical/multicultural/antibias phase* refers to the extent to which the reader or listener critically reflects and sees the often subtle ethnocentric or gender-based biases hidden within text. For example in this book, much is written between the lines, basically to encourage critical reflection. Each reader will make this book what it needs to be in her own life.

4. In the *creative/transformative phase,* the learners take the new knowledge and/or insights and use them for self- and social transformation. When you read this book, the creative/transformative phase takes place when you turn the last page and close the book. At that point, the real work begins for you. What will you do in your own world?

Discourse

Remember when discourse was—well, what in the world was it? Perhaps we remember discourse as something that we studied with rhetoric in college. Was it something more serious and more important than a discussion? Interaction? Something that carried status and power and was somehow related to profound speeches?

It turns out that discourse is not just the use of words. Rather, it is the use of loaded words that establish who is on which rung of the ladder. And it turns out that there are lots of ladders, or discourses. Discourses reflect a certain place; they are all socially and culturally grounded. For example, I am not at home with the discourse of statistics; I can do statistics and talk it and think it, but the truth is, I am just not at home with that particular discourse. In fact, when I find myself in that place, I have been known to invent language to make meaning of that context. I have a friend, Debe, who thrives on the discourse of statistics; I think she talks funny, and she thinks I talk funny in that environment. We see and know in very different ways when it comes to the discourse of statistics. She is central to a group of my friends who love statistics; I am "the other." On that ladder, she is several rungs above me.

Today discourse can sound like dialogue, but in discourse, the words carry subtle (and not so subtle) messages about power. It seeks to establish the hidden rules for who speaks and who listens, what knowledge is good and bad, whose words have more power and whose words are marginalized.

As I reflect back to thirty years ago, it seems that the meaning has changed—yet another change. I remember my first conscious experience with discourse. I don't remember what it meant, but I remember the professor who taught the class. I remember his name, his class, his walk, his eyes. I remember the fear we felt in the class. I remember reading, writing, and entering into discourse in the class. I remember how passionately he felt about discourse; it mattered to him. As the semester and nervous stomachaches continued, I remember that I began to feel more confident, more important, more (dare I say it?) elite. I had status and privilege. I think the word *discourse* for him was more in line with rhetoric and even oratory. As I reflect on the unspoken feelings of that class, I can now see that even then, the messages that we received were filled with messages of power and lack of power. Through this vehicle of the discourse class, we were assigned status, power, and prestige. I was rewarded with an A for my conformity. I hope the meaning of discourse has changed!

The power of discourse, or disempowerment in this case, can be seen in the use of the word *limited*. To label any student *limited* is to limit how that student is institutionally perceived, how that student feels about her capabilities and potential, and how peers feel about that student. But to articulate the various levels of limitedness is to socially sort students' status, as can been seen in the following class filled with teachers:

> *The graduate class had several discussions about the hidden language we all use to produce and reproduce social status and power. We had focused on words such as*

LEP *(limited English proficient)*, LES *(limited English speaker)*, GATE *(gifted and talented education)*, challenged, disadvantaged, at risk, *and* minority. *We had recently learned of a school with a program for potential dropouts. After much discussion, we had agreed that to place a student in this program would send a negative message about our expectations for the student. The class had dialogued about the importance of critically reflecting on our own language; therefore, we were all a little surprised at the following discourse, which emerged unexpectedly in class.*

We were discussing how assessment of bilingual children often does not lead to programs that serve the needs of these students.

"But in our school, we even have two levels of ESL instruction. One section is for the high-limiteds, and the other class is for the low-limiteds," a graduate student proudly told us. "I teach the low-limiteds."

Silence hung in the room as we internalized the meaning of discourse.

Recently, a conversation with a friend and colleague provided an unexpected opportunity to reflect and act on the importance of discourse. As professionals, our language does make a difference, as seen in the following conversation. My colleague and I had been discussing the evaluation of a third colleague whose annual evaluation had not been successful.

JOAN: Do the written evaluations indicate that he has had any successful experiences with students?

T: Oh, yes, he does okay with normal students.

JOAN: With normal students? Who would that be?

T: Well, okay, I mean with regular students?

JOAN: With regular students? And who would that be?

T: Well, okay, what word do you want me to use?

JOAN: I don't know. Use an adjective. Who are you talking about?

T: Okay, I mean with Anglo, English-only students.

My colleague recognized the power of language. When one group was labeled *normal* and *regular*, other groups in our program immediately were marginalized. This is how the norm is normalized, the regular is regularized, the standard is standardized. And for professors to use this type of discourse, no matter how unintentional, is to lower the value of one group of students and to raise the value of another.

My family, friends, and I have been spending quite of bit of time on our ranch on the plains. This has provided many opportunities to think about being admitted to the discourse of the prairies. We immediately know when we are admitted membership and when we are denied membership. Dean, my husband, has gained entrance into the Prairie Club because he looks like the other members of the club. He wears the same clothes, knows about cows, and gives the same one-finger wave as he passes lone trucks on the highway. He is hardier than the average, friendlier than the average, and taller than the average. When he speaks with the Prairie

Club members, he uses the same quiet, reserved language that establishes credibility and respect. The Club affects him, and he affects the Club.

Some friends from California came to visit on the ranch in January. Although they are the antithesis of every California stereotype, it was clear that the locals resisted allowing them to join the discourse of the rural and isolated plains. I noticed that my neighbors, each with a twinkle in her eye, would periodically ask how our California friends were enjoying the Midwestern winter. It was clear that the hardy plains natives assumed that the California couple were suffering, which, in addition, provided a little entertainment for the charter members of the Prairie Club. Our California friends always responded simply and positively to questions about the cold weather, but it remained obvious that the Club members were reserving discourse membership for the natives.

On one particular day, it was 0 degrees, and the wind was blowing. The wind chill was probably 30 below, and the howl of the wind created a forlorn sound across the prairies. My friend Sharon went with us in the cattle truck to feed the cows. En route to feed, we stopped to visit with some neighbors in the small grocery store/post office, which is the heart and soul of the Prairie Club. As Sharon blew through the front door, all eyes were on her. The store owner said what the others were thinking: "Well, what do you think of this weather?"

"Sure is crisp," Sharon calmly responded, slowly drawing out the sound of each consonant. A moment of silence hung in the air as the Prairie Club members stared at her and mused on how to handle this most acceptable, stoic, and understated response. Finally, the store owner, a respected, high-status member of the ranch discourse community, said, "Yes, you are right. It sure is crisp."

With that brief discourse, Sharon was granted preliminary membership to this particular rural discourse community. If she had said, "Whoa, it's so cold! How do you people stand it?," the door to membership in the discourse of ranches would have slammed shut permanently.[2]

Hegemony

Hegemony is the domination of one group over another with the partial consent of the dominated group. It is the control of knowledge and literacy by the dominant group. In the following scene, a high school teacher shares with us how one type of cultural knowledge was affirmed and validated in her presence and another type of cultural knowledge was denigrated.

> *"Rap music and break dancing are not allowed at our school," Mr. Smith, the principal, announced as he stormed into my classroom. He grabbed B.J. by the ear, literally pulling him out of the class. I was not physically strong enough to prevent the principal from dragging B.J. out of class and down the hall. I turned my attention back to the other students. After they were settled and working on their assignments, I walked down to Mr. Smith's office to check on B.J.*

"B.J. has been suspended. He has broken our rules. Perhaps this will set an ex-
ample for the rest of the students that we set the rules, and when we do, we mean busi-
ness," Mr. Smith told me.

I just walked back to class shaking my head, but I couldn't help but reflect on
the fact that Mr. Smith's (elevator) music was playing in the office of this school,
which was located in the middle of the African American community in town.

To be completely true to a definition of hegemony, B.J. would partially have
to support Mr. Smith's action, even if B.J. did not recognize his own involvement in
the process. We could say that B.J. began to reject rap music in favor of elevator
music. The truth is, that didn't happen. However, B.J. did get very angry and is
now considered a problem in school.

Enriched programs can be used as a hegemonic tool to groom one group and
to marginalize and silence another. The following conversation between a school
secretary and a director of assessment took place in the front office of an elementary school:

"This is a request for an assessment for the gifted program," the secretary said to the
director of assessment.

"Really? Who for?" the director responded.

"José."

"A minority in Gifted? Those tests are in English. He doesn't know anything,"
the director said with a dismissive wave of her hand.

Hidden Curriculum

If we think of curriculum as the river running through (Apple, 1999), the hidden
curriculum is the dark undercurrent, dangerous and unseen, which can pull us
down before we even realize it.

The *hidden curriculum* is the unexpressed perpetuation of dominant culture
through institutional processes. McLaren (1998b) defines it as the pedagogical un-
said (p. 45). The hidden curriculum is covert and insidious, and only a critical lens
will bring it into view. It teaches what is assumed to be important. It defines the
standard for the dominant culture. Critical pedagogy asks: Whose standard?
Whose culture? Whose knowledge? Whose history? Whose language? Whose perspective? Critical pedagogy seeks to make pluralism plural: standards, cultures,
knowledges, histories, languages, perspectives. Society has a tendency to domesti-
cate students into believing the dominant view.

Sometimes, the hidden curriculum becomes such a part of the curriculum
that no one notices it. For example, Vicky teaches in the Northwest. She is located
in a very rural area that has a history populated by Native Americans, their culture,
their language, and their ways of knowing. When she started teaching the junior
high students, she noticed that the history of the local Native Americans was never
studied or even mentioned. The week before Thanksgiving, she asked a Native

American eighth grader what Thanksgiving was all about, and his response was "The white man taught the savages how to plant." The room, filled with European Americans and Native American students, nodded in agreement. Only Vicky, the teacher, realized the devastating nature of the hidden curriculum.

The hidden curriculum can been seen in schools when little boys are called on more than little girls, when only Eurocentric histories are taught, when teenage girls are socialized to believe that they are not good in math and sciences, when heroes but not heroines are taught, and when counselors track nonwhites to classes that prepare them to serve.

Literacies

Remember when literacy was reading and writing? Remember when we thought that it was simple? It turns out that we were wrong. Perhaps our traditional assumptions of literacy were not just simple but maybe even simplistic. The world has changed. Schools have changed. Students have changed. Now we are coming to know multiple types of literacies: *functional* (languages of the streets and of life), *academic* (languages of schools and universities), *workplace* (languages of our jobs), *information* (languages of technology), *constructive* (languages we construct with the printed word), *emergent* (languages constructed with the text before we are really decoding), *cultural* (language that reflects the perspective of one culture— guess which one), *critical* (languages that take us deeper into more complex understandings of the word and the world), and, finally, *literacies* as a new type of literacy that provides a foundation reflective of multiple experiences. Literacies are reading, writing, and reflecting. Literacies help us to make sense of our world and do something about it.

I should have known that literacy would be more complex than my traditional assumptions. I have watched many students develop (and not develop) their literacies in multiple ways. These kids have forced me to expand my understandings of literacy to be far more inclusive of all types of literacies.

All these literate processes have one common characteristic: They all are derived from social practices. Literacies are socially constructed, often with our friends, in specific contexts, for specific purposes. Literacies do not develop in isolation; rather, literate processes grow from families, from schools, from work, from cultures, from knowledges, from technologies, and so on.

If the new and more complex meanings of literacies begin to slip away from you, go back to the section on discourses and start again. It is a very similar concept. Debe was one to frolic in and relish every level, every facet, every dimension, every implication of the literacies of statistics. On the other hand, my literacy in that world could never have been considered plural; it was barely singular, which reflects my tiny understanding of statistics. Do not be fooled into thinking that the term *literacies* is just specific vocabulary for one particular context. It is not. It is the underlying ways of knowing, thinking, and making complex meanings. Each of us brings our own world when learning to read the word and reread the world. I thank Jim Cummins (1998) for reminding me of Moffett's critical definition of literacy:

> Literacy is dangerous and has always been so regarded. It naturally breaks down barriers of time, space, and culture. It threatens one's original identity by broadening it through vicarious experiencing and the incorporation of somebody else's hearth and ethos. So we feel profoundly ambiguous about literacy. Looking at it as a means of transmitting our culture to our children, we give it priority in education, but recognizing the threat of its backfiring we make it so tiresome and personally unrewarding that youngsters won't want to do it on their own, which is of course when it becomes dangerous. . . . The net effect of this ambivalence is to give literacy with one hand and take it back with the other, in keeping with our contradictory wish for youngsters to learn to think but only about what we already have in mind for them. (Moffett, 1989, p. 85)

Critical Literacy: Reading the Word and the World

Yes, *critical literacy* is reading and writing, but it is much, much more. Critical literacy involves knowing, lots of knowing. It also involves seeing, lots of seeing. It enables us to read the social practices of the world all too clearly. Critical literacy can push us into the zone of "all this learning really isn't so great." Critical literacy means that we understand how and why knowledge and power are constructed by whom and for whom.[3]

Critical literacy is linked with liberty (Tozer, Violas, & Senese, 2002). Critical literacy builds on the students' languages and provides them with the ability to be in control of all the words they need (Searle, 1998).

Reading the word means:

To decode/encode those words

To bring ourselves to those pages

To make meaning of those pages as they relate to our experiences, our possibilities, our cultures, and our knowledges

Reading the world means:

To decode/encode the people around us

To decode/encode the community that surrounds us

To decode/encode the visible and invisible messages of the world

Traditionally, literacy has been reading the word (to paraphrase Freire and Macedo's title), or decoding sounds and letters. Critical literacy is reading the world, or encoding the power structures and our role in these processes (Freire & Macedo, 1987). Critical literacy recognizes that reading does not take place in a vacuum; it includes the entire social, cultural, political, and historical context.[4] In what follows, I introduce you to a variety of people who have sadly read the world.

Many five-year-olds do this before they ever enter school. From TV, from their family, from trips to the store, they understand power. They read who speaks and who listens, where, when, and to whom.

> *Five-year-old José and his family nervously entered the school for the first time. They found the office and entered to begin the enrollment process. The secretary greeted them in English and handed them a packet of papers, all of which were written only in English.*
>
> *"Fill out these papers, please," she said to José and his family. As they looked nervously at the papers, Jane, the secretary, walked around the counter, took José by the hand, and walked out into the hallway. En route to a kindergarten class, she was joined by two teachers.*
>
> *"Whose class will he be in?" one of them asked.*
>
> *"Put him in Special Ed. He's from Mexico; he doesn't know anything," the other replied.*
>
> *Defeated and with his head down, José entered the classroom.*

José cannot yet read the word, but he has read the world very clearly. José started school the same day as Carmen, his teacher. Together, Carmen and José taught me many things, including the meaning of critical literacy. It was not long before José was engaged actively in reading and learning with Carmen in her classroom.

Orate and Literate Communities

We in North America put much faith in literate communities. We place high status on literacy, or reading and writing. Status and prestige are not assigned to those who are *illiterate*, a word that carries heavy connotations of *less*. *Illiteracy* has become a loaded, value-laden concept that is used to deny access to power. For example, when we say, "They are illiterate," we often mean much more than just not being able to decode. However, this is not true in much of the world (Skutnabb-Kangas, 1993). Many people in the world carry their knowledge in their heads and not on paper. Important people carry important knowledge in their heads. Instead of being literate communities, these are called *orate communities*.

The most vivid example of orate knowledge is a mariachi guitar player I knew. He carried the entire history of the Mexican revolution in his head, and he could sing and play it. After taking lessons from him, I learned the difference between orate and literate communities. I now have boxes and boxes of Mexican music with all the verses that I have transcribed from the tapes I made of him singing. These boxes are dusty and in my garage. His orate knowledge is still in his head and can be retrieved at a moment's notice.

So much of our knowledge serves us better when we carry it in our heads and not on paper. For example, when I am in the grocery store or on a plane and people ask me questions about education, multilingual education, or critical literacy, they don't want me to get out my papers, my books, and my transparencies and answer their questions. They just want me to tell them in plain language something that is understandable.

   If you are a teacher, there is a fun way to learn about orate and literate communities with your students. Start your class by explaining that for today, the time will be spent doing a big review of all that has been learned. Tell your students that they will need a blank piece of paper. Watch carefully what they do; they will immediately begin looking for papers with notes, for books, for old journals—anyplace where the knowledge is contained. Tell them, "No, no, no. Use your brain; just brains, no books, no notes, no charts, no index cards. Just brains." Just orate literacy. Begin your review with some leading questions of what has been studied. You and the students will learn together that much of our knowledge is not carried in our heads; it's in our books, and we only access it—we don't know it. I suspect there is a lot we could learn from orate people who are often referred to as *illiterates*.

Pedagogy

Pedagogy is the interaction between teaching and learning. I used to think that pedagogy was only about teaching: how I taught, what I taught, and why I taught it. I thought pedagogy was a vehicle by which I drove ideas into the heads of students. I thought that if I taught in the "right" way, my pedagogy would be "perfect," and obviously the students would learn "perfectly." At least that is what I thought until I starting teaching. You can well imagine my shock when I discovered that the students had more to teach me. Pedagogy is not just about me, teaching. Pedagogy is the process of teaching and learning together. It is fundamentally about human interactions,[5] the joy of playing with new ideas, and the challenge of integrating those ideas in the real world.

Praxis

These stories are my praxis. My theory and my practice have joined together in the creation of the stories in this book. The stories reflect practice in classrooms that is grounded in theory. The theory is to be discovered in the practice. The stories reflect how beliefs become behaviors in the classroom and how we can reflect on our beliefs by critically examining our behaviors. I am one of those teachers who focused only on practice for many years. I didn't even realize that in those years of teaching, I was building theory. It was only after I went back to graduate school that I discovered, to my great joy, that there were books about what my students had been teaching me for years. To this day, I see former students' faces when I read theory, talk about theory, and reflect on theory. I came to theory through practice. Some do it the other way around.

   Praxis is the constant reciprocity of our theory and our practice. Theory building and critical reflection inform our practice and our action, and our practice and action inform our theory building and critical reflection.

This semester, I am teaching a methods course that is designed to assist English-dominant teachers who are working in a multilingual context. We focus on methods, on practice, and on the how-to, even though that is hard for me. After years of practicing practice, my bias is now on theory. The *why* is more interesting to me than the *how*. However, this is a methods course, and we practice various methods. One night in class, I slipped a little why into the class. After class, a teacher was walking out and said to me, "A little theory never hurts." Yes, I thought, and a little practice never hurts. That is what praxis is: practice grounded in theory and theory grounded in practice.

Problem Posing

Problem posing is much more than just a method or a series of methods. Problem posing ignites praxis and leads to action. Problem posing brings interactive participation and critical inquiry into the existing curriculum and expands it to reflect the curriculum of the students' lives. The learning is not just grounded in the prepared syllabus, the established, prescribed curriculum. Problem posing opens the door to asking questions and seeking answers, not only of the visible curriculum, but also of the hidden curriculum. Problem posing is very interested in the hidden curriculum, which is why many are uncomfortable with it. Problem posing causes people to ask questions that many do not want to hear. For example, in the following description of a family meeting, there is problem solving, which brings about a feel-good sensation, and there is problem posing, which causes some to feel uncomfortable. Both problem solving and problem posing are occuring simultaneously with very different consequences. This family meeting took place in the school of Rainey and Carmen, whom you have previously met.

The problem to be solved was that parents had stopped coming to the family meetings. Families felt alienated, teachers blamed them for not attending, and the state agency was asking why families were not involved in the education of their children. The problem for the district was to get the families involved. They needed to solve this problem, or state funds would be cut. The school had a new principal who actively worked with Carmen, Rainey, and all the teachers to find ways to make the families feel more welcome and more involved. At this point, only Carmen was making visits to the students' homes. Soon, the principal started making visits with Carmen; eventually, she felt confident enough with her limited Spanish to make the visits alone. The families, of course, responded very positively. Other teachers began to visit the homes instead of sending messages home telling the parents to come to school. Soon, the teachers thought there was reason to believe that they could have a family meeting and the families would come. The first meeting was scheduled. Invitations were sent to the families in their language; a door prize was offered; and the children were prepared to share during part of the meeting, which was scheduled to be held in the school auditorium.

The parents arrived and sat in the back rows. The teachers arrived and sat in the front row. Three empty rows of auditorium seats separated the parents and the teachers. The parents were welcomed by one of the teachers, and the children performed. A guest speaker from the state agency spoke to the families about the importance of their involvement in the education of their children. Her presentation to the parents was articulate and forceful. She encouraged the parents to turn off the TV and talk with their children. She explained to the parents that what they teach at home is as valuable as what is taught in school. She followed this by talking about the transferal nature of language: What the kids know in Spanish, they will know in English too. I could see the parents nodding their heads in agreement. She encouraged the parents to ask questions, and not just who, what, and where, but also why.

The meeting lasted a little more than an hour. When it was over, the parents began to gather their tired children. Among the teachers in the first row, there was general agreement that the meeting had been a success. They had solved their problem. The families came.

Why did I seem to be the only one who was disappointed? Very little meaningful interaction had taken place between the parents and the teachers. No one had asked the parents how they felt, what they needed, what their concerns were. The entire evening had been a monologue; the families had been talked at. I had hoped for a dialogue.

However, not all problems are so easily solved. Sometimes, problem posing spins off of problem solving. As the teachers were smiling among themselves and the parents were beginning to gather their children, an older man, who looked more like a grandfather than a parent, stood up and faced the stage of the auditorium. Very seriously and respectfully, he asked all of those in the front of the auditorium, "¿Por qué enseña a los niños en una lengua que no entienden, y entonces los retienen?" ["Why do you teach our children in a language that they don't understand, and then flunk them?"]

Silence hung in the room. No one answered him. Everyone silently left the auditorium. This is problem posing, as opposed to problem solving. The man had questioned the established processes, which were obviously failing. The children were not learning, and the state agency wanted to know why. So did this man. This was a real problem, based on his lived experiences, which mattered to his family. He posed the problem, and many in the room came to understand that it is sometimes easier to solve problems than to pose problems.

To Groom

It all seemed so simple when all I had to worry about was teaching that *to groom* was an infinitive. Critical pedagogy enables us to think about what it means in the real world. For example, I was groomed to be a teacher, a secretary, or a nurse. No one ever specifically said that to me, but I received the message in multiple ways; I read my world. Very early, I understood that I didn't want to be a secretary or a nurse, so that left just one choice. I really never questioned it. And as I reflect on those who groomed me, I am sure that they were not aware of it, or they were doing what they thought was right for the time. My brother was never groomed to be a teacher, a secretary, or a nurse.

Grooming is preparing one group for a high-status place in life. Grooming is akin to putting one group on a superhighway and the other group on a rough and bumpy road. When the group on the highway arrives first, they assume that they got there because they deserved to, because they worked harder, because they are smarter. For my age group, it is particularly easy to understand grooming when we consider our own experiences. Little boys were groomed to be bosses; little girls were groomed to be secretaries. I think, as a society, we have developed more complex understandings of this process.

I literally had just written that sentence when an outraged Dawn, our daughter, called and read this article to me:

> Despite three decades of affirmative action, "glass ceilings" still keep black women and minority groups from the top management ranks of American industry, a bipartisan federal commission said Wednesday in the government's first comprehensive study of barriers to promotion. White men, while constituting about 43 percent of the work force, hold about 95 of every 100 senior management positions, defined as vice president and above, the report said.
>
> The Glass Ceiling Commission, which spent three years studying the issues, noted that 97 percent of senior managers in Fortune 1000 industrial corporations are white males, and only 5 percent of the top managers at Fortune 2000 industrial and service companies are women, virtually all of them white. Two-thirds of the overall population and 57 percent of the work force are female or minority, or both. ("Glass ceiling intact," 1995)

I guess I was wrong about us developing more complex understandings about boys being groomed to be bosses and girls being groomed to be assistants. What a waste of talent, what a waste of resources when only a small part of the population is allowed into positions of authority. I do not believe that 95–97 percent of the men are smarter and more productive; I do believe that they were groomed for these positions by hidden institutional and societal processes that we have failed to recognize.

Grooming still exists in overt and covert ways. Race, class, and gender are variables that determine your path: the superhighway or the dirt road. Those of us who have bumped into the "glass ceiling" have a moral mandate not to let others behind us have the same experience. Have you ever visited Washington, D.C.? It is frightening to see the grooming of white people to rule and the grooming of brown people to serve. It is a tragic contradiction of life that in the assumed center of democracy, it is so easy to see which race has been placed on the superhighway and which race has been placed on the bumpy dirt road.

Sometimes, these processes of grooming are an inherent part of specific lesson designs. For example, in the following activity, who is being groomed?

"Around the World" is a great name for a not-so-great math activity. The overt objective is for students to have an opportunity to practice a skill or to memorize a fact. The objective in this particular class was to review addition by using flashcards. The real objective was to win. This is what happened on the day that I watched this activity.

> Rainey, the teacher, sat on a chair in front of the room; the children were seated at four groups of tables. Two children stood up, and Rainey held up a flashcard with an addition problem. The child who said the correct answer first, as determined by Rainey, was the winner. Then that child would move on to compete with the next child. The loser sat down. I studied the individual faces as they won and lost, stood up and sat down. The winners received cheers and applause from their peers and moved on for more practice. The losers sat down and did not get to practice. Thus, the ones who needed less received more, and the ones who needed more received less.
>
> Despite my apprehension about this, the activity appeared to be a resounding success. All the children were squealing with glee. The principal passed the door and glanced in with an approving look on his face. The lesson certainly appeared to be student centered and very interactive, not to mention fun. However, the primary focus of the activity was on the winning, not learning. Several students in particular caught my eye.
>
> First, I noticed Irma, the cheerleader, who was a consistent loser. Each time someone said the numbers faster than she did, she had to sit down. She must be an amazingly resilient child because, each time after she sat down with a very dejected look on her face, she would quietly stare at the floor for about two minutes and then begin cheering wildly for the others again. I still do not know whether Irma can add, but I'm not sure that it mattered in this activity.
>
> The second child who caught my eye was Rosio, the loser who can add. Now how could this happen? At the beginning of the game, I did not know Rosio, her math abilities, or her level of fluency in English. But I did notice that throughout the game, she was very quiet and still. When it came her turn to stand, she did so slowly and always was immediately forced to sit down because she didn't say anything. It appeared that she could not add, but later I learned that she could add very well.
>
> When the math activity ended, I asked Rainey whether I could take Rosio to a little table and work with her. We began in Spanish, and Rosio communicated very little with me. I asked if she knew English, and she said yes. I asked her if she wanted me to use English or Spanish. She immediately replied, "English." Rosio answered 80 percent of the addition problems correctly. When she had trouble, she would count the beans we had on the table, and then she had 100 percent accuracy. Why then didn't she win some of the rounds of competition? Rosio is a very quiet and shy girl. She thinks carefully before answering.

This activity was designed to reward those who think and speak quickly and loudly; it also grooms those who know and eliminates those who need to know (Wink, 1991). Despite its great name, this activity benefits those who least need it. Those with the most get the most. Those who need this type of structured practice stay in their seats. Sometimes these classroom activities are even more subtle but just as deadly, because you have to be able to cut through sentimentality to understand the dynamics of power that are being constructed for one person or one group.

To Name

To name is to call an *ism* an *ism:* racism, classism, sexism. Naming is talking about the corruptible colonization, the damnable domination, the insidious supremacy that many marginalized groups have experienced, but have been conditioned not to mention. The A Team gets huffy when they hear the B Team name. The A Team responds with sentences that begin with "Yeah, but. . . ." Naming is talking honestly and openly about one's experiences with power and without power.

Naming is more than just articulating a thought; it is more than just talking and labeling. Naming occurs when we articulate a thought that traditionally has not been discussed by the minority group or the majority group. Naming takes place when the nondominant group tells the dominant group exactly what the nondominant group thinks and feels about specific social practices. To name is to take apart the complex relationships of "more" and "less" between the two groups. For example, when little girls tell little boys (or when women tell men) that they hate the "glass ceiling," they are naming. When women say that they hate it that men, 43 percent of the workforce, hold 95 percent of the senior managerial positions ("Glass Ceiling Intact," 1995), they are naming. And when ethnic minorities say that they hate it that the remaining 5 percent of those managers are women, and only white women, they are naming. When African Americans say that they hate it when blacks in public sector jobs earn 83.3 percent of the median income of whites (Bancroft, 1995), they are naming.

A friend, Verena, who lives in one of the northern states, wrote me a long letter about a school at which she had found a job. She had discovered terrible racist policies that were hurting the Native American and African American students. Because she desperately needed this job, she was upset about what to do. She wrote, "I have to make a choice to teach and play the game, or expose what is going on. If I do that, I am sure that I will eventually lose my job." If Verena decides to expose the racist policies, she will be naming. And if she doesn't, it will be because she has a fear of naming.

When I went to college, I pretended that I couldn't type, although I was very good at it. I didn't want to end up typing (as a secretary) for a man (as a boss). At that time, I didn't have the language to articulate and name the gender-specific role that I could easily see might be assigned. And even if I had had the thought and the language to be able to talk about why women shouldn't type for bosses, I would never have done it. Even if I could have named, I would have been afraid to name. I still struggle with this, but I am improving. We must have courage and patience.

To Marginalize

To marginalize is to place someone or something on the fringes, on the margins of power. To be marginalized is to be made to feel less. Sometimes teachers marginalize specific groups of students. Remember when I told you about my colleague who labeled some students *normal* and *regular*? That is marginalizing. What group has been devalued in the following phone conversation?

> **TEACHER 1:**   Hi. This is Amy Jones. I understand that you are going to be my substitute tomorrow. I didn't leave any special plans. I want to tell you a little about my class and what you'll be doing tomorrow.
>
> **TEACHER 2:**   Great! I'm glad you called.
>
> **TEACHER 1:**   My room is way in the back of the school, Room 42. It's a sheltered English class. They are third, fourth, and fifth graders. Several languages are represented in this group.
>
> **TEACHER 2:**   Oh, I remember your class. I substituted in Room 43 yesterday, which is the special education class. I brought one of the students to your room so he could paint with your class. You may remember me.
>
> **TEACHER 1:**   Sure, I remember you. But listen, my kids are great. They are normal. They aren't stupid or crazy like those kids next door.

Certain trigger words often give you a hint that marginalizing is coming—words like *normal, regular, those people,* and *them.* When you hear these words, you can almost be assured that someone is going to be marginalized.

In another context, a secondary teacher was struggling to understand *marginalized.* Finally, her face lit up as she was able to connect that word on the page with her own school. "Oh, I get it. Marginalization is when only the GATES and IB (International Baccalaureate) students get to have a textbook at home and a class set at school. Every year the administration promises us that we will have a class set of books and another copy for the students to keep at home, but so far it has not happened."

In the following statement that a teacher made to me during a staff development day, can you see which group has been marginalized?

> **TEACHER:**   Give me one of those Asians with glasses any day before a Mexican!

Schooling, or to School

Schooling refers to the hidden educational processes by which schools impose the dominant ways of knowing on all. We have been schooled to think in traditional ways. One problem with this is that we now often have schools filled with traditional teachers and nontraditional students.

For example, I have mentioned that I was schooled to write in a traditional way; it was linear, dense, distant, neutral, and boring—none of which I am. I wrote in academese; I hid behind my jargon. As I reflect on my old writing, I can see more and more of my male professors in every sentence. My old writing reflects them very well. My writing of today reflects me. It is everything I was schooled not to do: tell stories, be circular, be passionate, use real language. More than anything else, I was schooled to believe that I was writing for someone else; it had never entered my head to write for me, to write to make sense of my thoughts.

I must not be the only one who had this experience. My grad students initially think that they are writing for a grade in the grade book. They want to know exactly what I want; they want to know how many pages. I just want them to write and make meaning of ideas that are bouncing around in their heads. I want them to write and to get smarter. I will respond as I come along for the cognitive ride. Who knows what we will learn, but we will learn. Recently, I was reading Sandy's journal. Sandy is a young grandmother who is back in college.

I have been *schooled* to believe that my thoughts did not matter. For example, I have been *schooled* to believe that I should not share a thought unless I could cite the authority. I am learning now that my thoughts matter. This is so new that it can be scary. Being asked to think for myself and then commit it to paper is a challenge: It flies in the face of everything I have ever been conditioned to do. Schooling is alive and well in me.[6]

To Silence

I struggle with silence. Men can silence me more than any other group. The old socialized patterns run so deeply that it is hard for me to break them even when I understand and can articulate the dynamic. Breaking the old domesticated patterns of silence is still a struggle. However, now I *see* silencing. Previously, when I was silenced, I did not know it; I did not understand it; I did not recognize it. In fact, I bought into it and supported it with my behaviors. When I was silenced, I cooperated and perpetuated the process. Now when I am silenced, I understand what is happening. Now I can name it. However, I still struggle with my fear of naming. Sometimes, when I am in university committee meetings filled with full professors, I am painfully aware that the insidious dynamic of silencing is controlling the agenda; I am painfully aware of my own fear of naming. The invisible agenda of who speaks and who listens often takes my mind from the visible agenda.

I am always aware of the delicate balance between courage and patience as we move critically together toward a more democratic society. In my own context, I have noticed that (a) most full professors are men; (b) some are aware that they are silencing others, and others are not aware; (c) the few full professors who are women do not silence me. I know that this tells a lot about my sociocultural context and about me. (I told you early in this book that I don't always like learning—for example, right now.) However, my experiences have taught me that this social dynamic of silencing plays out every day in all contexts. Sometimes we just don't see it. I guess my message is that we should see silencing and stop silencing.

I watch in amazement in my grad classes when certain students speak freely, but I am particularly aware of those who are still silenced. They feel as deeply;

they know as much. I watch which individuals are silenced by others. I watch which groups are silenced by other groups and have noticed that silencing has a certain pattern:

> Often,
> those who have more, silence those who have less;
> those who are from the dominant European American culture silence
> those from non-European American cultures;
> boys silence girls;
> men silence women.

> Often,
> men don't know it;
> boys don't know it;
> European Americans don't know it, and
> those with more don't know it.

Silencing is usually a quiet and insidious process. Sometimes those who are being silenced know it, and sometimes they don't. Those who are doing the silencing rarely know it.

Responses to the previous editions of this book demonstrate clearly that there were two places in this book that triggered the most reactions. This is one of those pages. The reactions I have received clearly run along gender lines. I simply could not tell you the number of people who have challenged this page. And I simply could not tell you the number of people who have said, "They do too know it." Multiple perspectives, the voice of the other, naming, power: These are all inherent in the concept of silencing. I think that is why it triggers such strong and opposite reactions. The other page in the book that always triggers a reaction is the metaphor of an A Team and a B Team.

If at this moment you are experiencing strong negative or positive reactions, this is an example of "otherness out loud," in which a narrative facilitates an awakening of the consciousness (Romo, Bradfield-Krelder, & Serrano, 2004). We can be silenced by others, and we can also self-censor and self-silence, which is equally harmful. I have also been guilty of that. To give me courage with this internal battle, these words are never far from me:

> *You must do the thing you think you cannot do.*
> —ELEANOR ROOSEVELT

To Socialize

Society sends many messages to each of us. Sometimes we hear those messages, and sometimes we don't. However, when we consciously or unconsciously accept those messages and live those messages, we are being socialized.

This took place in a fourth grade classroom when the teacher announced that the students would clean out their desks on Friday. Throughout the week, the students waited patiently for the Great Cleaning Day. When Friday finally came, papers, books, and giggles filled the room—except for one boy, who did not take part. This boy comes from a culture that believes that boys do not clean; girls and women clean. His mother came after school to clean his desk because this was work not befitting a young man.

This example is quite vivid and easy to see. Many times, we do not recognize, see, or understand the hidden socializing that is taking place. For example, from the point of view of this little boy and his mother, he is not being socialized; it is just the way things are. From the point of view of the teacher who told the story, it was an outrage. It is not really so different from the way I was socialized as a child. I cleaned; my brother did not.

Another example of socializing happened to us when we had an exchange student from Mexico. Laura was from Mexico City and came from a very enriched background that included ideas, books, laughter, love, and lots of money. Her family had many servants to make life easier. She left the urban confines of Mexico City and came to the desert ranch to live with us.

Suddenly, we realized that she had never done any of the indoor or outdoor chores that we had socialized Dawn and Bo to believe were part of everyone's responsibility. Washing and ironing clothes presented a particularly sensitive area. Bo and Dawn were in junior high and high school, respectively, and had been doing this for themselves for years. Dawn, as a grade school feminist, was quick to make sure that if she did her own clothes, her little brother sure would do his. So Bo grew up believing that if I washed his treasured T-shirts (a.k.a. rags) and jeans, they would be ruined with hot water or a hot drier. I socialized him to believe that only *he* could take care of *his* clothes. So now, suddenly, both of our kids were very eager to see whether I would wash and iron Laura's clothes. They understood my vulnerable position as it related to justice, equity, and culture, and they relished every minute of my dilemma. After reflection, I realized that I couldn't undo all of my socializing of my own kids and that Laura would have to learn to wash and iron her own clothes. I can still remember all three of the kids standing in the washroom while Bo and Dawn smugly taught Laura how to wash. Laura did all of her own washing; she never did iron, but then neither did Dawn and Bo. Laura is back in Mexico City now and no longer washes her own clothes. She is now socializing others to believe that it is their job.

Voice

Walk into any classroom, any teachers' lounge, any school office and see whether you can tell who has voice. Who uses voice to express their perspective? Their viewpoint? Their way of knowing? Whose voice is promoted and valued? Whose voice is discredited with a wave of the hand? Courage is related to voice; it takes courage for some to express their voice. *Voice* is the use of language to paint a picture of one's reality, one's experiences, one's world. I am more interested in the voice that traditionally has not been heard.

The voice of those who traditionally have not been heard is usually embedded with varying degrees of resistance, rage, and a hint of resolve. I vividly recall standing as a little girl in a rural, isolated spot where the gas station/general store was the hub of the community for many, many miles. I remember the two out-houses behind the store. One had an old sign that said "Whites only," and the other had an old sign that said "Indians." I remember looking at the signs and knowing something was terribly wrong, but I said nothing. I had no voice. I remember being asked to carry moldy bread onto the Sioux Indian reservation to the various families. I can still feel the shame I felt handing the bread to the women who answered their doors. But I would never have dreamed of expressing myself. I had no voice. My resistance, rage, and resolve were silenced. Most of my life has been dominated by the voice of one powerful group. This *monovoice* has been very limiting for many. As we near the end of the century, more and more voices are being heard. Multiple voices are moving us forward. The broader the diversity of voices, the better the quality of society. Our society is becoming more vibrant, more enriched, and more exciting. It represents more of us. This traditional monovoice is transforming itself into a new *multivoice,* and not everyone is happy about it.

The following voice comes from Sheila, who is discovering hers as she prepares to be a teacher:

> *I wonder how much voice I will have when I'm teaching. I have recently left a career in management to become a teacher. During my years in management, I became one of the top employees where I worked: top in responsibility, not in authority. It seemed to me that the "voices" of women were not valued because the system was "just fine."*
>
> *The majority of teachers are women, but their voices are just whispers. Women and minorities need to be at the top levels of school systems, and we need more men at the elementary teaching level.*
>
> *Cummins (1989) said, "Unless we ourselves are empowered, we cannot be involved with any other processes of empowerment. To be voiceless is to be powerless. If we view ourselves as helpless, we are." I thought that it must be easy for him to say. He is a man, not teaching in the elementary school with others holding his future in the palm of their hands.*

Critical pedagogy has helped me to understand what teaching should be about: encouraging teachers to be complete professionals, intellectuals, and, above all, people who own their own experience and humanness.

As Sheila is discovering her voice, she is "voicing" one of the most difficult questions of the study of critical pedagogy: Why so few women? Why so many men? Critical pedagogy has caused me to reflect seriously on the moral mandate that falls to those of us (women and minorities) who have survived a career of trying to change the system. My experience teaches me that many women see and know in critical ways and are moving to voice. I note with interest that we are in good company when we move into relearning and unlearning. In a dialogue, Donaldo Macedo is asking Paulo Freire how he would respond to his omission of the voice of women in his earlier works. Freire responds by saying, "I believe that the question feminists in the United States raise concerning my treatment of gender in *Pedagogy of the Oppressed* is not only valid but very timely" (Macedo, 1994, p. 106).

The purpose of this chapter has been to focus on one central question: What in the world is critical pedagogy? My intention has been for you to discover meaning based on your own experiences and knowledges. My purpose has not been to provide a list of definitions for you. However, on the very day on which I was finishing this chapter, I found the following paper among a large stack of graduate students' work on my desk. This piece of paper was from a student and was entitled "Scribble Notes." The first paragraph seemed like a powerful definition of critical pedagogy for those who would like to have it. As I say, sometimes these definitions just fall from heaven. Lily, a teacher, wrote:

Critical pedagogy is a process of learning and relearning. It entails a sometimes painful reexamination of old practices and established beliefs of educational institutions and behaviors. Critical pedagogy causes one to make inquiries about equality and justice. Sometimes these inequalities are subtle and covert. The process requires courage and patience. Courage promotes change and democracy provides all learners equal access to power.

What in the world do you think critical pedagogy is? It is certainly more than is written in this chapter, and it is as much as we allow it to be in our own ways, in our own communities. Critical pedagogy is more than the sum of its parts; it is more than a list of definitions of the words that have come to be associated with it. Lily, wisely, did not fall into the trap of seeing only the separate words of critical pedagogy. She put it together holistically after much reading and reflection. She made meaning of all the parts on the basis of her experiences in life and in schools. Critical pedagogy is a process that enables teachers and learners to join together in asking fundamental questions about knowledge, justice, and equity in their own classroom, school, family, and community.

In this chapter, the language of critical pedagogy has been seen in real classroom experiences with the hope that it will help readers to generate and expand their own meanings for critical pedagogy. In the next chapter, I will share my understandings of critical pedagogy and tell you how I came to know in this way.

Looking Ahead for Your Thoughts and Language on Critical Pedagogy

What are your own words and ideas?

Practicing Pedagogy Patiently

In this chapter, we looked at the language of critical pedagogy, word by word. In what follows are activities to do with students when they are encountering new and challenging language. For each of the following two activities, you have two guidelines: The more words, the better. The more difficult the words, the better.

New Words, New Friends

First, begin with new language, which is daunting for the learners. If you are doing this as a prereading activity, choose words from a specific reading assignment, which they will be assigned later. If you are using this activity following an independent reading activity, ask the students to choose the words they do not know. The bottom line is that you need a group of words that students do not understand.

Second, pass out "New Words, New Friends" (Figure 3.1) to each student. Ask the students individually and privately to place all of the new words in the column to the left and fill in the "Before Reading" column with A, B, C, or D.

FIGURE 3.1
New words, new friends

	New Words	Before Reading	After Reading	After Talking with New Friends
1.				
2.				

A—Not a Clue

B—Only a vague hunch

C—Knew it but couldn't explain it

D—Knew it and could explain it

Learning new words with new friends

Word	My Guess Is . . .	Context Clues	Dictionary Definition	My Friends Say . . .

Third, assign the reading assignment, which includes these new words. After reading individually, each student is to fill out the next column, "After Reading," on the chart. In class, do all of the reading activities you would normally do. At the end of the entire assignment, whether it has taken an hour, a day, or a week, ask the students to fill out the final column, "After Talking with Friends."

Many students will see that their letters on "New Words, New Friends" moves from A to D instead of the opposite. Students have told me that this helps to debunk the weighty connotations of A, B, C, and D grades—not to mention that students generate real knowledge of new language and possibly even make some new friends.

Post-it Patterns

This is another activity which can be used for prereading, post–independent reading assignment, and vocabularly or spelling list activities (see Figure 3.2). The following activities work well with the most esoteric and abstract words, and it works well with at least fifteen words at one time; more is better.

First, place the students in small heterogeneous groups. For this particular process, I always place students who do not know each other well together, thereby

FIGURE 3.2   **Post-it patterns**

Post-it Patterns

Purpose

The purpose of this activity is for students to generate knowledge of new language in a specific reading assignment. This prereading activity works well with "New Words, New Friends."

Preparation

1. The instructor will provide Post-it Notes, index cards, or small pieces of paper; using three or four different colors enhances the activity but is not necessary. If using index cards, change the name to Card Categories. If using papers, change the name to Paper Patterns.
2. Choose the challenging words from a specific reading assignment. Write the words on the chalkboard.

Procedures

1. Seat the students together heterogeneously at a table. Pushing desktops together will also work.
2. Students write words on Post-it Notes, one word per Post-it.
3. Students together create a pattern with all of their Post-it Notes and words. The patterns are to demonstrate the linkages and relationships between and among the words. Students are encouraged to talk with their teammates about the meanings of the words.
4. Each small group eventually shares with the whole group the rationale for the pattern they created with the Post-it Notes.

demonstrating that we can also make new friends as we learn new words. Try it. Yes, I do this with adults, and they do come to know and respect more of their colleagues in class. Each small group needs to be at a small table or have their desks shoved together to make a smooth working surface. Give each group several colors of small Post-it Notes. As a group, they are to write a word on a little Post-it Note. When each new word has been written on a Post-it, simply tell them to talk about the words, guess their meanings, and make a pattern of the Post-it Notes. They can use shapes and color to demonstrate the rationale for the pattern of Post-its. Leave the students alone, and let them talk about the words. You will be amazed at the different patterns that will begin to emerge on the tabletops. Next have each small group explain their pattern and the rationale for the pattern to the whole group.

I have done these two activities in conjunction many times with groups of learners who are new to the language of critical pedagogy. It can be noisy, fun, and productive. Not only will the patterns be surprising, but also students will generate a lot of knowledge about the language of critical pedagogy.

NOTES

1. For definitions of the language of critical pedagogy, I refer to the books that are surrounding my computer chair at this very moment: (a) several by McLaren; any of his three editions of *Life in Schools: An Introduction to Critical Pedagogy in the Foundations of Education*; (b) Giroux (1988); (c) Harris and Hodges (1995); (d) Kanpol (1994); (e) Leistyna, Woodrum, and Sherblom (1996); and (f) Darder, Baltodano, and Torres (2003), an edited book, which has several good overviews of the language. The truth is that there are marvelous definitions in these various books. I love some of them. I strongly encourage you to reflect on others' definitions. As you do, you will notice that the definition of critical pedagogy varies with each person, each page, and each book. How could it not? Experience is inherent in critical pedagogy. These books and others to which I refer throughout this text will provide definitions that move you to other levels of complexities of understandings. Remember, one of my not-so-hidden goals in this book is to lead you to other books. Perhaps you might like to start with the glossary in the back of deMarrais and LeCompte (1999).

2. Gee (1992, 1996) provides very thorough and meaningful perspectives on discourse in these two books. His image of discourse as an identity kit is helpful for many who are struggling with this concept. In addition, he weaves tight connections between discourses and literacies. In fact, I would suggest you read Gee (1990 and 1992) and McQuillan (1998b) at the same time; they are guaranteed to make you think more critically about literacy.

3. If you are intrigued with the concept of critical literacies, I strongly recommend that you read Lankshear and McLaren (1993), Macedo (1994), Freire and Macedo (1987), and Edelsky (1991), Kellner (2000), the entire issue of *Language Arts (79)*5, 2002, and Darder et al. (2003). The topic of critical literacies is just too deep and too wide for the confines of this little book.

4. An example of this is Jeff McQuillan (1998b), who uses his own critical literacy to deconstruct the popular notion of a literacy crisis. In addition, he demonstrates how this notion makes it easier for us to ignore the serious pedagogical hurdles that students face in their literacy development. This book may very well be an unlearning experience for some readers. Remember, this is good.

5. Cummins (1996 and 2001) says that human relationships are at the heart of school (p. 1). He then expands the concept to demonstrate how these relationships that we teachers establish have the power to open the door for students to grow and develop freely or to wither and fade painfully.

6. Parker Palmer (1998, p. 18) tells a wonderful anecdote about assigning an autobiographical essay. One student asked whether it would be okay to use "I" or whether that would knock off half a grade point. In fact, Palmer never mentions critical pedagogy, but his ideas extend this discussion to a broader context of humanness, justice, equity, and morality grounded in critical pedagogy.

4 What in the World Do I Think It Is?

"You need only claim the events of your life to make yourself yours. When you truly possess all you have been and done . . . you are fierce with reality."
—FLORIDA SCOTT-MAXWELL *(1983, p. 82), an octogenarian*

In Chapter 3, I asked you to define critical pedagogy. The purpose of this chapter is to tell what I think critical pedagogy is and to tell how I came to this understanding. We are not alone in our struggle to understand critical pedagogy. Weiler (1988) writes of a *struggle for a critical pedagogy*; Greene (2003) writes of the *search for a critical pedagogy*. Experience, reflection, honesty, action: These are all part of critical pedagogy. I take courage from Scott-Maxwell as I share the experience of a student-led discussion of what I mean by critical pedagogy.

"What does she mean by *critical*?" Elizabeth asked her colleagues of international education as she began to share her learning after her first encounter with a previous edition of *Critical Pedagogy: Notes from the Real World*. Elizabeth and I, both midway through life, had lived vastly different experiences. However, we had more in common: a love of learning, life, family, and friends.

"Does she mean critical thinking? A critical essay? A critical person? A critical moment? In critical condition?" she said with a twinkle in her eye, as she quickly wrote each of the concepts on the chalkboard in a vertical line. I sat as quietly as I could, trying hard not to react to each comment. We were all a bit nervous, and Elizabeth was in an awkward situation as she began to share her reflections on my book. In addition, Elizabeth, thus far in class, had appeared very quiet and even shy. It was early in the semester, and the students, all experienced teachers, did not have a sense of who Elizabeth was. Already, they began to rethink their assumptions: Elizabeth might be shy, but she is also courageous.

Elizabeth continued trying to understand my use of *critical*. She systematically eliminated each of her initial hypotheses, drawing a red line through each as she did so.

"Critical as in *critical thinking,* as in careful evaluation?" she said. She stopped and stared at her writing on the chalkboard as she reflected with the rest of the class. Finally, she rejected that meaning and drew a line through *critical thinking.*

"Critical as in *critical essay,* as in of or relating to criticism?" She drew a second line through *critical essay,* indicating her rejection of that meaning also.

"Critical, as in a *critical person,* as in one who is inclined to judge severely?" she questioned and finally crossed it out on the chalkboard.

"Critical, as in a *critical moment,* as in something significantly important? Nope." Another line streaked across the board.

"Critical, as in a *critical element,* something crucial or essential?" she questioned before eliminating that also.

"Critical, as in *critical condition,* as in a crisis," she said with an inflected certainty, which indicated that she had found her answer.

The class warmed to her subtle form of humor and sat spellbound as the quiet student gently prodded the instructor to be more clear in her writing. I squirmed.

"Initially, I was sure that she must have meant the first, *critical thinking,* or something which is marked by careful evaluation. However, at the end of the book, I thought, "Holy cow, she means the last one, *critical condition,* as in a crisis."

Yes, Elizabeth, I do think that education is in critical condition. I would like to see more democratic processes. I would like to see teachers, students, and families be more in control and be mandated less. I would like to see more books and fewer worksheets. I would like to see more for kids who have less. I would like to see less time testing and more time learning. I would like to see less teacher and student bashing in the daily papers. I would like to see the longitudinal body of educational research read, respected, and implemented. I would like to separate ideology from research. I would like to see people in schools run schools and people in business run businesses. I would like to see less blurring of the lines between the federal government and big business, particularly as each relates to schools. Actually, Elizabeth, I dream of setting up accountability tests for people in business and the federal government; first I could create the tests, sell the tests, score the tests, and, finally, report the scores in the newspaper. In addition, if they did not do well on my standardized test, I like to imagine taking money from them as a punitive measure and giving it to schools. In my wild and crazy dreams, I would give it to the schools that really need it. For example, in a school near me this spring, maggots were falling from the ceiling onto the kids' heads and desks. As you can guess, Elizabeth, this school is in a very impoverished neighborhood, and the school will soon be even more impoverished, as money will be taken from them because the kids did not score well enough on the new standardized test. Incidentally, maggots did drop on a stack of the tests too.

Kuhn (1970) posits that the paradigm will shift when we are close enough to the edge of a crisis and when there is enough critical mass insisting on change. Surely, Elizabeth, we must be close to that point, even if you count only the people I know who want this change. However, more than anything, your presentation with your colleagues tells me that I need to clarify just exactly what I mean by some of the language of critical pedagogy.

So What Is Critical Pedagogy?

In Chapter 3, I challenged you to understand critical pedagogy and the language that surrounds it on the basis of your own lived experiences. Now I share some definitions, followed by how I came to these understandings. Instead of embedding definitions throughout the narrative, as I did in previous editions, here I will simply write my understandings of critical pedagogy, although they are still embedded throughout the text. I am indebted to several readers and graduate students who, as a form of academic sport apparently, have generated lists of embedded definitions from previous editions and shared the lists with me. Thanks to each of you, particularly to Shahin.

Let's begin with pedagogy, which is the interaction between teaching and learning. Critical pedagogy means that we see and articulate the entire critical context of teaching and learning. We are not afraid to say what we see, and we move to take action. Critical pedagogy is teaching and learning that transforms us and our world for the better. Critical pedagogy gives us the courage to say what we have lived. Critical pedagogy challenges us to question our long-held assumptions.

Critical pedagogy is learning, relearning, and unlearning. It often involves rethinking our histories and rewriting our world. The notion of learning-relearning-unlearning has had different meanings through the years. Relearning can be uncomfortable at first, but eventually, it becomes doable. For example, most of us have to relearn a lot of pedagogy while we teach. We think we understand pedagogy (teaching/learning) when we begin teaching, but we come to understand that *teaching is learning*. Unlearning, however, is something very different from relearning. It is fundamentally more painful. It involves a complete reexamination of philosophy, beliefs, and assumptions. It means that we each must look seriously within, never a simple task. Unlearning calls us to critical reflection. Unlearning is jumping across the great paradigm. Unlearning took place for me when I moved from behaviorism to transformational teaching and learning. It took decades, and not every moment was wonderful. Unlearning means that we unpack and begin to learn and relearn again: the great cycle of pedagogy.

Critical pedagogy encourages us to find the magic of personal discovery based on our own lived experiences. Cummins (2001) and Ada (2003) each describe critical pedagogy as transformational education. Freire and Macedo (1987) describes critical pedagogy as a process that challenges us to name, to reflect critically, and to act. These definitions can be very helpful as you begin to build your own understandings.

I came to critical pedagogy student by student, word by word, book by book, and person by person. I slowly built my own internal glossary; certainly, McLaren and Giroux were the first to challenge my language—and thus my thoughts—as I struggled to understand their definitions. Now the search for meaningful definitions is instantly facilitated by the use of a good search engine on the Internet. For example, simply type in "critical pedagogy," and more resources with definitions than you can possibly use will emerge. Glossaries can be good, too; try www.glossarist .com and/or www.questia.com.

Defining critical pedagogy is not easy; however, living it is harder. I see critical pedagogy through the lens of Paulo Freire (Friere & Macedo, 1987, p. 157), who describes it as a radical pedagogy that makes concrete the values of solidarity, social responsibility, creativity, and discipline in the service of the common good and critical spirit.

How I Came to These Understandings of Critical Pedagogy

It was a long journey, but basically, I came to critical pedagogy through former students and teachers. My tendency to define critical pedagogy through real people is because that is how I lived it. The Benson kids played a major role, as do the students and teachers I work with today. The path was not direct: first Spanish, then bilingual education, then critical pedagogy.

I grew up in an English-only world on the prairies. When I was a senior in high school, I took my first Spanish class with Mrs. Johnson. I remember entering the class and feeling embarrassed and chagrined, as all of the other students in the class were sophomores; however, when Mrs. Johnson entered the room and started speaking Spanish, I knew at that moment what I would do when I grew up: anything with Spanish. I have never wavered. The saying "We never know when we are making a memory" became real for me at that moment. I went on to be a high school Spanish teacher, and Spanish has been central to all of my professional work. I had no idea that this would eventually lead me to write a book on critical pedagogy. However, when you love languages as I do, you eventually begin to see that languages are not just about diagramming sentences; you soon come to a point at which you realize that languages are really about power.

My Journey: First, Spanish; Next, Bilingual; Finally, Critical Pedagogy

It began in Mrs. Johnson's high school Spanish class, but I did not know it then. For me to generate my own understandings of critical pedagogy, it took my entire career. First, I had to spend several years becoming, in a Freirian sense, "wet with the waters" of teaching high school Spanish. Next, I spent several more years relishing in the embattled world of bilingual education. Finally, my years in the classroom started to make sense to me as I entered the world of critical pedagogy. Of course, I recognized very little of this while it was happening, as I was usually too busy being passionate about pedagogy and people, some of whom are in my own family.

I started teaching in 1966, and, yes, I used to be a *nice* Spanish teacher; now I am a bilingual professor, and things aren't always so nice anymore. Now, when I am in the grocery store and someone asks me yet again to explain bilingual education, I often muse on how in the world I ended up in this exhilarating, infuriating, exhausting world of bilingual education.

When I first began to think about bilingual education, I was teaching Spanish to a group of high school students in a rural town in the desert Southwest. At that time, I was sure that I knew a lot about second language education. I had studied French, Latin, Spanish, and English—I loved languages. I had a couple of state Spanish teacher credentials; I had a master's in Spanish. Certainly, I knew second language acquisition. It turned out that I didn't know as much as I thought. When I unknowingly began to enter the world of bilingual education, everything seemed very upside-down to my right-side-up.

Many of the students in my Spanish high school classes were Mexican-American. Spanish was their first language and still the language of their families. None of the students had experienced good bilingual programs, and there was much of the core curriculum that they had not learned in their grade school years. When they were in the early grades, they couldn't understand the language of the class and the language of their teachers, which was English. Many of these students did not learn what the teachers were teaching, although I know that they were good teachers. The problem was that the students couldn't learn what they couldn't understand. Me either.

The students' literacy developed more slowly in their second language than did the literacy of their English-only peers. When many of these students were in middle and junior high school, they were frustrated, angry, and sometimes behaving badly. When I met these students, their cumulative folders were filled with labels such as *underachiever, slow reader, very limited, behavior problem*. At that time, I intuitively doubted those labels, but now I hate those labels. As I learned by teaching, these students were not limited; rather they had experienced limited pedagogy.

It was my job to teach these students Spanish in high school. Think of the irony. They had been in a system since grade school that had tried to rid them of their Spanish—now I was it to teach them! Most of the students still had more Spanish than I did. I learned a lot from the students.

One of the most important things I learned from this group of bilingual students was the importance of bilingual education. It would be too simplistic to say that they taught and I learned. These students had no idea what bilingual education was. They only knew what they had experienced and what they now needed. It was the first time that I was aware that the students and I were experiencing a new (to me, at least) type of pedagogy. We were learning and teaching together. None of what we were doing was in our Spanish language scope and sequence; none of it was in the Spanish grammar texts; and certainly, none of it was planned.

In retrospect, it seems that we were all a bit unarmed and unafraid. I remember that the whole process was thrilling, messy, and mysterious. I remember that it took a long time before I was able to articulate what was happening. I just knew that it seemed to work for the students and me. I knew that I was learning by teaching, and we knew that the students were teaching by learning. It was at this time that I seriously began to ponder my own pedagogy.

Although many of the students had a history of underachievement, in my Spanish language classes, they knew more Spanish than the English-dominant students, and many knew more Spanish than I did. Think about it: In life, we are sometimes in a position of knowing and sometimes in a position of not knowing. Which feels better to you?

This particular group of students had a pedagogical history of a system that consistently placed them in a position of not knowing. English-only students were traditionally placed in a position of knowing. Suddenly, in Spanish class, their pedagogical context turned upside-down. The English-dominant students were in a position of not knowing, and the Spanish-dominant students were in a position of knowing. I was somewhere in between, trying hard to understand.

However, I slowly began to notice that when they had a test approaching in another class, they all were feeling that they were in a position of not knowing content. It mattered to all of them. If they were going to have a world history test, all the students would talk about it, worry about it—some even studied for it. The English-dominant students had the advantage of learning the content in a language they understood. I could see that it was more difficult for the Spanish-dominant students to access the content in their new language. The playing field was not level.

Meanwhile, my scope and sequence (and certainly the dreaded teacher's manual) were telling me that I had to teach the indirect object pronoun to all the students, and I had to do it this week. For those of us in that classroom, there was a clear disconnect between teaching and learning. What I was supposed to teach simply didn't matter to the students. What mattered was the approaching world history test. One of the things that we teachers get to learn again and again as we teach is that if it doesn't matter to the learners, it doesn't matter.

Spontaneously, one day, I told the students to put their pronouns away. We went to the library, and we read about world history. Some read in Spanish, and some read in English. I stood back and was amazed at how interested they were in reading world history. We returned to the classroom, and we talked about world history in Spanish. It was one of my best teaching days, and I did nothing—except learn. They all did well on the test, and we celebrated in Spanish class, in Spanish. For those of you who might still be agonizing over the fate of those poor pronouns, I noticed in our conversations that we were using pronouns properly and, dare I say, meaningfully.

It astounded me. It was more meaningful for them, more fun for them, and far more interesting for all of us. They began to do better on their tests in the other subjects. As the months and years progressed, we continued with this practice. Our gorgeous Spanish texts were always in sight in the classroom, but basically, we tried to focus on what was meaningful for the students. Of course, during this time, I agonized and felt like a heretic. What would people think if they knew what we were doing in those Spanish classes? There we were—having fun and learning lots *of*

Spanish by learning lots *in* Spanish. The students' grades improved; they did well on the annual achievement tests; they won multiple awards in Spanish contests in the state; the administrators and the families supported us even when they didn't understand. How could they? We didn't either. We only knew that it was working. Many of these students who had originally been labeled as *limited* graduated with two honor cords: one for their work in all their courses in English and a second for their work in Spanish. I cannot tell you the pride we felt at their graduation.

It was at this time that I started to do some serious pondering about my own pedagogy. I was not doing anything that I had been taught to do in my educational programs. I still thought of myself as a Spanish teacher and didn't think too much about bilingual education. Now I realize that we were well into bilingual education before we ever knew it. We provided meaning in a safe environment, and the students were motivated. They learned the content, and the language came along free for all of us. They continued to learn English and to learn in English in their other classes. Their self-image soared. As we focused on content (and not grammar), my Spanish language improved in ways that I had never dared to hope it could.

Those students are the ones who gave me the courage to enter a master's program in bilingual education. When I was a Spanish language graduate student, I used to think that I never could be good enough to enter the world of bilingual education. I looked at the professors and the students and wanted to be in that magic world, but I was too intimidated by all that I did not understand. I feared the unknown.

When I finally found the courage to begin the program, in one of my early classes in the program, I was the only Anglo in the room and took the seat in the back of the room closest to the door. Within the first five minutes of class, the professor said, "I see we have a blue-eyed devil among us." If it hadn't have been for all of those high schools students who had taught me so much, I would have left the room. After class, a group of Latina students from the class asked me to go to coffee with them. In the next class session, this group of women surrounded me and included me throughout the entire class. The professor never bothered me again. It made me wonder, "Does gender trump ethnicity?"

To those high school students and those women (you know who you are), I send you my most heartfelt thank you. And to Mrs. Johnson, thank you is not enough for opening the world for me.

My own discovery of critical pedagogy has had many pivotal moments. One was when a professor in Texas said in exasperation, "Joan, at some point you are going to realize that language isn't just about words."

"Huh?" I replied as he stormed toward the office door. Just before he huffed and puffed out of the room, he tossed me one more book, *Literacy: Reading the Word and the World.* I spent the next several hours reading and becoming "wet with the waters of words." Oh, those words.

> *"Reading the world always precedes reading the word, and reading the*
> *word implies continually reading the world"*
> —FREIRE & MACEDO (1987, p. 35)

"All my life I had read the world all too clearly," I thought to myself, "but I just had never connected to the written word. Suddenly, I could see that reading my own world, even the pain of my own world, is what kept bringing me to words even when I was afraid of those words. And finally, those words opened my world even more. The union of my world through words is how I finally came to critical pedagogy.

The Word Universe

In a Freirian sense, the "word universe" (Freire & Macedo, 1987, p. 35) refers to the words of our own unique world. They are words filled with hope, anger, anguish, and dreams; I knew those words from my own world, but until I came to critical pedagogy, I denied them. Words matter because they have the potential to transform our world.

> *I am my language.*
> —GONZALÉZ *(2001)*

Susan, a teacher, had students in her classroom who spoke many different languages at home. Susan took it on herself to learn one new word from one of the other languages each day. The students blossomed. The language came from their own "word universe." However, in the course of the busy classroom, Susan forgot about the new words each day. One day, one very shy Hmong student slipped the following note onto Susan's desk: "You said you wanted to learn my language. Div means dog in my language."

"Now I try very hard never to forget to learn these new words from the students every day," Susan told me. "I can see that their words have helped me to understand their worlds much better."

The word universe of critical pedagogy is too easily dismissed as jargon. However, these words and thoughts of critical pedagogy are as significant as *div* is to the little Hmong girl and her teacher, Susan.

The word universe of critical pedagogy continues to grow, change, and reflect the world. For example, when Theresa, a teacher, discovered the word *corporatocracy,* she explained to me that it was the coming of a word that reflected the new reality of our world. She explained to me that although she could not yet find *corporatocracy* in a dictionary, she knew from her world that it meant the silencing and the marginalization of education by corporate America and its curriculum-selling companies.

History Helps: Three Perspectives

History helped me with my understandings of critical pedagogy also. We are a reflection of all that has gone before us; we are indebted to the people and the ideas that have preceded us. When I started teaching, the world was a very different place.

I do things very differently in my classes now, but I know that what I do in classes every day is touched by all the teaching, learning, and believing that have preceded me. Looking back historically can illuminate our present as we run to catch the future. In what follows, we will examine three approaches that represent unique educational perspectives. These are not the only three perspectives in education, but they are three communities of thought that most of us have experienced. Understanding the theory and practice of these three perspectives helped to bring me to my understanding of critical pedagogy.

Transmission Model

The teacher is standing in front of the classroom, and the students are at their seats, which are in rows. They listen to what she says and write it down in their notebooks: "A carrot is a root. We eat many roots. It is orange, and it is good for you. Other roots we eat are onions, beets, jicama, and potatoes. Class, are you writing everything that I tell you? Today I will classify plants into those you can eat and those you can't. Make two columns on your paper, and be sure to get every word I say for your homework. You will have a test on these exact words tomorrow. Who can name some other roots that we eat?"

I suspect that every one of us has had a similar experience. Were you taught this way? Do you teach this way? Why? For centuries, the vision of the teacher in front of the class pouring knowledge into students' heads guided the image of pedagogy. In this instructional model, the teacher has the knowledge, and the students receive that knowledge. The teacher's job is to transmit knowledge. The teacher controls who knows what; power has always been a part of pedagogy.

I began my career in much the same way; I taught the way I was taught. In fact, I was a true eight-year-old direct instruction specialist, maybe even a zealot. I made my girlfriends sit on the basement steps, and I stood on the cement floor below, and I taught. Oh, did I teach! I spoke; they listened. I had the knowledge in my head, and all I had to do was transmit it to them. What power! I could control their knowledge. For evaluation, they had to give it back to me exactly the way I gave it to them. Why in the world did they ever come to play with me? Fortunately, since the days of stair-step pedagogy, we have learned a lot about teaching and learning, not to mention the fact that the world has changed too. Politically, economically, scientifically, ecologically, culturally, demographically, those days are gone. That was then; this is now.

Today, we have more complex understandings of who students are and how they learn. This new knowledge has raised questions about the traditional way of transmitting previous knowledge. Educators and researchers increasingly recognize the role students play in constructing knowledge and accessing new knowledge. The teacher-directed lesson too often lacks opportunities for students to interact with one another and with the ideas that they are studying. In addition, in linguistically diverse classrooms, the teacher-directed lesson is often incomprehensible to students who are still learning English. We can't learn what we don't understand.

To address these problems, more and more educators focus their pedagogy on discovery, exploration, and inquiry. While intrigued by these ideas, many teachers find themselves at a loss in terms of how to structure these kinds of learning experiences in their crowded, assessment-driven classrooms.

Generative Model

Now imagine a classroom with small groups of students clustered around various learning centers. At each center, students are exploring the properties of edible roots. One group is cutting a potato, a carrot, and an onion and dropping iodine on the pieces to see whether they contain starch. Another group is sorting through an array of vegetables to determine which are edible roots. At still a third center, a group is setting up jars to sprout potatoes. The teacher moves around the room, quietly observes, and periodically interacts with various groups. The teacher moves to the group that has jars for sprouting potatoes. "I see your group has used different amounts of water in your jars. Can you predict which potato will sprout first? Why?"

The generative model maintains that students must actively engage in their learning process. In this model, students come together and construct or build their own knowledge. Learning is not passive. Students generate meaning as they integrate new ideas and previous knowledge. Simply put, students are participants in their own learning. The teacher's job is to structure and guide classroom experiences that will lead to student learning.

Transformative Model

Now let's visit another classroom that is also studying carrots and onions and roots. The educational model that is being used in the following classroom is historically rooted in the transmission and generative models. However, this model reflects, not only the changing world, but also our more complex understandings of meaningful teaching and learning. This model reflects today and prepares for tomorrow.

In this class, small groups of students are outside working in their garden, which they planted several months ago. The students are digging the potatoes, carrots, and onions and weighing them. On the basis of their production costs, the students will determine their price per pound later in math class. The group has decided in their class meeting that they will sell a portion of the vegetables to earn money for the scholarships for a field trip. The remainder will be donated to the local food kitchen (Wink & Swanson, 1993).

In transformative pedagogy, or critical pedagogy, the goal includes generating knowledge but extends from the classroom to the community. Good constructive pedagogy often stays inside the classroom. Critical pedagogy starts in the classroom but goes out into the community to make life a little better. Some would say that this group of students is doing critical pedagogy.

Transmission to Transformative: An Example

Recently, I had an experience at the postsecondary level with these three approaches: transmission, generative, and transformative. My goal was to share that immersion has many simultaneous and contradictory meanings often resulting in misinformation or disinformation[1] and harmful consequences for many language minority students. The public doesn't understand this. Many educators are confused about these multiple meanings, which result in very distinct programs and theoretical underpinnings.

This particular group of adult graduate students had already been working hard for several hours with me, so initially, I explained that I had one more concept I wanted them to understand. It was important. If they were too tired, we would wait until the next day. No, they were ready—let's go.

I am sure that some would describe this as an anticipatory set from the five-step lesson plan. Some would say that I was working to establish motivation. Maybe. However, I believe that learning is about ownership. It is about making meaning together. It is about socially constructing knowledge. It is about experiencing. It is not about being talked at. If learning is not meaningful to students, it is irrelevant what the teacher does. Students have taught me this through the years. So did Dewey. So did Vygotsky. By the time I began the following lesson, the students owned their learning and were ready to experience a new idea.

Previously, I had made a chart to capture the three models of immersion and other dual languages programs, as seen in Figure 4.1. I reflected on various pedagogical approaches I could use.

First, I knew that I could use the transmission model. It would be fast (for all of us) and efficient (for me). I could simply lecture on the information or give them the handout and tell them to read it. Then they could memorize what I had given them, and I could test them on the knowledge. I knew that they would all get good grades on such a test, but I also knew that the information would not be meaningful and relevant, nor would they remember it.

Second, I thought about a more interactive approach. I wanted the students to be socially constructing meaning as we worked our way through immersion. I wanted them to talk to each other, to ask questions, to slow me down. I decided to use a generative or constructive approach to sharing the information. I had a very large and very long piece of paper that covered the entire front of the wall. On this paper, I had drawn the chart as seen in Figure 4.2; however, I drew only the framework of the chart.

I drew it all with a black marker. Under the program column, I wrote "French Canadian immersion" in red, "bilingual, dual, or two-way immersion" in green, and "structured immersion" in blue. Because immersion models were the focus of this lesson, I wrote the other program models in black. I did not fill in the information on goals, students, teacher preparation, or time for any of the program models. The empty spaces were waiting for us to generate or construct the knowledge together.

Of course, I was hoping that the class would also begin to generate other dual language models after they understood the three immersion models. First, I was interested to see whether they would discover the parallels between dual language immersion and maintenance bilingual education. Second, I wanted to see whether they would discover the difference between French Canadian immersion and dual language immersion.

Let the dialogue begin.

FIGURE 4.1   Dual language models

Program	Goals	Students	Teacher Preparation	Time
French Canadian immersion	1. English and a second language (bilingualism/ biliteracy) 2. High academic achievement	Language majority population	Credential	K–6
Bilingual, dual, or two-way immersion	1. English and a second language (bilingualism/ biliteracy) 2. High academic achievement 3. Positive cross-cultural relations	Language majority and minority populations	Credential	K–6
Maintenance/ enrichment bilingual education	1. English and a second language (bilingualism/ biliteracy) 2. High academic achievement 3. Positive cross-cultural relations	Language majority and minority populations	Credential	K–6
Structured immersion	English only	Language minority population	English only	Nine months
Structured sheltered English immersion	English only	Language minority population	English only	Nine months
Transitional bilingual education	English only	Language minority population	Aide/English only/bilingual	Short as possible

K-W-L

We began with a K-W-L approach. What did the students know (K)? What did they want (W) to know? How might they learn (L) it?

- *K (know):* The students talked in small groups about what they knew about immersion. They shared with the whole group. We recorded their prior knowledge on the chart and were able to fill in some of the blanks.

FIGURE 4.2   **Constructing the models**

Program	Goals	Students	Teacher Preparation	Time
French Canadian immersion				
Bilingual, dual, or two-way immersion				
Maintenance/ enrichment bilingual education				
Structured immersion				
Structured sheltered English immersion				
Transitional bilingual education				

- *W (want to know):* They wanted to know about the empty blanks. They wanted the information about immersion that they couldn't generate together.
- *L (learn):* Usually, students learn in various modes: from books, interviews, videos; on the Internet; at the library; from conversations with their families and friends; by collecting their own data; and so on.

Given the context (remember, we had all been working very hard together for several hours, it was late, and I knew that I was exhausted), we decided that I would share the information with them as I have experienced all three of these models. When we were finished, our chart reflected the following, as seen in Figure 4.1:

1. *French Canadian immersion* is a term used in the United States to refer to a program that serves language majority students. The goals are English *and* a second language (bilingualism/biliteracy) and high academic achievement in seven (K–6) years. The teachers are credentialed or certified bilingual or multilingual teachers. It has a long, successful history in Canada.

2. *Structured English immersion* (or, as it has more recently been called in California, *sheltered English immersion, structured English immersion,* or even simply *English immersion*) is very different from the Canadian model. It is designed to serve language minority students. The goal is English dominance within one year. Teachers or paraprofessionals need not speak the language of the students, and the language of instruction is overwhelmingly in English (Krashen, 2003). Although this model is programmatically and philosophically the exact opposite of the French Canadian model, the public often thinks that they are the same. In addition, some politicians perpetuate this myth for their own political agenda, as happened in California in June 1998 with the passing of Proposition 227, "English for the Children." The public was asked whether they wanted their children to speak English. Of course, they did. However, if the proposition had been written differently—for example, asking whether they wanted their children to speak English *and* receive primary language support in content areas while learning English—perhaps the results would have been different, as is reflected in Krashen (1998b).[2] For me, this seems to be a classic example of taking a very complex (social-cultural-pedagogical-linguistic-educational-political) issue and presenting it in a simplistic manner. It all reminds me of the old saying "For every complex issue, there is an answer, which is obvious, simple, and wrong."[3]

3. *Bilingual (dual or two-way) immersion* is designed to serve majority and minority students. The goals are English *and* a second language (bilingualism/biliteracy), high academic achievement, and positive intergroup relations in seven (K–6) years. The teachers are credentialed or certified bilingual or multilingual.

Together, the students had generated the knowledge on the three immersion programs, and they had gone beyond the immediate learning objective to also generate their own knowledge about all dual language programs. When we finished, the graduate students/teachers in this group immediately pointed out two things to me. The first was that the bilingual immersion model is very similar to the French Canadian model. It differs in one profound area: In contrast to the French Canadian model, the bilingual immersion model is designed to provide biliteracy for *all* students, not just the majority language students. The second thing my students pointed out was that the structured immersion model is essentially the old "submersion" model: Sink or swim. We also discussed the fact that I could have handed them the copies of the completed chart (see Table 4.1) and told them to read it. They were confident that the more generative/constructive way, although it took longer, was more effective. They felt that they knew the materials.

Of course, I wish for this to be transformative learning for the students, but I can never control what students do with their own learning. Transformation requires that we shift from being passive learners to active professionals and intellectuals in our own communities.

In summary, these three perspectives are not the only ways of teaching and learning. Of course, there are many ways of understanding complex processes such as teaching and learning. I very much like Sonia Nieto's (1996, p. 319) advice to always keep the number 17 in mind, as it reflects so well multiple perspectives on complex realities. Make no mistake about it: The interaction between teaching and learning, or pedagogy, is very complex. However, these three approaches (transmission, generative, and transformative) do provide a framework for us to reflect on our own pedagogy.[4]

1. In the traditional classroom, instruction outcomes are often quite narrow and specific (memorized concepts, vocabulary, and skills); in the transformational model, student outcomes are as complex as the complexities of our diverse society. The problem that students study and the range of possible solutions reflect the dilemmas of the larger society, and the complexity of society is mirrored in both the instructional strategies and content of classroom discourse.

2. The transformative lesson, or doing critical pedagogy, distinguishes itself in two ways from the generative, or constructive, lesson. First, it is designed so that the students act on and use their generated knowledge for self and social transformation. The socially constructed knowledge of the classroom is to be applied in the social context of life. Second, this lesson design is inherently grounded in democratic principles.

3. The transformation model of education is another name for critical pedagogy. In this case, the teacher and the students are not only doing critical pedagogy, they are also living critical pedagogy. The fundamental belief that drives these classroom behaviors is that we must act; we must relate our teaching and learning to real life; we must connect our teaching and learning with our communities; and we must always try to learn and teach so that we grow and so that students' lives are improved, or so self- and social transformation occurs.

Practicing Pedagogy Patiently

Corri Does Dialectics in Secondary Science

In the following activity, we begin with Corri's reflection on how she discovered this learning activity. This is followed by the activity. I want to note that Corri has continued with her study of the theory and practice of dialectics in a secondary class for her M.A. thesis, and it all began simply one Friday afternoon.

During my first year of teaching, I presented the students with a list of ethical questions while we were studying genetics. I talked to the class about being respectful of others' opinions. I asked them to choose one issue and give their opinion to the class. I encouraged each student to give the reason behind his or her opinion. After each student gave his or her opinion, other students were welcome to comment on their feelings on the topic. The results of the activity were exciting. I thought this was going to be a simple Friday activity. It seemed that all we were doing was sitting around and talking. I was not presenting new material, and we were not doing a lab. I knew that some students might get their feathers ruffled, but I never expected it to turn into the learning experience that it did (both academic and otherwise). Through the discussion, some students showed that they understood the material (better than they ever could on a multiple-choice test), while others figured out the part of a given concept that they had been confused about. Everyone got to hear opinions that differed from theirs, and they got to hear the reasons behind these opinions. A few students who hardly ever spoke up in class were raising their hands and eagerly giving their opinions.

Because of the surprising way the activity went, I knew that it was much more than a fluffy Friday activity. I decided that I should spend time learning more about other teachers' experiences with opinion-based ethical classroom discussions and adding structure to the activity. Therefore, I have developed the ethical dialectic method.

Ethical Dialectic Method

The ethical dialectic method is an approach to learning in which students are involved in ethical discussions with a dialectical approach (thesis, antithesis, synthesis). I developed this method for application in the secondary, multicultural classroom. I have used this method in the science classroom, but it could easily be applied to other content areas.

1. *Teaching the concepts.* Present a unit, chapter, or concept as you would normally teach the material.
2. *The ethical questions.* Present the students with a list of four to eight ethical questions that apply knowledge from the concepts that have already been covered. For example, imagine that one woman agrees to have a child for another woman who cannot do so. After the first woman has given birth, she changes her mind and decides to keep the child. A judge rules that she can do this. Is this a fair decision?
3. *The position paper.* Have the students write a short paper in which they take a position on the ethical question that they feel the most comfortable discussing with the class. This helps the students to organize their ideas before they have to present them.
4. *Setting the environment.* Establish a respectful and comfortable environment for student discussion.
5. *The ethics discussion.* Start with the first ethical question, and have each student who chose that question give an opinion. When each student speaks, he or she should be given the chance to express himself or herself without interruption. When each student is finished, the rest of the class should be given the chance to express their opinions (whether they agree or disagree). Follow the same pattern with the rest of the ethical questions. During this process, the

teacher should refrain from giving her own opinion; rather, the teacher should encourage student involvement and interest and the application of relevant concepts.

6. *The dialectical paper.* Each students should write a second paper that includes an original opinion (thesis), opinions that were in contrast to her own (antithesis), and her final opinion (synthesis).

7. *The final presentation.* The students should briefly speak to the class about the conclusions they came to in their dialectic paper.

NOTES

1. Although the word *disinformation* is used in many other contexts, it is also used to refer to false information that is spread (knowingly or unknowingly) by opponents of bilingual education. For more on how this happens, I refer you to Chapter 8, "Disinformation in the Information Age: The Academic Critics of Bilingual Education" in *Negotiating Identities: Education for Empowerment in a Diverse Society* (2001) by Jim Cummins. This book is available through California Association of Bilingual Education, 660 S. Figueroa Street, Suite 1040, Los Angeles, CA 90017 (www.bilingualeducation. org). For more about the deliberate misrepresentation of education and language, see Goodman (1998) and Taylor (1998) as listed in the Bibliography. All three of these books might push you into that uncomfortable unlearning zone and therefore are important to read.

2. Krashen (1998a), "Is 180 Days Enough?" in *Bilingual Basics*, 1(2), pp. 1–4, which is published by TESOL (http://www.tesol.edu/) This very short article is a review of literature that overwhelmingly demonstrates that children do not acquire enough English in one year to do grade-level work in mainstream classrooms. Another way to answer this question is simply to reflect on how long it has taken you, or would take you, even with your high level of literacy and rich academic experiences. Structured immersion is a programmatic model that has rarely been used, except in isolated cases, particularly in Texas in the 1980s. However, many classrooms are de facto English immersion programs for the majority of language minority students with disastrous consequences for these students. For those who favor English-only initiatives in schools, it is already the reality for most language minority students. The educational and social consequences have had a profound negative effect for the students who are directly involved and for all of us who care about schools. For more on this, read August and Hakuta (1997). Flood, Lapp, Tinajero, and Hurley (December 1996/January 1997) provide another concise overview of the debate swirling around immersion.

3. Krashen, S. (1998b and 1999a), "Why Did California Voters Pass Prop 227? They Thought They Were Voting for English." *TABE Newsletter* (Tucson Association for Bilingual Education), August, pp. 3–4. This article, often referred to as "The Crawford Question," demonstrates that, contrary to popular opinion, California voters do support primary language support for students in the process of acquiring English. A *Los Angeles Times* (April 13, 1998) poll shows that 63 percent voted for Proposition 227 because they thought they were voting for English; only 9 percent polled felt that bilingual education was not effective. In the same poll, 32 percent were in favor of "English-only," and over 60 percent supported the idea of using the first language as support for learning. The *Dallas News* (June 28, 1998) produced nearly identical results. A third poll conducted by Steve Krashen and James Crawford in the Los Angeles area supported the findings of the *Los Angeles Times* and the *Dallas News* and further demonstrated that few people knew what was in Proposition 227, and if they had known, 71 percent would have voted against it (Crawford, 2004; Krashen, 2003). Unfortunately, much misinformation and disinformation were made available to the voters. McQuillan (1998a) looks at the early data on student achievement since the passage of the English-only mandate.

4. Others have used different language to describe these three approaches to teaching and learning. Of course, there really are more than these three approaches; there is a continuum from

transmission to transformation. For further reading, I encourage you to see Freeman and Freeman (1994) *Between Worlds: Access to Second Language Acquisition,* published by Heinemann of Portsmouth, New Hampshire. In that book, they adapt the language of Lindfors (1982) and describe these three approaches as student as plant, builder, and explorer. The student as plant relates to the transmission model of education in that the teacher provides the students with all that the student needs. The idea of the student as builder reflects the constructive and generative approaches to knowledge and literacy. The student as explorer moves on the continuum toward transformational teaching and learning.

Cummins (1996, 2001) describes these three somewhat typical approaches to teaching and learning: traditional, progressive, and transformative.

5 Where in the World Did It Come From?

Throughout this text, I hope to make critical pedagogy more meaningful by sharing questions about critical pedagogy: What is it? Where did it come from? How do we do it? And why does it matter? The spirit of inquiry that is fundamental to critical pedagogy has caused me to seek answers for these questions. In this chapter, we will follow the roots of critical pedagogy from the Latin voice to the European voice, the Eastern voice, and finally the multiple voices of North America. I realize that when I begin to speak of the critical voices of North America, I will inevitably omit someone. Therefore, in this chapter, I will direct my comments to the critical theorists who have most directly influenced my own experiences and thinking. My purpose is to tell the big story that lies behind those big words and ideas. Darder et al. (2003), in particular, provide an informative overview of the history of critical pedagogy. The historical roots of critical pedagogy, as seen in Figure 5.1, spread to many parts of the world. As I paint this picture, I will ground it in the reality of teachers' voices.

It would not have been possible for us to engage in the kind of curriculum work we do if past members of the field had not struggled mightily.
—APPLE *(1999, p. 45)*

The Latin Voice

Freire: The Foundation

Let me introduce you to the Paulo Freire I love. I have a tiny tape recorder that often can be found on my windowsill above the kitchen sink. When I begin to lack courage or when I need more patience, I play only one tape: Paulo Freire (1993). This is a recording I made of him speaking to several thousands of people in southern California. When I listen to this tape, I still feel as though he were speaking only to me. During this presentation, he spoke of two concepts: teaching and learning. As I listened, the seeds for this book were planted. As we were walking away, Dawn said, "Mom, he's just like Gandhi, only with clothes on."

For me, Freire is the quintessential teacher and learner. He has taught many things to many people all over the world. When I read his words, when I hear his words, I learn and relearn to focus on teaching and learning that is rigorous and

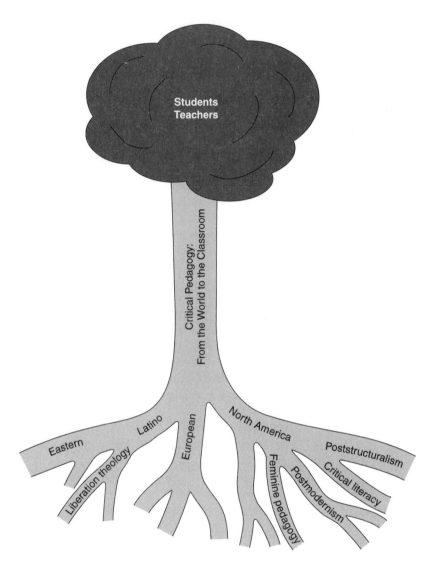

FIGURE 5.1   Critical roots

joyful (Freire, 1994; Gadotti, 1994). When I walk into a class or a presentation, I am thinking, "Rigorous and joyful, rigorous and joyful, rigorous and joyful."

In the section that follows, I share parts of the transcription of the audiotape of Freire. During this presentation, he spoke passionately of the transcendent power of teaching and learning. Please remember that this was given to a very large audience and he spoke largely without notes. During the presentation, the audience was extremely attentive, and Freire connected with many. After the presentation, he shook hands and greeted individuals until there was not a person left in the huge conference room. I know, because Dawn and I were among the last to shake his hand.

Freire's Voice: A Transcription of an Audiotape

There is no possibility for teaching without learning.
As well as there is no possibility of learning without teaching.
—*PAULO FREIRE*

My friends, first of all it is a pleasure for me to be here. It is a pleasure to say something about education to you. Of course I have had in my life experiences all over the world in talking to such a quantity of people, but from time to time, I feel as if I am lost.

I ask myself: What can I say? Sometimes it is good to say to the young people that a man like me, with many experiences of speaking and writing, also sometimes does not know what to say and even becomes afraid. Right now, for example, I am afraid, and it is good to acknowledge this.

I asked my wife when we were coming, "You know, I feel like I am forgetting about the things which I taught in San Paulo."

"Why don't you speak about teaching and learning?" she said.

"Yes, I will talk about the difficult task of teachers and learners here [in the United States]," I responded to her.

The first point I want to make is that there is no possibility for teaching without learning. As well as, there is no possibility for learning without teaching. The two tasks are so united and so contradictory also. It is absolutely impossible to teach without learning and to learn without teaching. Let us try to think about this kind of relationship. How is it possible to dichotomize them [teaching and learning]?

The Teacher, the Learner, the Content

Teaching implies, or demands, the existence of two subjects. By subjects, I mean [you have] the educator, and on the other hand, [you have] the educatee. However, there is another [part of this process]: the object to be known. We also speak about the object to be taught, learned, or known as the content. If I teach biology, for example, biology is the object to be taught, learned, known; then biology is the content of my practice.

What Is the Role of the Teacher?

Let me speak a little bit about these three elements. First, the teacher: What is the role of the teacher? When we ask ourselves this question, we discover that there are different answers for this question. I don't want to refer to the problems of methodology, for example, the methodology for teaching mathematics or teaching history. These things really are objective things.

Teaching Is Not a Neutral Process

What is really important is to discover that teaching is not a neutral process. It's not a neutral action.

A Progressive Teacher

This is a teacher who has a progressive vision or understanding of his or her presence in the world; a teacher whose dreams are fundamentally about re-building of society. [A progressive teacher is one] whose dreams are dreams of changing the reality to create a less ugly society.

The Opposite of a Progressive Teacher

We also have teachers whose dreams are to keep society as it is—that is, to keep a discriminatory society. To keep society crushing the so-called minori-ties, which prevents the possibilities of the children of minorities from be-coming themselves.

If you ask the first kind of teacher, the progressive teacher, "What do you mean by teaching?" and if you ask the second [kind of] teacher, we will have different, contradictory, antagonistic responses.

It Is the Love of the Progressive Teacher

I think we still have people who become stupefied when we say that educa-tion is political, but it is. It is a question of the [very] nature of education [which I will address]. I ask you to forgive me because I am not interested in describing the role of the reactionary teachers—that is a question for the re-actionary philosophers, not for me. I will stay in the field that I love. It is the love of the progressive teacher.

What Is Required of Progressive Teachers?

Teachers need to be humble. Why does the process of teaching demand the teacher to be humble? It is necessary for the progressive teacher to be humble precisely because of the impossibility of separating teaching from learning. If the teacher is not humble, the teacher does not respect the students. It is as if the students have nothing to do in the process of learning but just to listen pa-tiently to the voice of the teacher. This is precisely a totalitarian teacher. The totalitarians do not need to be humble.

Teaching: Research-Based and a Political Choice

One of the requirements for us to be good [progressive] teachers is very in-teresting because [the knowledge of] teaching is research-based, and on the other hand, teaching is a political choice.

Another condition [requirement] of [progressive] teachers is that they recognized that we are always becoming, because we never just are. We are always becoming.

[However] the first condition for us to become a good teacher is to be sure that in spite of all, in spite of the school, in spite of the experience of all the other teachers, when students come to us, [we need to realize] that they already know many things. Unfortunately, we are [sometimes] bureaucratized by the institution. We assume that before entering schools, students know nothing. It is assumed that the only place for us to know is only in school. We assume that the knowledge of the streets is not important. To think this is a terrible mistake.

When kids come to school, they are already able to read the reality. Before reading the words, kids already read the world. The first condition of being humble is to begin to understand the finality [importance or primacy] of our task as teachers. We have many things to do. We need to discover that in teaching, we learn.

By teaching, I learn how to teach. It is fantastic that there exists the possibility for me to know much better what it means to teach, precisely because I am teaching. In eating, I learn how to eat and what to eat. In teaching, I learn, first of all, how to teach, but secondly, I learn much better what I am teaching. Why? Because of course we can only teach what we know.

Can you realize the contradiction of someone teaching something that he or she does not know? It is impossible; nevertheless, we have many examples of this.

At the moment, I am teaching something I already know. When I teach what I know, to students who supposedly do not know, I am also teaching to the curiosity of the students. Their curiosity teaches me. It teaches me to re-know what I already knew.

Is it clear? It is not a mechanical process. It is a dialectical process.

To Become Wet with the Waters: Knowing and Memorizing

In order for us to understand this process, we must enter into the dynamism of language. The words need to become wet with the waters [of meaning]. The teacher grows by teaching the object to be grasped by the students. If the students don't grasp the object with their bare hands, the students only memorize the description, but they don't *know* the object.

Knowing is not a question of memorization. It is a question of acquiring the object. [Sometimes], we try to memorize first, in order to know secondly. This is the way some students do for tests. I will memorize it today, and tomorrow maybe I can write about it. Next week I will know nothing.

Knowing is something different. It is kind of an adventure. Knowing is a reinvention of the object being known. It is a recreation. It is a mutual process of teaching and learning. The more the teacher refuses to learn with the students, the less the teacher teaches.

The Passion of Teaching

Another dimension of this process is something which I will call passion, without which I cannot teach. How can a [progressive] teacher ever become a bureaucrat? And when I say bureaucrat, I am not making reference to a [school] administrator. No, [that type of bureaucracy] is important. Schools cannot be without bureaucracy, [schools need an administration]. When I said bureaucratic [in this context], I am talking about a teacher's mind becoming bureaucratized. These are people who do exactly what they were told [to do]. People who follow exactly [the bureaucratic orders of others], even though maybe they could die by doing that. He or she does it because they were told to do so.

No Fried Eggs at Three O'clock in the Afternoon: An Example of Bureaucratization of the Mind

I will tell you a very interesting example of the bureaucratization of mind. Years ago I was in Los Angeles in the airport, as I was preparing to leave for New York. It was three o'clock in the afternoon, and I went to the restaurant and ordered fried eggs, orange juice, English muffin, and a coffee.

"I am sorry, but it is not time for breakfast," the young woman very politely said to me.

"But look," I said, "I love fried eggs, English muffin, orange juice and coffee. If I can't have breakfast at three o'clock in the afternoon, I would like to ask a favor of you. Please go to the boss and say to him that there is here a Brazilian professor who loves eggs. My question to him is whether there is in the American Constitution anything which prevents us from eating eggs at three P.M. If there is no such thing, then I insist I want to eat fried eggs. It is simple. You cannot deny me my eggs only because it is no longer time for breakfast. Please do that."

And she went, and in five minutes she came back smiling. She said that the boss said nothing in the U.S. Constitution says that you can't have fried eggs at three o'clock in the afternoon. Fortunately, the young woman and the boss were not totally bureaucratized. This is for me a beautiful example of the human perspective. The example [demonstrates] that even if/when there are structures of society which work to bureaucratize the minds, there is always the possibility for us to be saved.

I only needed to ask the question. The young woman and the boss were touched by the challenge of the question. Maybe they realized that there is no such an item in the Constitution, and at that moment they became again human beings and not machines. It is for me a fantastic example.

My friends, please don't allow yourselves to fall into the trap of bureaucratization of the mind. React against it so that you to may continue to be human.

Another Example of Bureaucratization of the Mind: The Schedule Is Greater Than the Speaker

Look, we organize the schedule, and when we finish the organization of the schedule, we become less than the schedule. Do you see this is an absurdity? I had this experience when I was with Nita in Sweden. I had been invited to a very important meeting, and I wrote the paper for the presentation. However, I am a Brazilian and very independent and rational. As I wrote, I did not consider the time for reading, as the text was in Swedish. I had only ten, maybe fifteen minutes to finish the speech. However, the woman who [organized the schedule] approached me from behind with a gift, while I was still speaking. She is a specialist and very qualified to organize meetings like this. My wife saw all of this and worried that I might become angry. The woman walked to me [as I was still speaking] and handed me the gift.

"I am supposing that I am to stop?" I said to her.

"Yes," she replied to me.

"I will obey. I will stop. Nevertheless before stopping, I have something I have to tell you," I replied to her. Then I spoke about the bureaucratization of mind. I made another speech, maybe fifteen minutes more.

Look, don't think I am against principles, against discipline, against order. Without these things, we have nothing. However, we are greater than the time, which we organize. If we don't do that, we become machines. Please don't do that.

When I had finished the [extra] fifteen minutes, I said that the organization paid for very expensive tickets to bring me. Do you see the irony? First, when they asked me, they invited [only] me. Nevertheless, I told them that I don't travel alone. I have to go with my wife. Secondly, it is not a bourgeois demand, it is a question of survival. I am seventy-one years old. I am not a tourist. I am a thinker. When the bourgeois created first class, the bourgeois did not know what she was doing. It is a fantastic way to travel. Finally, I told them, you have to pay me because I am not ashamed to receive money because if I don't receive money, I cannot eat.

The Question

Look, what I cannot understand is how it is possible for you to spend lots of money to bring me here and then prevent me from finishing my speech? That does not make sense. This seems to be the bureaucratization of the mind. The more we, as teachers, do this, the less students are free to risk.

Freedom and Risk

Look, my friends, there is no possibility for greater achievement without taking risks. Without freedom, you cannot risk. When you are not free, you have to risk in order to get freedom. Teaching is not [like] spending a weekend on a tropical beach. It is to be committed to the process of teaching, the adventure, and to the students.

Education Is Testimony

We have to bear witness for students. For example, how is it possible for me to speak about risk if students discover that I never risked. How is it possible to speak about the seriousness of teaching and learning, if the testimony I give is the lack of seriousness? Education is, above all, testimony. If we are not able to give testimony of our action, of our love, we cannot help the students to be themselves.

Freire's Conclusion
Then, my friends, I am sure that I must stop, but not because of the bureaucratization of mind. Of course, if you ask me if I could speak another hour or two, I would say yes, because my life is completely devoted to this. We never can exhaust the issues [of teaching and learning], but I must also respect the need for those who listen. They have to rest, too. The best speech finishes when the people would still like to listen. I know that there are still some more moments for me to speak. [Therefore], I stop now. Thank you very much.

This speech was given in 1993. Freire died in 1997.

Much of multicultural critical pedagogy in North America today stands on the shoulders of this giant, Paulo Freire. He taught me the difference between reading the word and reading the world. During the 1960s, Freire conducted a national literacy campaign in Brazil, for which he eventually was jailed and exiled from his own country. He not only taught the peasants to read, he also taught them to understand the reasons for their oppressed condition. The sounds, letters, and words from the world of his adult learners were integrated and codified. Ideas, words, and feelings joined together to generate a powerful literacy that was based on the learners' lived experiences. The Brazilian peasants learned to read the words rapidly because they had already read the world, and their world was the foundation for reading the words. Traditionally, literacy has been the process of reading only the word. Emancipatory literacy is reading the world. Freire was not jailed and exiled because he taught peasants to read the word, but because he taught the subordinate class to critically read the world (Freire & Macedo, 1987). Freire taught the peasants to use their knowledge and their literacy to examine and reexamine the surrounding power structures of the dominant society.

Freire teaches that no education is politically neutral. Traditionally, teachers (that would include me) have assumed that we don't have to bother with politics; teaching is our concern. I see on my resume that one of the first state conference presentations I ever gave was entitled "Teaching, I Love. It's the Politics, I Hate." I now think that I was pretty naive, and maybe even elitist, to think that teaching and learning could possibly take place in a vacuum. Every time we choose curriculum, we are making a political decision. What will I teach, and what won't I teach? The social, cultural, and political implications are great. After reading Freire, a local teacher wrote me this note in e-mail:

> *Freire left me with a new insight. I had never thought about the role of passivity. Before, I did not look at passivity as being active. This oxymoron is new to me. I am learning that these contradictions are confounding and enlightening.*

Schools are social; they are filled with real people who live in real communities and have real concerns. People with multiple perspectives send their children to schools. Teaching and learning are a part of real life, and real life includes politics and people. Schools do not exist on some elevated pure plain of pedagogy away from the political perspectives of people. If two friends sit down for a social visit, politics is a part of it. If hundreds of kids from a neighborhood come to school, politics is a part of it. Paulo Freire recognized this before many others in education. If educators state that they are neutral, then they are on the side of the dominant culture. "Passivity is also a powerful political act," a student said to me. Teaching is learning.

Traditionally, the strong voice of school has been very homogeneous along the lines of race, class, and gender. Historically, the strong have been the A Team, and the weak have been the B Team. The weak have been underrepresented and not heard. This is changing, and change is hard. Twenty-five years ago, I wrote in a private journal that I thought we would go "kicking and screaming" into a multicultural society at the turn of the century. I remember feeling rather neutral, distant, and clever when I wrote it. I had no idea how difficult it would be for us as a society to change. Change can make the strong feel weakened and the weak feel strengthened.

I recognize that words such as *A Team, B Team, strong,* and *weak* can be very jarring and disquieting. I also realize that sometimes that is what it takes to trigger critical self-reflection—at least for me. I have not always been known to immediately welcome and embrace new ideas, new challenges, and new perspectives. Sometimes, words and experiences had to disturb me to my deepest core before I could think new thoughts and take new actions. Power is never conceded easily; things shake, rattle, and roll first. I suspect that this is true for a great many of us.

> *I am always ready to learn although I do not always like being taught.*
> —WINSTON CHURCHILL

Demographically, the world has changed, and nowhere are those changes experienced more profoundly than in classrooms today. Many classes are filled with traditional teachers and nontraditional students, conventional teachers and nonconventional students. The past is past; it is not necessarily bad, but it is past. We all must move forward. We cannot continue to use old answers for new questions. The questions have changed, and together, we are seeking new answers for new questions. Critical pedagogy has helped me to rethink old questions, and Paulo Freire has helped me to search for new answers.

Recently, I had an experience in the Minneapolis airport that demonstrated to me how much change has taken place. I had three hours to wait, and I spent the time walking, looking, and trying to enjoy myself. I was very aware of a most uncomfortable feeling; I felt out-of-sync, vaguely apprehensive and uneasy. As I became more and more aware of my feelings, I tried to analyze why I was feeling that way. After a couple of hours of strolling and musing, it hit me like a ton of bricks: Everyone looked just like me; it was like a world full of Joan clones. One generation ago, a homogeneous world was the only world I knew. It made me reflect on how much had actually changed and how we change with the changes. It is moments like these that give me hope.

Labeling Freire.   Paulo Freire has been labeled "the most labeled educator." He has been labeled *Marxist, idealistic, liberal, national-developmentalist, new schoolist, inductivist, spontaneist, nondirectivist,* and *Catholic neoanarchist* (Gadotti, 1994, p. 126).

My spell-checker has trouble with some of these labels; I do, too. I have heard him called a communist, a revolutionary, a philosopher, and a genius. Lots of labels. He has been called the authentic intellectual in our world, an ancient sage, and, in his own words, humble warrior of the spirit (Gadotti, 1994). Of all the labels for Paulo Freire that I have heard, the one I love the best is the one my spell-checker uses: *Freer.* Yes!

Reflecting on Paulo Freire now reminds me of a story I heard Maxine Greene (1998) tell. The last time she was with Paulo Freire before he died, they had lunch together in New York. Nita's (Paulo's wife's) ten-year-old grandson was with them for the lunch and kept trying to jump into the conversation. "We hotshots," Maxine said, "continued to talk and ignored the little boy's questions."

The young boy continued to interrupt, and the adults continued to ignore his comments. Finally, Paulo halted the adult conversation and called attention to his young grandson with these words:

"Be quiet," Paulo said, "Every time you ignore a person's question, you dehumanize him."

This statement hit me like a ton of bricks. I hope I never forget that quotation when I am teaching a class. I hope that I never forget that quotation when I am anywhere.

Labels I Love to Hate.   Paulo Freire and Tove Skutnabb-Kangas were two of the first voices I read who made me stop and think about our use of labels in North American educational institutions. It was one of those hey-I-never-thought-of-that experiences for me. For example, think of the word *minority.* From Freire (Freire & Macedo, 1987), I learned that it is often laden with connotations of less of something:

> Do you see how ideologically impregnated the term "minority" is? When you use "minority" in the U.S. context to refer to the majority of people who are not part of the dominant class, you alter its semantic value. When you refer to "minority" you are, in fact, talking about the "majority" who find themselves outside the sphere of political and economic dominance. In reality, as with many other words, the semantic alteration of the term "minority" serves to hide the many myths that are part of the mechanism sustaining cultural dominance. (pp. 124–125)

Recently, a teacher was complaining that her students "weren't intelligent" and "couldn't learn." However, she was particularly annoyed because "most are minorities." Wait. Most are minorities? Then wouldn't they be majorities? Traditionally, we used to use the words *minority* and *majority* in a numerical sense. *Minority* meant "less"; *majority* meant "more." Something has changed. If not numbers, then what in the world are we talking about? More and more, my sense is that when schools complain that they have so many "minorities," the hidden message is that the "minorities" have less value than the "majorities."

No one has been more personally involved with my own unlearning than Tove Skutnabb-Kangas. And, yes, not every minute of my own unlearning has been fun. It has happened again since the first edition. Skutnabb-Kangas (1998) demonstrates that when we (that includes me) in North America stop using the word *minority*, we deny students their legal protection under international agreements. She reminded us that when we use terms such as *linguistically diverse students* and other nice euphemisms, we actually rob students of the only protection they have in international human rights law. Linguistically diverse students have no protection in international law; minority students do (Skutnabb-Kangas, 2000).

Ouch. Critical pedagogy teaches us to name, to reflect critically, and to act. Tove named, I have reflected critically, and now I must act. In public, in policymaking, in publishing, I will use the word *minority*. However, my respect and love for Tove is superceded only by my complete disdain for the way I have heard the word *minority* used by some educators in schools to completely discredit the experiences, the cultures, and the languages of students who (a) have not yet acquired English, (b) come from cultures other than European ancestry, and (c) are often the numerical majority in the school. Therefore, I know I will continue my attempt to find language that describes students, if that information is necessary to add meaning to the context. For example, if they are bilingual and that information fits the context, I often say *bilingual*. Now, even *bilingual* has been expunged from the language by the term *English language learner*, which, of course, makes me use *bilingual* more. I repeat: Being bilingual is not bad; actually, it is very good for all. The world seems to understand this; the United States seems reluctant to acknowledge it.

Cummins (1996) writes in his preface of the same difficult issue. He generally tries to avoid *minority* and *majority* because of the pejorative connotations and inaccurate reflection of schools in the United States. However, he notes that in the European and Canadian contexts, the term *minority* is generally not laden with negative connotations; in fact, its very use guarantees certain legal and constitutional rights, as Skutnabb-Kangas noted.

The legacy of Paulo Freire is pushing me to unlearn other labels. I know of a junior high school that proudly boasts of its "Potentially At-Risk Program." I can almost guarantee that all the kids who are placed in that program will end up "at risk." Labels can lead to tracks, which are an insidious form of social sorting. Sometimes, we don't like to be bothered with this issue of labels. I think we need to bother ourselves more with the hidden implications of our language. What we say matters. The rationale of "that's the way we've always said it" just doesn't work for me anymore. However, sometimes the issue of labels and their devastating effects is exceedingly clear for almost everyone to understand. For example, a teacher told me that she was visiting another classroom in her school. Within the first half hour of her visit, the teacher of that class pointed out the "losers" in his room. Every student in the class heard his comments, and she noted that every one of the "losers" was either brown, black, or poor.

The European Voice

Critical pedagogy also has been influenced by voices from Europe. In the following, I will trace the roots of multicultural critical pedagogy in North American schools back to social and political contexts of other places and other times. The theory of reproduction, which started as an economic, political, and social idea, continues to thrive in schools today, but it is much more difficult to see and to understand than it was when it was a faraway idea in the history books. This part of the chapter will look at the early ideas of resistance that are alive and well in critical pedagogy of today.

Gramsci

The word *hegemony*, the domination of one group over another, can be traced to the Italian social theorist Gramsci.[1] He felt that hegemony was how societal institutions maintained their power, even by force if necessary. Gramsci (1971) thought that it was important for educators to recognize and acknowledge the existing oppressive structures inherent in schools. Power is a fundamental societal issue. As Western industrial societies grow more sophisticated, power is less likely to be used in a physical manner and more likely to be used in subtle ways that are harder to see because even the dominated group is partially supporting the process. Hegemony takes place when the B Team smiles and keeps quiet because (a) it is the polite, appropriate way to behave; (b) they have been schooled to behave that way; and/or (c) it is safe. These hegemonic smiles take time and emotional energy. I know. When the dominated group behaves this way, the dominating group often thinks of them as "respectful." Counterhegemonic behaviors are filled with risk, insecurity, and not many smiles. They also take lots of time and emotional energy. I know.

Hegemony occurs when twelve- and thirteen-year-old girls suddenly begin to do poorly in math and science courses. It is not that girls are less intelligent; it is that they are partially supporting the process of believing that boys know more about numbers and problem solving. Hegemony takes place when Spanish-dominant families support English-only processes. Hegemony takes place when one of the Hmong American graduate students in our program comes into every class and sits toward the back of the room and remains silent throughout the class. Many of the majority students think that he is the nicest, most "respectful" colleague. It is only during my office hours, when the door is closed, that I hear of his anger. He hopes that he can move into counterhegemonic behaviors in his lifetime. But then what will his former colleagues think? He is beginning his doctoral program now, so I suspect I will learn.

Hegemony and counterhegemony are painful concepts. Critical pedagogy calls us to name. In my precritical pedagogy days, when I was a nice Spanish teacher, I avoided words like *hegemony*. I just lived it. Now in my post–critical pedagogy time of life, I try not to be a part of hegemonic processes. I am sure I slip sometimes. And when I enter into counterhegemony, it is not easy, but it is honest and authentic, based on my lived experiences. From Gramsci, I have learned that in subtle and insidious ways, we can all be a part of maintaining myths.

Gramsci (1971, pp. 57–58) defined hegemony as a dialectic between force and consent. The threat of force, even if not used often, makes hegemony even more destructive for the B Team, who support their own domination because of that very force. This explains subordination without taking agency away from the subordinated. Artz and Murphy (2002) suggest that the construct of hegemony is an effective tool for understanding some of the more challenging questions surrounding diversity.

Marx

The economic and social ideas of Karl Marx form important roots of critical pedagogy. Marx believed that education was being used as an insidious vehicle for institutionalizing elite values and for indoctrinating people into unconsciously maintaining these values.

Marxist thought challenges the way in which the dominant ideology is reproduced through the use of myths (Macedo, 1994), which offer a sound bite to legitimize processes of oppression. One is the prevailing myth of a classless America: "We're all alike and all have equal access to opportunity in this great land." I have noticed that people who believe this tend not to hobnob with the folks who know that it isn't true. Myths are used as tools so that the have-nots will affirm and support the processes that benefit the haves. A glaring example is the way George H. W. Bush in 1988 campaigned on the notion of a classless America while at the same time he fought for a capital gains tax to benefit the rich and threatened to veto a tax cut for the middle class (Macedo, 1994). The gulf between the social groups continues to widen, although some people would have us think that the gulf is not even there.

Marx's ideas of reproduction are reflected in every classroom with subtle and hidden processes in which social classes are classified and grouped. Schools call it *tracking.* Sometimes social classes suddenly are acknowledged even by those who have traditionally denied them. They are publicly identified if they can be used to legitimize processes that hurt other groups of students. For example, during an in-service teacher education workshop, a group of teachers was discussing what they could do to serve more effectively the needs of bilingual children. The principal of this school, who had been a very reluctant participant throughout the in-service, could stand it no longer and suddenly announced in a loud voice to the group, "Oh, we don't have any LEPs in our school. The problem we have is poor white trash."

The teachers passively hung their heads—I think with shame—but they did not challenge her. My hunch is that the "poor white trash" in this school will be tracked for as long as they can stand to stay in school.

Whereas Freire had many labels, I think it would be safe to label Marx a Marxist. So the questions are "What is a Marxist? What does it feel like to be in a Marxist classroom?" I recently had the opportunity to ask these questions of students in a writing composition class.

What does a Marxist, the teacher in this classroom, look like? A lot like several hundreds of others teachers whom I have known. He was sitting in a circle with twenty-five students who had lots of books on their desks and appeared (to me) to be eager to learn, which I later found to be true. The teacher explained to me that the class was not studying Marx; rather, they were simply teaching and learning with a Marxist approach. My original question began to change a little: "What is a Marxist approach to pedagogy?" The students jumped right into the dialogue and told me.

> *A Marxist Approach to Pedagogy*
> "It reignited my desire to learn."
> "It forces me to think."
> "Anyone can ask and answer questions."
> "We take time to learn."
> "It is applicable to my life."
> "It connects me to my imagination."
> "It always seeks other views."

The students discussed their frustration with other classes in which they had to write down everything the professor said and then regurgitate the same knowledge on a test. They spoke of their yearning to know of multiple paths to teaching and learning.

Freire and Marx provide deep roots for critical pedagogy that are reflected in learners turning their beliefs into behaviors for self- and social transformation. The ideas we grapple with are not just for the safe confines of the four walls of the classroom. The whole idea is to improve the quality of life for ourselves and for others in our community. The mere momentum of the status quo will keep us in a vacuum unless we walk out the door and seek other ways of knowing.

These students in the composition class were actively engaged with new ideas; they were socially generating new knowledge; they were cogitating; and they were reading challenging books. This all seemed good to me. So I asked them, "If this pedagogy is working so well, why is Marx the bad guy to so many North Americans?" "He messes up the control," one young man quietly said. His classmates nodded their heads in agreement.

I have noticed that when the subject of Marx comes up, a confrontation often follows. Confrontation is great sport for some, particularly those who have more control and power. Confrontation is more difficult for others, particularly those who have less control and power. Marx hands us a mirror and makes us look at our traditional patterns of control in schooling, patterns that run along the lines of race, class, and gender.[2]

The Frankfurt School of Critical Theory

The Frankfurt School of Critical Theory of the 1940s believed that schools were a vehicle for reproduction (a.k.a. "tracked for life") whereby the workers who were needed in the existing power structures of society were prepared. These critical theorists postulated that the schools reproduce not only what society needs, but the corresponding social and personal demeanor as well. Gee (1990) updates this notion and shares his perspective:

> Schools have historically failed with nonelite populations and have thus replicated the social hierarchy, thereby advantaging the elites in the society. This has ensured

that large numbers of lower socio-economic and minority people engage in the lowest level and least satisfying jobs in the society (or no jobs), while being in a position to make few serious political or economic demands on the elites. Indeed, the fact that they have low literacy skills can be used (by themselves and the elites) as a rationale for them to be in low-level jobs and the elites in higher level ones. (p. 31)

Reproduction is easier to see at some times than at others. Tracking is often one of the institutionalized processes that is very visible, but the reproduction of the status quo and the existing power structures is more invisible. In one district I know, they have the usual tracks: snob track, poor-white-trash track, Spanish/Portuguese track, and a new one that I just recently became aware of: the middle-class track. Remember, I do not make up these stories; these are words I repeatedly hear. The students who are tracked through these colored institutionalized processes reflect and reproduce themselves again and again.

TEACHER 1: Yes, it's yellow for the Asians, red for the Mexicans. It's the way they segregate the kids.

TEACHER 2: Yeah. That way if an Asian moves to another school, he'll be on the same track.

TEACHER 3: Yes, that's how they segregate at our school, too. Yellow for the Asians, red for the Mexicans, and green for the white trash.

Tove Skutnabb-Kangas

Let me introduce you to Tove Skutnabb-Kangas, whom I know and love. She often brings out a strong response when people meet her, and the same was true for me. I had read her works for years, so I was prepared for the power of her thoughts, but I was not prepared for her personality. No one had ever told me.

Since the day I met her, the Easter Bunny and Malcolm X will forever be wedded in my mind. Let me explain. We were in a county school office presentation room; tables, chairs, and teachers filled the room. When I walked in, I noted a general air of excitement and happiness. I recognized the sound I heard: the happy hum of learning. Tove was moving among the teachers as they worked at tables; I could hear thoughtful questions and chuckles of joy throughout the room. I stood in the back of the room for about ten minutes and simply enjoyed watching and experiencing the entire environment. "So this is the famous Tove Skutnabb-Kangas," I thought.

Tove is of medium height and build; she has curly blonde hair that does exactly what it wants to do and she has round, round cheeks with the pinkest skin I have ever seen. Not white, but pink. The minute I met her, I thought of the round little nose and cheeks of the Easter Bunny. When she smiles, her face lights up the room. On that day, she was wearing brilliant colors with a long flowing skirt that had sequins sewn in so there was a kind of twinkle and reflection as she walked. She had on a fuchsia T-shirt, with a multicolored scarf and a darker jacket. For me, there is this aura of a cuddly Easter Bunny about Tove. A very powerful Easter Bunny, indeed.

She came to our campus and worked with teachers and learners in the area. While she was here, she met and talked with one of my male colleagues who had previously heard me describe her. When she left, he said, "Easter bunny, huh? Maybe a pink Malcolm X." Her ideas are strong, and her love is soft. When I see her, which is never often enough, I am filled with joy. We laugh and hug, and hug and laugh. Then we begin to discuss powerful ideas.

I have noticed that not everyone reacts to Tove the way I did during my initial encounter with her. In fact, sometimes the power of her ideas gives people a tummy ache. Sharon, a teacher/grad student, shares her story:

> *I first met Tove at a conference in San Francisco. I sat in the front row of the enormous auditorium. I didn't want to miss a word, an inference, a smile.*
>
> *Soon an official of the conference introduced Tove Skutnabb-Kangas, and I immediately noticed her rosy cheeks. Everyone applauded as Tove stepped up to the microphone and began talking loudly about education and language. Where was this soft, cuddly bunny rabbit I had heard about? I was so confused. I sat up in my chair so I could try to grasp the words. What? I, as a teacher, was cutting off the native language of my bilingual students? Me, who is so dedicated? My preconceived notions exploded! Well, yes it is true, I speak only English, and I don't know the language of my students.*
>
> *I sat up even straighter and thought seriously about leaving the room. How could I get out of here? And my professor was sitting two seats away. This message was not comfortable for me to hear. I mean, how could I be hurting children?*
>
> *I listened painfully and quickly left the room when Tove finished. I was enraged, hurt, confused, and angry. Later that week in class, we talked about the conference. My professor began talking about how wonderful it was to listen to Tove. All of a sudden she said, "Sharon, tell your colleagues about Tove." I could feel my face turning red, and I had to say, "Well, I really didn't care for her. I thought she was very loud and angry."*
>
> *For the next year, I read, reflected, mused, read, reflected, mused before I came to terms with my feelings. Tove was not saying that I was a bad teacher, only that I was not meeting the academic needs of multilingual students in their primary language.*
>
> *Yes, I could teach them in English, I could give them love and build their self-esteem. I could not, however, give them what they really needed to succeed in an English-speaking world: literacy and cognitive development. Even as I worked with the students on the oral English development, they would start to fall behind their classmates cognitively and linguistically.*

Now you have met two Toves—or at least one very complex person. You will have to draw your own conclusions. Let me share with you a more formal introduction to Tove Skutnabb-Kangas, the internationally known Finnish linguist. She is a critical theorist with deep roots in many parts of Europe. She has worked throughout the world as a sociolinguistic and a change agent. However, because of her numerous trips to the United States, many people (like me) have come to know her almost as if she were a part of the North American voice. She has challenged many of us to think and rethink in critically relevant ways. She consistently asks us to look again at the processes by which the norm gets normalized.

In her writings and her presentations, she has raised the issue of linguistic genocide in our schools. Students enter our schools speaking languages from all over the world; twelve years later, they leave our school, speaking only English. Then we immediately want them to go to college and study *foreign* languages. Tove asks us to rethink this practice, and she asks us to consider why it is taking place. Other countries often use direct and brutal tactics to prevent minority languages. In the United States, our methods are indirect and more effective. When students are not served in the mother tongue and when students are not allowed to use their own language to construct meaning, we are all part of the process that normalizes the majority use of English and disenfranchises all other languages. Or, as Tove has repeatedly said, "We kill languages every day in our classes."

I cannot imagine what it must be like for a five-year-old to go to school and learn that this language of family love—of mom, dad, grandma, and grandpa—is bad. What must it feel like to be a small child and feel shame about one's own mother's language? Five-year-olds read the world well and understand quickly that their family's language is bad. This is why they learn to say, "I don't speak Spanish." Shame does terrible things; anger follows shame. (This unlearning is not always comfortable.) I think that when Tove raises this question with schools in the United States, she is moving us institutionally to problem posing. Traditionally, the dominant culture does not respond well to this type of probing, thoughtful activity.

Declaration: Kids Need to Learn.   Tove continues to campaign for the United Nations to adopt the Declaration of Children's Linguistic Human Rights. Before I share it, let me explain something about Tove. English is not her first, second, or third language. Every time I ask her how many languages she speaks, reads, writes, and understands, we never get to the end of the answer; she always starts telling me stories about the languages along the way. But I have noticed that she needs more than her own ten fingers to do the counting. Even though English is not her first language, she is highly sensitive to gender-specific language that had, until recently, been so entrenched in the English language. In her writing, she has long used only the feminine pronoun as a little prod to help us move to a more equitable approach to gender-free language. I have some male friends who are very sensitive to this and really offended by it. It feels good to me.

Tove, like many of us, believes that children need to learn. She noted early in her writing that we don't learn what we don't understand. Therefore, she is an international leader in persuading the United Nations to adopt the following declaration:

Declaration of Children's Linguistic Human Rights
1. Every child should have the right to identify with her original mother tongue and have her identification accepted and respected by others.
2. Every child should have the right to learn the mother tongue fully.
3. Every child should have the right to choose when she wants to use the mother tongue in all official situations.

One of the best experiences I ever had with this declaration happened with the departmental secretary/assistant. Sheri and I see and know in very different ways, but we laugh and have a great time learning together. Two years ago, I remember when I first hung a laminated copy of this declaration on the wall above my desk. On more than one occasion, I was aware that Sheri was musing on it but not mentioning it. Then one day, as I was walking out the door, Sheri looked at it and quietly said, "Makes sense to me, Joan." I smiled and thought a lot about patience on my way home.

A Team and B Team.   Another idea of Tove's that has affected critical pedagogy in North America is her concept of the A Team and the B Team. Tove speaks to the issues of power with this construct. The A Team, which controls the power and material resources, continually invalidates and marginalizes the voice of the B Team. This is how the A Team socially constructs knowledge and maintains its own power. Many of us, at one time or another, have been on the A Team or the B Team without ever realizing it. However, some people tend to be only and always on the B Team. For example, recall the Benson kids who taught me so much; many of them had only and always been on the B Team. When they graduated with honors from high school, they shocked some of their former A Team classmates. Another example from higher education follows.

Pada is a young Hmong American woman. She has successfully finished her undergraduate studies, she has her teaching credential, and she is now a graduate student. She told me a story about discovering the A and B Teams when she arrived in the United States:

> When I started high school in the United States, my achievement was high, and my command of the English language fairly good. However, I was still terrified of all the tests the schools gave upon entering school. The first battery of tests was to determine which track was best for me: ESL track, B track, or A track. I was placed on the B track, which was designed to prepare students for a vocational career. I felt like the teachers thought I was incompetent. They gave us very little homework and hardly any real reading and real writing. I remember having to memorize lists of words and their definitions. I could see that the students in A track were always doing more interesting work; I could see that the A track was used to prepare people for college, which was my dream. Every time I tried to get into the A track, my counselor would remind me about my initial entry scores on the exams. I was achieving on B track, but that didn't seem to matter to anyone.
>
> During my second year of high school, my counselor finally allowed me to try the A track. However, he continually discouraged me and made me bring letters of support from teachers in order to make the transfer. At that time in my life, I did not understand the meaning of words such as socialization practices, schooling, and teacher expectations, but I could understand that I was being programmed for less than my dream.

Obviously, a society to which stratification into separate classes would be fatal must see to it that intellectual opportunities are accessible to all on equable and easy terms (Dewey, 1944/1916, pp. 88–89). In spite of this early warning from Dewey, tracking continues.[3] I wanted the students to read Dewey, to understand Dewey, to experience Dewey, so I decided to consciously create an A Team and a B Team on the first night of one of my classes. The experience was so powerful that it took us a few weeks to recover.

The class of thirty-eight arrived at 5:00 P.M. We were in a large room with all of the chairs screwed to the floor in straight rows, which would surely horrify Dewey if he were alive today.[4] The teachers/grad students drifted in and greeted each other. Those who knew me and had been in my classes before began by hugging friends, visiting, renewing friendships, and mostly moving toward the chairs in the front to the room. Before everyone was seated, I announced that those who had been in my classes before should sit in the front chairs and those who had not should sit toward the back. Everyone immediately complied. The front of the room continued with happy noise; the back of the room became quieter. We started class, and I consciously directed my comments to those in the front of the room; those in the back received only token attention. For the next two hours, we continued like this: I would initiate an idea or a thought and ask the students to discuss it. After their discussion, I would ask for whole-group sharing, but I mostly called on only those in the front. I consciously tried to assign status, power, and prestige to those in the front. I behaved as if they knew more and as if their knowledge was more valuable. They thrived. The back of the room became quieter and quieter. Soon I was able to see angry, frustrated looks. During the small group activities, I could tell that they were sharing their anger with each other; I ignored it and walked among the students in the front of the room, who couldn't understand why I was making the new students feel so bad.

After two hours, I couldn't take it any longer. The front of the room was confused; the back of the room was angry. I asked how many of them were teachers; there were thirty-eight teachers in the room. I asked them how many of them were involved with tracking in their class; thirty-eight were involved with tracking. I asked why. The front and back explained to me that they had to do it because some students were *ahead of* and *knew more than* other students. They still did not see the connection to our class. I asked the names of the various tracks: yellow, red, green, blue. They all knew which students went in which track. I asked them whether their assumptions about students made a difference in their students' achievement. The front and the back agreed: Their tracks reflected what the students knew.

Although I could tell by looking at their faces, I asked the back of the room how they were feeling: furious, angry, worthless, and finally, ready to drop the class. The front of the room still could not understand why I was making the new students feel so badly. Finally, I told them that I had created an A Team and a B Team so that they could experience it. *Experiencing* is different from *knowing about*. The students in this class are all teachers who know about tracking, but when they experienced it, they did not like it.

Tracking is so institutionalized in the geographic area where I live that the very thought of challenging it is considered almost heresy. Even the B Team in class that night wanted to legitimize it and rationalize it. Hegemony had reared its ugly head again. It took three more classes of dialogue, reading, and writing before I felt that the class had come together as a whole and could see that I had manipulated them and the context into the haves and the have-nots. I had consciously reproduced a reflection of their world and their individual classrooms. I had socially sorted on purpose to make a point that A Teams and B Teams always work to the advantage of the A Team. Five-year-olds know the difference between the buzzards and the blessed. It doesn't matter what color you label the track.

Lucille, an African American grad student, always knew that her elementary teachers thought she was on the B Team. But when she was in junior college, she was amused to find that she had been placed on yet another B Team. Only this time, it had a new name: the Lazy Tongues. Although English was the only language she knew, she was placed in an ESL phonics class with Spanish, Chinese, and Japanese speakers; the professor referred to them as LEPs; Lucille and the other African Americans were the Lazy Tongues. Lucille now believes that this is the way her institution reproduced the existing superstructure, or the A Team and the B Team.

What in the world does reproduction of the existing superstructure have to do with classroom teachers? Critical pedagogues often speak and write about schools maintaining and recreating social status and power. For example, if one group of students is labeled *gifted* and another group is labeled *limited,* which group benefits? I know a school that divides the limiteds into *low limiteds* and *high limiteds.* Apparently, the high limiteds would be the A Team of the B Team in this case. I think that we teachers often don't realize the role we play in this. We have a tendency to think that others do it, but not us. However, if we are creating (consciously or unconsciously) A Teams and B Teams in our classes, we are also a part of reproducing the existing social, cultural, and political power bases.

A Teams and B Teams are just another name for tracking, a practice that was deconstructed by the work of Jeannie Oakes. Often schools continue tracking because of false assumptions. Ryan (2003) articulates the ways in which these assumptions are erroneous, in that we now have a large body of consistent research that demonstrates that heterogeneous groups best serve all students. Ryan continues with an alternative to tracking, which includes both a pretest of reading on the first day of school and posttest of reading sixty days later. However, in between the two tests, he calls for specific curriculum and methodology. For curriculum, Ryan challenges teachers to use only the most enriched: anything from Shakespeare to Angelou to Homer to Villasenor. Classroom rules are reduced to two: Arrive on time and work hard for the entire session. All other extraneous, phony rules are gone. For methodology, Ryan posits that teachers need to follow three steps: explain, apply, and synthesize. However, above all, teachers must inspire, a construct posited also by Searle (1998), "imagination in teaching is the great motivator" (p. 2). Ryan asks that we try his suggestion for sixty days, and then he challenges us to discover, on the basis of the reading test, that students who read and write do indeed learn to read and write.

How does this history of critical pedagogy relate to the everyday life of a classroom teacher? Look around your own school, and ask yourself these questions:

1. Who is on the A Team and who is on the B Team? What part might I be playing in the reproduction and maintenance of the two teams?

2. Which students are meaningfully and purposefully interacting to generate more knowledge?
3. Who is doing fill-in-the-blank dittos? Why?
4. Am I unconsciously taking part in the selection and maintenance of the A Team at my school because of my silence?
5. Do we track? Why? Which track is best? Why?

Critical pedagogy relates fundamentally to every teacher and to every student every day. These are basic questions and issues that we live every day. However, many times, we have been so schooled, so institutionalized as to believe that we are helpless to make a difference in our own environment. If not us, who? Schools R Us? Critical pedagogy enables us to stop the "yeah, buts" and to begin to recognize our own power as professionals. Critical pedagogy gives us the power to understand that we must do the very best where we are today. We cannot fix every educational problem in the world, but we can live our own beliefs in our own communities. Critical pedagogy is the power that leads us from silence to voice.

I will conclude my introduction to Tove Skutnabb-Kangas with one last story. She and I keep a running list of who can find the most damaging, dreadful, despicable label. I have a new one that she has not seen but will when she reads this. I recently read a document that left our university and went to a state agency. In the document, I found a new label under the category of diversity: It was *differing gender*. I guess that would be Tove and me, and it would place us on the B Team. Top that one, Tove!

I have a suspicion that A Team/B Team is one of those metaphors that force us to confront our own assumptions and our own experiences. We can agree on this: None of us supports the idea of the A Team and the B Team. However, I choose to acknowledge that it exists in multiple ways, and I will not deny that it has a long and painful history for some people. Critical pedagogy calls on us to name—to throw it on the table and then provide a safe place where *all* can reflect on it, can talk about it, can begin to deconstruct it. Only after this can we take action and build a more just society for all. Let the dialogue begin.

Since the previous edition of this book, the dialogue continues regarding the metaphor of the A Team and the B Team. Unexpected e-mail messages pop onto my computer monitor, as you, the reader, challenge me to relish in more unlearning. I have been particularly inspired by a graduate student, Richard, whom I have never met. In our ongoing dialogue, he asks that we replace the A Team and the B Team with the WE Team. I shared with Richard that Freire (1970) wrote that authentic education is not carried on by "A" *for* "B" or by "A" *about* "B," but rather, by "A" *with* "B," mediated by the world.

As I write this, I am reminded of the famous quotation by Frederick Douglass: "Power concedes nothing without demand. It never did, and it never will."

The Eastern Voice

One critique of previous editions of this book was that I did not include the Eastern perspective on critical pedagogy. However, Lava D. Awashthi, a doctoral student who is studying with Tove Skutnabb-Kangas, has generously shared his perspective on critical pedagogy through the filter of his life, grounded in Eastern philosophies.

Reflections from the East

In relation to critical pedagogy, it is important to note that the "West" appears to show more interest in "analysis," whereas the "East" tends to focus on "synthesis." In other words, people in the West have analytical minds, while people in the East seem to have synthetic minds. Owing to these reasons, the West has gained successes in the material world, which perhaps is the by-product of its inherited analytical skills. On the other hand, the East has gained supremacy over the West in its inherited integrating skills due to synthesizing characters. Perhaps that is why in the East, efforts have been made to synthesize nonmaterial and material worlds, and elements of spirituality have been integrated in the critical pedagogy. Also, it has been seen that in the East, the establishments have always been challenged and redefined to reestablish a new world order. This is what we call *incarnation* or a *chakra* (a wheel, representing life cycle). For example, Krishna as an incarnation challenged the establishment and employed the Bhagavad Gita as a vehicle for his critical pedagogy. Likewise, Gautama Buddha gave a new insight into people's lives and challenged the caste-based hierarchical society through his critical teachings on enlightenment. Similarly, Guru Nanak and Mahabir Jain used their critical wisdom to create a new world order for social equity and justice.

Mahatma Gandhi is a unique example of how the East has followed a path of critical pedagogy through a synthesis of a world within (spirituality) and a world without (a material reality). To reflect on Gandhi's vision of critical pedagogy here, I would like to give a couple of examples:

First, Gandhi raised a question whether the goal of our education is simply to get employment. He further elaborated that if this is so, the dream of a nation can never be realized. Talking about the education system of the time, Gandhi warned that we are being reduced to a state in which we are losing our own identity without acquiring anything new.

To address this problem, Gandhi emphasized that education should aim at developing an individual's body, mind, and soul. For him, body is important for earning a living, mind is important for bringing in creativity, and soul is crucial for building character. He saw education as an integrated whole of life, creativity, and character building.

Peace Education

One way in which the Eastern perspective is represented in the United States is through peace education. It is fairly common in many parts of the country for peace education to be reflected in various writing processes. In our local area, students are involved in writing about their unsung heroes and heroines for peace. In this case, peace is understood to mean not only an absence of hostilities or war, but also a state of harmony existing between people, groups, or nations. Sometimes countries go to war in an attempt to bring peace by military means. Yet throughout history, many other people have worked for peace and justice through nonviolent and nonmilitary means. As a framework for you to recreate a similar process, I share the specific directions.

Peace Essays in Secondary School
500- 1,000-Word Essay
By talking with others and researching, discover someone who has worked for peace and justice through nonviolent and nonmilitary means. Your essay will consist of two parts.
In the first part of your essay, describe:

Who the person is or was and how he or she has worked for peace and justice

What prompted the person to choose to work for peace

Why you think what the person did was important in creating peace and justice in our world

In the second part of your essay, explain why you think what the person did was important in creating a more peaceful and just world in which to live.

Peace Essays in the Middle Grades
By talking with others and researching, discover someone who has worked for peace and justice through nonviolent and nonmilitary means. Your essay will consist of two parts.
In the first part of your essay describe:

Who the person is or was

How he or she has worked for peace and justice

What prompted the person to choose to work for peace

In the second part of your essay, explain why you think what the person did was important in creating a more peaceful and just world in which to live.[5]

The North American Voice

When the critical perspective arrived in the United States, it was nourished by two schools of thought that had a long history in North American educational theory: reconstructionism and progressivism. A critical educational approach had a waiting audience of those who believed that the purpose of education was to continually reconstruct society. Critical theory and Freirian thought joined with democratic ideals, which were central to progressivism. Social reform was inherent in the improvement of schools. The critical perspective shared with the progressivists a belief that all of education is value-laden and morally grounded. Dewey's progressive ideas were fertile ground for the seed of critical theory from Europe and Latin America.[6] Dewey's idea connected tightly not only with critical theory, but also with democracy.[7] Dewey saw the connections between democracy and pedagogy. Democracy was not a subject to be studied, but rather a value to be lived. Dewey believed that the theory and practice of democracy should be nourished by the power of pedagogy. Books are filled with personal stories of Dewey[8] that bring him to life.

What follows are a selected few of the North American critical perspectives. I cannot include all who have contributed, but I can highlight a few significant contributors. More thorough analyses are acknowledged throughout this text in the hope that you will move on to read them also. We begin with the legacy of Dewey as it might actually be experienced in schools today.

Dewey

Dewey said it best: "Accept the child where the child is." The critical pedagogy of today in North America is grounded in this legacy from Dewey. If we could all remember this simple educational principle, how much better our system would be. But sometimes we forget. The following is a description of a family night at the beginning of the school year for the first graders. During the evening, one of the parents asked the teacher:

> PARENT: Where do you begin? Do you begin with what the students know?
>
> TEACHER: Oh, no, we start with Chapter 4. The first three chapters are just review, and I don't want to waste my time with that. If the students aren't there yet, they don't belong in my class.

Run, families, run! And I know that this teacher studied Dewey in her credential program. But she forgot. We continue to forget another lesson from Dewey: "Accept the child as the child is."

> TEACHER #1:   I just don't know what else to do. Esmeralda just sits there. She never says anything. She never takes part in any regular activities. She would rather sit alone in her seat all day, I guess.
>
> TEACHER 2:   Well, she would do better if she could speak English.
>
> TEACHER #1:   All the students would do better if they came to school speaking English. In any case, our jobs would be easier.
>
> TEACHER 2:   Still, you would think that Esmeralda's parents would teach her English. But I guess that's supposed to be our problem, too.

Accepting who the students are is sometimes very difficult for teachers. Sometimes teachers don't want the students of today; they want the students of yesterday. This is not going to happen. I think that Dewey meant for us to accept the whole child, whatever the child's race, class, gender, language, and culture. When teachers cannot accept who the child is, they sometimes want to blame it on others—such as the child or parents. I think this tells us more about the teacher than about the child and the parents.

Every educator has studied the effects of progressivism and reproduction on the educational system. These are not abstract, historical ideas that can be relegated to a history book, placed on a shelf, and forgotten. These ideas are alive and well today in a new form with a broader historical, cultural, and political base.

Oftentimes, simultaneous and conflicting ideologies move through history together. Today, we would call this *polarization;* however, it is not a new phenomenon. During the days of progressivism and reconstructionism, very divergent ideas existed at the same time. Critical pedagogy often refers to oppositional views as the "other," which is reflected in the way in which schools were historically used to control and maintain the existing power structure. This is not a new concept on the North American continent. As early as the 1850s, schools were considered to be the most effective method of Americanizing the many immigrants who were coming to the New World for freedom and democracy. Many believed that it was the responsibility of the schools, with their European American philosophies, to test the loyalty of new immigrants, who were the groups that tended to come from southern and eastern Europe and Asia. I immediately can think of several new immigrants I know whose loyalty is being tested today. Can you? Ellwood Cubberley of Stanford was an eloquent leader of this movement. He thought that to Americanize was to Anglicize. It was the duty of the schools to assimilate the new immigrants as part of the American race (Cremin, 1964). American race? What in the world is that? "Americanism is not, and never was, a matter of race or ancestry" (Franklin Delano Roosevelt, as cited in Carnes, 1995).[9]

The social interactions of power that take place in schools every day mirror the power relationships of society. It seems we, in schools, are trying to do the same thing. Bowles and Gintis (1976) wrote that there is a simple correspondence between schooling, class, family, and social inequities. Schools are mirrors of society.

The idea of schools reproducing inequalities of society is a part of the critical theory legacy to North American school of today. It is not always an easy or welcome topic for discussion; sometimes it causes great resistance. However, I would only ask that we follow the advice of Goodlad (in Goldberg, 1995), who, reflecting on the words of John Dewey, said, "What the researcher in education must do is to get immersed in the complex phenomena, then withdraw and think about the issues" (p. 85).

Ada

Alma Flor Ada has influenced multiple classrooms and families with her critical approach to teaching and learning. Her influences are particularly felt on the West Coast.

I know we aren't supposed to say this, but Alma Flor Ada empowers me. After I am with her, I am braver, smarter, and nicer. She lives her beliefs daily and somehow makes it okay to be whoever you happen to be. In addition, I never go in front of a group to teach unless I have her methodology (Ada, 1988a, 1988b) safely tucked away in the corner of my brain. She calls it the creative reading method, which is far too narrow a description for me. I have found it to be effective in any teaching/learning context.

Instead of the five-step lesson plan, try her approach:

- *Descriptive phase.* Information is shared by teacher, text, media, and so on.
- *Personal interpretation phase.* Students grapple with new information on the basis of their lived experiences.
- *Critical phase.* Reflection and critical analysis are invited.
- *Creative phase.* Theory is connected to practice; learning flows from class to the real world of the student.

I find that these four phases are effective whether I am with five-year-olds, fifteen-year-olds, or fifty-five-year-olds. Of course, it need not be a lockstep, linear approach. Rather, it ebbs and flows as students acquire and inquire into new knowledge while they (and we) continually move through the learning-relearning-unlearning process. This pedagogical process ends with creation or action and then begins again. The students find ways to live the ideas, create more ideas, or take the ideas to their own real world. It is an approach that any teacher can begin to-morrow. If you are accustomed to lecturing or only following a perspective lessons design, this teaching/learning experience only requires two things: courage and pa-tience. As we enter into transformative pedagogy, it is often difficult to know ex-actly where to start. Alma Flor's process of the descriptive, personal interpretive, critical, and creative phases provides classroom teachers with a framework in which to discover their own praxis. Try it. However, when you are teaching and learning with this approach, remember what Alma Flor answered on March 20, 1998, in Seattle, Washington, when asked how to do critical pedagogy: "I am going to quote my daughter, who says that the only way to do it is to deeply, deeply be-lieve in the learner.[10]

McCaleb

How many times have we heard educators say, "I schedule parent conferences, but the parents won't come. How do we 'do' parental involvement?" Sudia Paloma McCaleb (1994) is helping educators to build community and build books. She asks educators to look within and examine their own assumptions about fam-ilies and literacies. Recently, a secondary teacher read this book and said to me, "I used to think that "these" families were illiterate and didn't care. Now I know that my assumptions contributed to keeping the families from coming to visit with me."

For McCaleb, transformative educators are those who view the role of a teacher not as the all-knowing instructor, but rather as a coparticipant in the learning process with students. A Spanish-English bilingual secondary teacher described this situation:

> *I held parent conferences last year, and not a single parent came. I thought I had been accessible to parents. However, McCaleb made me realize that the families were actually isolated by the appointment system, yet another hidden gatekeeping process. There I sat in my room alone while Spanish-speaking families were to make appointments in the front office with a secretary who spoke only English.*
>
> *This year I contacted all the parents and invited them to our first family night. I promised them I would get all notices to them in Spanish, and I gave them the name and phone number of a Spanish-speaking secretary. During the next conference schedule, more than 50 percent of the families came to visit during class, and three parents called later. My goal is get all the parents to come.*

Giroux

I have written of the importance of courage and patience in our study of critical pedagogy. You will need both when you begin to read Peter McLaren and Henry Giroux. I was reminded of a raging river on a stormy day when I first read these two critical theorists. Behind those big words, you will indeed find big ideas.

The first time I ever read the words of Henry Giroux, I actually thought the book was vibrating. I had never read that type of language, but I must have been ready for those powerful ideas. I could not put the book down. Even as I remember it today, it is like an almost physical and metaphysical experience. I finally got it! We, as teachers, are not to be passive, robotic technocrats who can't do anything because of the administration, or the texts, or the parents, or the students, or the tests. We are to be intellectuals and professionals who take control of our own teaching and learning. Perhaps we can't control society's perception of teachers as less, but we can control how we perceive ourselves. My suspicion is that as we begin to come to know ourselves as intellectuals and professionals and turn those beliefs into behaviors, society will begin to change its perception of us.

Giroux's idea of correspondence, which states that schooling functions to reproduce the class structure of the workplace, reaches back to the thinking of the Frankfurt School's theory of reproduction and to the economic production ideas of Marx. Giroux suggests that even though our roots are in the theory of reproduction and resistance, it is time to move to the possible that lies within each of us. He focuses his critical lens on curriculum, which is generated by the students and teachers and reflects their real world. Building from the Freirian concept, Giroux (1988) states that curriculum is never just a neutral body, a warehouse of knowledge. Rather, curriculum is a way of organizing knowledge, values, and relationships of social power. Every time I hear a teacher say, "Yeah, but the curriculum we have to use is so bad," I hear the words of Giroux in my head. He challenges us to challenge ourselves. We are not passive technocrats devoid of power over curriculum. If the curriculum needs to be challenged, challenge it. If not us, who?

McLaren

Peter McLaren challenges teachers to be courageous moral leaders who understand how knowledge, language, experience, and power are central to society and our classrooms. He asks us to look again with new eyes and see how literacies are used to support the A Team. His theory crystallizes the concept that what we do as teachers is morally and ethically grounded. Students' lives are at stake daily in our practice. It matters what we do, and we can do a lot. McLaren's words are an echo of Dewey, who stressed the acceptance of the children on their own terms. Many have written of the teachable moment, but only Peter has described the *teachable heart*.

In the works of McLaren and Giroux, we continually find an underlying current of the potential in each of us. If you are courageous and patient enough in your reading of their ideas, you will find the hidden "Yes, we can" message they are sending us. It is this idea that transforms teachers to take action and causes the shift to social and self transformation. They open the door to Freire's conscientization. How ironic that Giroux and McLaren, who are often viewed as theorists, can be the trigger to help us turn our own theory into action.

When I first heard McLaren (1994) mention the idea of the teachable heart, I thought, "Yes, that is the by-product of good teaching and learning." I would like to say that he taught this to me, but really what he did is just affirm what I had previously learned from José of Tucson phone book fame.

You will remember that José was one of that group of students who taught and learned with me for six consecutive years in Benson. The first year I met José, he was in seventh grade and didn't say a word all year; José was very much like an ethnographer in that he participated in and observed everything. José was—and is—a quiet, private, and reserved person. In the eighth grade, José started to talk. In the ninth grade, he spoke and students in the class began to listen. In tenth grade, students in other parts of the high school started to listen. In eleventh grade, the students in student government started to listen. In twelfth grade, the entire community started to listen when he graduated with honors in two languages.

In the spring of his senior year, the students chose to take a standardized national honors test in Spanish and in English so that those with high achievement could be given college credit for their knowledge.

One of our most memorable teaching/learning experiences had taken place when José was a freshman in high school. One of his classmates had innocently asked how to say "I love you" in Spanish, in French, in German, in Swahili, and the list went on and on. This was a turning point for all of us because we stopped whatever we were covering and began to research answers for the questions. For the next several weeks, the students went to libraries, interviewed travelers, and visited with families who had come from other countries. The students could not collect enough information to satisfy them; I was almost running to catch up as I tried to understand what was happening. Of course, we learned more about languages, cultures, and geography than anything else could have taught us. The students also established a list of twenty-five different ways to say "I love you." They relished practicing in and out of class. Since that time, I have never been afraid to follow the natural curiosity of students.

Although this activity had not been mentioned in class since their freshman year, when José and his classmates sat down to take the national test, I wanted to include some part of the activity as a reminder of our very special time together. On the final page of the very long test, I had written in bold letters down the middle of the page:

Translate into as many languages as you can:

I love you. _____

I love you. _____

I love you. _____

I love you. _____

I love you. _____

I love you. _____

I love you. _____

I love you. _____

I love you. _____

I love you. _____

As the students came to the end of the test, I could tell by the look on their faces that I had found the perfect parting memory for us. José was sitting in the middle seat of the middle row. As I quietly walked the rows during the test and came up behind him, I looked down at his paper and saw that he had written:

Yo sé.

Yo sé.

Yo sé.

Yo sé.

Yo sé.

Yo sé.

Yo sé.

Yo sé.

Yo sé.

Yo sé.

Yo sé in English means "I know."

From that moment on, I have understood the importance of the teachable heart. José had one; he learned not only what was taught, but also much more. And along the way, he taught us all.

Cummins

Jim Cummins's concept of empowerment (2001), which has been used and abused by many, still focuses us on the primacy of power in educational and societal issues. Cummins has taught us that unless we ourselves are empowered, we cannot be involved with any other processes of empowerment. To be voiceless is to be powerless. If we view ourselves as helpless, we are. We cannot control how others have traditionally perceived us, but we can control how we perceive ourselves. Critical pedagogy empowers our theory and action into a personal praxis that challenges the exclusive membership of the A Team.

Empowerment Framework.   Schools often ask, "What can we do?" I believe that Cummins's framework is vastly underrated and underused. Everyone talks about it as a marvelous theoretical construct, but very few use it. I suggest that it is highly usable—tomorrow! It doesn't cost anything; you won't need a mandate; you won't need a committee or another spiral notebook for your shelf. Just do it.

The beauty of this model is that it is highly adaptable in any context. As Figure 5.2 illustrates, Cummins provides guidelines along a powerful path of intervention. It is not a prescribed recipe. Teachers and learners need to bring their knowledge and experience to the model and adapt it to fit their own particular context. Schools and communities can begin the dialogue by examining their own perspectives on Cummins's framework. The following questions, which are all based on Cummins's four areas of the empowerment model, can be used for teachers, students, administrators, and/or community members. All you need to do is bring the community together and let the dialogue begin.

1. *Cultural and linguistic incorporation.* Are our theory and practice additive or subtractive? Why? What does that mean? How can we learn? Are all students encouraged to keep their family's culture and to learn more about other cultures also. What does *multicultural* mean? What does it mean to me? In what ways do we show respect for all cultures and languages? Do kids come into our schools speaking more than one language and leave twelve years later speaking only one? Why? Does our practice reflect our theory?

2. *Community participation.* Do all families feel included in the school processes? Who does? Who doesn't? How could we learn what families really feel about their inclusion or exclusion? What specific collaborative processes do we have? Who comes? Who doesn't come? Why?

3. *Pedagogy.* What does *pedagogy* mean? How can we learn? What type do we believe in? Why? Are those beliefs turned into behaviors in our classrooms? How? Do the students really get to interact and experience their own generation of knowledge, or are they just memorizing facts that might soon become dated? What can we do?

4. *Assessment of programs.* When we talk about the programs in our schools, do we find ourselves legitimizing or advocating? What is the difference? How can we learn? What specific programs make us feel like advocating? Why? We always as-

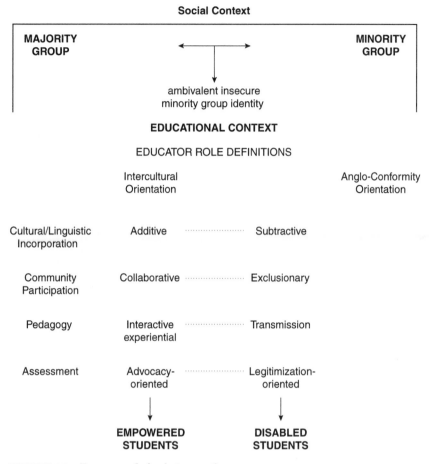

FIGURE 5.2   Framework for intervention

Source: From *Negotiating Identities: Education for Empowerment in a Diverse Society*, by J. Cummins, 2001, Ontario, CA: California Association for Bilingual Education. Copyright 2001 by the California Association for Bilingual Education. Reprinted by permission.

sess our students, but do we ever assess our own role in our local education? Should we? How? Why?

This process of reflection and action leads to empowerment. My only cautionary note for those who plan to examine critically Cummins's empowerment framework is as follows: Allow plenty of time and be supportive of each other and the process. This is not a three-hour in-service. Allow at least a year for the reflective phase and another year for the action. Things will change.

I suspect that there are two reasons why people don't actually do the empowerment framework. First, it seems too simple. How could that possibly work? Don't be fooled. The empowerment framework is not simple, nor is it simplistic. Its merit lies in the fact that it is grounded in highly complex theory and, at the same time, provides a clear picture of action. The four components force us all to confront ourselves as educators and to take the responsibility for our own educational actions. The second reason I think people tend to overlook this framework is because of the connotations of elite jargon that have developed around the "e" word. Okay, I'll say it: "Empowerment. Empowerment. Empowerment." Power is not something to be trivialized. I suggest that we put the power back in empowerment, as demonstrated in Figure 5.3. Jim Cummins has joined with Tove Skutnabb-Kangas to say clearly, "Power is, after all, what it is all about" (Skutnabb-Kangas & Cummins, 1988, p. 390).

The meaning of *empowerment* is not fixed; it is constantly emerging and redefining itself; its definition is daily informed by teachers and students as they explore its boundaries. However, the primacy of empowerment is power.

In the same way that Peter McLaren has consistently warned us of the insidious danger of critical pedagogy being reduced to nothing more than banal liberal education, Jim Cummins has warned us of the abuse of multicultural education as it becomes nothing more than celebrations of festivals and foods. I far prefer the directness of Cummins's antiracist, antisexist, anticlassist education, which forces all educators to confront the real issues of our own involvement in the hidden (and not so hidden) processes of institutionalized racism.

Cummins's concept of empowerment (1989) expanded (Cummins, 1996) to include the concept of negotiating identities, which is exactly what we do when we do critical pedagogy. Cummins has backed away from the term *empowerment* because of its patronizing use in some circles. *To empower* is not a transitive verb; it

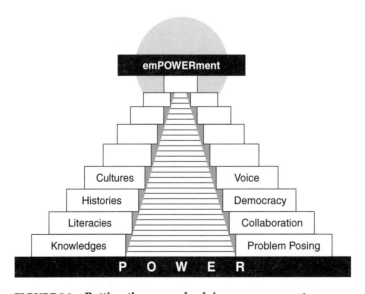

FIGURE 5.3   Putting the power back in empowerment

does not take a direct object. Think about it: if you say that you empower someone else, who actually controls the power?

Here is the point of negotiating identities: "human relationships are at the heart of schooling (Cummins, 1996, p. 1). What we do matters. The connections that we create in classrooms are central to students' growth as they negotiate their own identities, and, we, while learning with them, continually negotiate our own identities. These interactions trigger a process whereby students create their own sense of self. Furthermore, these human relationships can have a negative or positive effect. The implications throughout Cummins (1996) are clear: Students may be failing not because of who they are, but rather because of what is being communicated to them by their teachers. These human interactions are the ways we negotiate identities in our classrooms. These relationships are evident when students transform their own self-image and discover who they are and can be and thus create the future for all of us.

None of this takes place in a vacuum. These new and emerging identities are surrounded by the powerful relationships between teachers and students in your classroom and in my classroom. We are a part of our own personal pedagogy. It's true: We are in the classroom, too. It is not about *them;* it is about *us*. The vision of critical pedagogy makes clear our own human potential and that of every student in our classroom. Just as, in 1989, we all tried to understand and explain empowerment, so once again we will all now be called on to clarify negotiating identities. Cummins says that human relationships are the ways in which we negotiate identities in our classrooms. These relationships are evident when students transform their own self-image, discover who they are, and redefine themselves and thus create the future.

Collaborative and Coercive Relations of Power.   Cummins has continued to expand his ideas of power and empowerment with his concepts of coercive relations of power and collaborative relations of power (Cummins, 1994). We all have experienced coercive relations of power in which it is assumed that there is a limited amount of power; power is believed to be fixed and subtractive. If one person gets more, the fear is that someone else must get less. These assumptions are nonsense. Power and problems have something in common: There is enough for us all. I have noticed that every time I mention this to a group of educators, there is always a knowing smile of understanding on hearing that specific language. Well, let me be precise—most smile, a few squirm. What does that tell me? Who smiles? And who squirms? I think you know the answers to these questions.

When you have worked in a coercive environment, how did you feel? Were you effective? Productive? Not me. When I am in coercive environments, I do less, and I do it with anger. Collaborative relations of power assume that power is infinite; it grows and generates during collaborative interactions. When I have been in an environment of collaborative relations of power, I do more, and I do it better. The trick for teachers is to have the courage to negotiate their own power even when they are within the context of coercive relations of power.

Krashen

"Joan, why are you here for a reading conference?" he asked when he saw me at a large international airport.

"Yes, we thought you were working in bilingual education. Have you changed?" his friend added.

The airport was packed with teachers and principals all rushing to catch their flights after a large and very successful conference on literacy. It seemed that everyone in the airport was carrying the same colorful conference bookbag filled with the books and memories of a truly stellar conference. As I was running to catch my plane, I happened to meet two former colleagues who had known me in another time and place. They seemed happy to see me but were mystified: Why in the world would I be at a literacy conference?

Literacy is what it is all about, for all of us. If you are in education, any phase of education, you are involved with literacy. This includes those of us with a history in bilingual and multilingual education.

Steve Krashen has done more to bring us all together around books than anyone else I can name. Books are about literacy. If critical pedagogy is about self- and social transformation, Krashen is a critical pedagogue. His gentle, humorous, and persistent voice continues to link all educators—those from the mainstream with those from bilingual with those from immersion with those from ESL with those from special education with those from gifted programs. Pre-kindergarten, primary, elementary, middle school, high school, postsecondary, grad school—it doesn't matter. We are all involved with literacy development, which is the road to understanding, new knowledge, and the unknown future. Of course, I am involved with literacy. So are you.

A national debate is taking place about literacy: How do kids learn to read? Is it better to focus on parts (for example, sounds), or should we focus on the whole (for example, a story)? Which way is best? Well, it turns out that there is no one-size-fits-all; Jonathan and Wyatt taught me that. There is no one perfect way; my own kids taught me that. Just because I learned to read through phonics does not mean that it worked for them. In fact, it didn't. My children learned in the exact opposite way: They read books, borrowed books, and slept with books. They loved books, something that eluded me and my sound-centric approach until I started reading to them when they were babies. However, access to books is the bottom line. Children who have books have a far greater chance of learning to read and loving to read and continuing to read.[11]

In spite of this, some states and districts are now mandating a one-way-only-approach to reading. Some teachers are now required to give so many teeny, tiny parts that there is no whole, creating a hole in literacy development. It is possible now to walk into schools and hear kids in multiple classrooms making the same sounds, from the same page, at the exact same time of day. If I hadn't actually experienced this, I doubt that anyone could convince me of its reality.

"I can't believe I just told that student to stop reading and start doing the sounds with us," the teacher said to me. "She was sitting over in a chair completely enthralled in her book, and I stopped her from reading to do isolated sounds with us."

"Why?" I asked.
"Because if anyone walks by and see one student not doing sounds in isolation with us, it will be written on my evaluation," she sadly told me.

I will tell you, dear readers, that this is not an isolated example. I could cite many, many more from my own personal experience within the last academic year. If anyone had told me two years ago that it would come to this, I never would have believed it.

Yes, kids can learn to recite sounds, but can they read a good book? Do they want to read a good book? Do they have access to good books? Will they love to read? These are the important questions? Even more important, will they take a flashlight to bed with them?[12]

The Historical Evolution of Critical Pedagogy

The history of critical pedagogy continues to evolve; it is not a product, it is a process of development, and each person reading this page is a part of that development. For example, since the last edition, it is clear that connections have been established to the Eastern perspective. I predict that these will continue to grow and even flourish. Another omission from critical pedagogy has been the linkages with the African American historical roots, particularly in North America. Cooper (1892/1988), Du Bois (1903), Woodson (1933/1990), and Clark and Brown (1990) have all made significant contributions to the roots of critical theory. The construct of reading the word and the world is the undergirding of literacy, but particularly so for many people of color as they struggle to negotiate identity within a historically hostile macro culture. I am confident that we will have a much more complete understanding of race, racism, and racialization, particularly in U.S. schools and society. Critical race theory and critical pedagogy both focus a critical lens on the multiple ways in which inequalities are perpetuated through societal and institutional processes.

The Benson Kids

Critical pedagogy always begins with questions. In the search for my own unique voice within the framework of critical pedagogy, I asked, "Where in the world does it come from?" These philosophical roots originated in many areas of the world and from multiple voices. These voices of culture, experience, language, knowledge, and power provide us with a foundation for further learning. I have painted a picture of the roots, which extend south and east. In addition, I have written of critical roots that have touched my life. This picture is not all-inclusive, but my wish is that it is enough to pique your curiosity and make you run to buy or borrow another book.

However, if you really want to know where I learned about critical pedagogy, it was from those Benson kids. They were the ones who taught me all of this. The University of Arizona and Texas A&M think that they taught me this, but they only affirmed what students had taught me. I started out with the intention of teaching the Benson kids how to conjugate verbs; they taught me how to teach. These students challenged all the philosophy and methodology that I had previously been taught. Now, when I read roaring, raging books of theory, I see the faces of the students who taught me.

In the next chapter, I will ask the question "Critical Pedagogy: How in the World Do You Do It?" I suspect that the following chapter will require all of my courage and most of your patience.

Looking Ahead for New Leaders: You!

Our future together will need new leaders. What critical leadership qualities do you bring to the future?

Practicing Pedagogy Patiently: Civics, ESL, and the New Immigrants

When Bella Yakubovich, seventy-one years old, and her agemate Alexandra Sviridova spoke to the city council, they were not dressed as smartly as many in the room. The two immigrants from the former Soviet Union stepped to the microphone and spoke carefully to defend their English classes at a senior center against impending budget cuts. Their requests were what many reading this book might take for granted: We want to tell a doctor our problems. We want to understand TV. We want to talk with neighbors. We want to know history and culture. Help us to become complete citizens.

These two senior students are part of a growing teaching/learning experience in which English as a Second Language classes are tightly connected with literacy and civics. Often called English Literacy-Civics, these classes go beyond a curriculum focused on workplace skills, which took place in the 1990s. In these classes, fill-in-the-blank exercises and irregular verb memorization are replaced by active involvement within the community. The participants are involved with language that matters, or with their own "word universe." The goal is to replace the transmission model of teaching and learning with the transformative model. The goal is to make education meaningful in the real world of the students. The teachers and students together pose problems and seek solutions. For example, journals are used for students to record real conversations and words they hear on the streets; the Internet is used to research human resources within the community; letters are written to newspapers and public servants; students develop a voice and learn to have greater control over their own lives.

The connection between literacy and civics in the immigrant community has its roots in the legacy of Paulo Freire. In this notion of critical pedagogy, it is assumed that the students bring a wealth of knowledge into the classroom; the teacher acts as a facilitator who assists the students' articulation of their own knowledge as they learn to generate more knowledge within their new community. The purpose is to improve the quality of life (Nathan, 2003).

NOTES

1. You might have noticed that I enjoy knowing about the person while I am learning about his or her ideas. In this little book, I cannot tell all the stories about the people I mention. However, if you want to know about the amazing life of Gramsci, please read Csikszentmihalyi (1997).

2. For more on Marx and the concept of economic and social reproduction, please see deMarrais and LeCompte (1999) and any of the three editions of McLaren's *Life in Schools.*

3. Tracking. For further reading on this subject, read Oakes (1985). Tracking is also a recurring theme with Rethinking Schools, a marvelous Milwaukee group of teachers and their newsletters. (Rethinking Schools, 1001 East Keefe Avenue, Milwaukee, Wisconsin 53212; tel.: 414-964-9646; fax: 414-964-7220.) More recently (1995), *Rethinking Schools* (ISBN 1-56584-215-4) was published by The New Press, New York, NY 10110.

4. "Here Lies the Man Who Convinced Americans to Unbolt School Desks from the Floor" is an old joke about Dewey's headstone for his grave. For more on this, read Newman (1998).

5. This discussion of peace education has been informed by a dialogue with Pam Franklin, a teacher who is committed to peace.

6. For more on the connections between Dewey and Freire, I refer you to Campbell (2004).

7. Remember it this way: Dewey and democracy. For more on this, I refer you to Dewey (1994/1916).

8. Newman (1998) captures Dewey, the man and legacy, with his fresh look at memorable old stories that education students so often hear and tell.

9. Newman (1998) also reexamines Cubberley with a focus on relearning and unlearning some of our historical educational assumptions.

10. This quotation from Alma Flor's daughter is a direct reference to Freeman and Freeman (1992, 1994, 1998). The idea that teachers need to have faith in the learners is fundamental in their work. Freeman and Freeman (1998) have devoted their entire Chapter 10 to how to do it and why it matters.

11. For the most comprehensive information on real reading and the real stats on real reading, I refer you to the latest Krashen publications in the Bibliography and also to McQuillan (1998b). If critical pedagogy is about exploding myths (Nieto, 1996), and that certainly has been my experience, these specific references might very well explode a few more.

12. Finding my own kids in bed with books and flashlights was one of my most assuring parental experiences. I didn't know the research then, but I sensed that this was a "good" problem. Since that time, we have learned a lot about children and flashlights and books. Krashen (1993) finds that the data reflect that free readers have a chance. You might also like to read Quindlen (1998), who tells the story of the practice, not the theory.

CHAPTER

6 How in the World Do You Do It?

Always think about practice.
(a fundamental Freirian principle as expressed by GADOTTI)

Thinking about Practice

Here I sit, thinking about practice—thinking about what can't be written: how to *do* critical pedagogy. In the previous chapters, we discussed the meaning and the history of critical pedagogy. In this chapter, I will move to a harder question: How in the world do you do critical pedagogy? Is there a blueprint? A prescription? A recipe? Of course not, which will make writing this chapter fairly problematic. This must be how Mem Fox (1993) felt when she wrote about trying to teach what can't be taught. I am writing about what can't be written. I doubt I can teach someone how to do critical pedagogy. We do not *do* critical pedagogy; we *live* it. Critical pedagogy is not a method; it is a way of life (Jasso & Jasso, 1995).

However, my view of living critical pedagogy is balanced by the persistent voice of Dawn Wink, who keeps rolling her eyes and saying, "Yeah, but how, Mom?"

If you are one of the practitioners who constantly say, "*How?*," you will be glad to know that I have suffered a lot in the preparation of this chapter. Whenever I try to explain to someone that you don't do critical pedagogy, you live it, *how* just keeps creeping into the conversation. For example, when I told Dawn about self- and social transformation, emancipatory pedagogy, a spirit of inquiry, and problem posing, she sighed and asked, "How?" When I told her to have students interview their parents, she queried, "Yeah, but what about the parents who question me because my students don't get dittos like the other kids?" When I told her to record her student-generated questions on the board, she came home and asked, "Okay, now I have thirty student-generated questions on the board. Now what?"

The fact is that I love to play with the dialectic of living or doing critical pedagogy. The fact is that Dawn Wink is not as enthralled with this as I am. So for all the Dawn Winks, I hesitatingly offer these guidelines for doing critical pedagogy. I encourage you to take them and shape them to fit the needs of your students. All the following guidelines are based on Paulo Freire's concept of problem posing: **to name, to critically reflect, to act.**

The practitioners' voices in critical pedagogy must be as strong as the theorists' voices. It is always easier to state a theoretical concept than it is to live it with twenty, forty, or 240 students every day. A secondary teacher, who also is a graduate student in my theory class, teaches 240 high school students daily. Most of these students speak languages other than English. In addition, this teacher is a parent, and he consistently makes visits to the homes of the students, even though he does not speak the languages of some of the families. Certainly, he has much to teach me in my theory class. The voice of critical pedagogy must flow in both directions: from theory to practice and from practice to theory. My ongoing dialogue with Dawn has offered me the opportunity to relearn and unlearn as her practice informs my theory and my theory informs her practice. In the spirit of McLaren (2003), this is my attempt to pry theory away from the academics and incorporate it in educational practice (p. 167) as I have experienced it.

Carla: Reflecting on Her Practice

In what follows, Carla, an adult graduate student who is also a high school teacher is thinking about her own practice. She was inspired to think and write of her own practice after she read Freire (1996), in which he challenged his readers to think constantly of the complexity of the relationship between teacher and learner. Carla writes:

> *Masuda is a lovely girl: long black hair, an oval face with exotic eyes, rimmed with dark kohl liner. English is her third language, and she speaks carefully, enunciating clearly, with particular emphasis on the last syllables of words. She no longer wears the chador. (After September 11th, she feared retaliation.) She has a regal bearing, and she carries burdens far too heavy for her age. Her father was killed when she was an infant. Widowed at twenty-one, her mother has struggled to raise three children. Because of the practical matters of escaping from Afghanistan, Masuda did not attend school for many years. Masuda's oldest sister was kidnapped by her abusive husband— an arranged marriage—and taken to Pakistan. Masuda is often near tears.*
>
> *She signed up for an English elective this year because I was the teacher. She remembers the story that I told the class and has told me more than once how much it inspired her. Too much time has passed now for me to ask, "Which story?" but I think it must have been some version of Literacy as Liberation. During the time between her freshman and senior years, she kept me apprised of her progress. On the rare occasion that I wear something stylish, she compliments me on my clothes. She pauses every day after class to chat; that extra connection is critical to her. She even loves my car and has clearly fantasized about my life. She has placed me on a pedestal, and I am leery of being there.*
>
> *We have an appointment Monday to work on her personal statement—she plans on applying to U.C., and the deadline is looming. Here's the rub. As an English writer, she is still emerging. She has not mastered the complexities of writing in English, and I think she is too delicate for a large, impersonal school. I don't think she has a snowball's chance in hell of getting in. If admitted, she would be destroyed during*

the first term. I hesitate to say that going through this application process is a waste of time; I want her to believe that she can make it. But I don't want her damaged so that she retreats behind her chador and acquiesces to an early marriage, something she has been fighting since she was fifteen. She sees me as a beacon, someone who overcame adversity, and she is charting her course with me as one of her guides. It scares the hell out of me.

I do know what it is to be a little girl who watches an admired teacher, someone who actually went to that magical place called college. And I know what it is to be a woman looking back at the mirage. I desperately do not want to mislead her, and I know the power of a touchstone—an image that you can hold in your mind, some blind faith that powers all the plodding effort that promises sometime, somehow to pay off.

Yes, Paulo, teacher-student relationships are "fundamental and difficult" and you will be pleased to know that I struggle constantly.

Democratic Pedagogy

Democracy is at the heart of the transformative lesson. Schooling in the United States has historically prided itself on teaching democratic principles, but how many schools are truly democratic? If you would like to explore this question, the next time you are with a group of teachers, initiate a discussion of democracy. It's all the rage. Everyone is for it. Then ask them whether they work in a democratic school. I have done this on multiple occasions in large staff development groups with many teachers. I have consistently been amazed at the level of cynicism of teachers when they discuss the lack of democracy in their own schools. It would take more than one hand for me to count the social studies teachers I know who teach democracy but admit that they do not live and work in a democratic environment. Ah, these contradictions are confounding! It seems that in schools, we teach it well; apparently, we don't live it quite as well.

> A society which makes provision for participation in its good of all its members on equal terms and which secures flexible readjustment of its institutions through interaction of the different forms of associated life is in so far democratic. Such a society must have a type of education which gives individuals a personal interest in social relationships and control, and the habits of mind which secure social changes without introducing disorder. (Dewey, 1944/1916, p. 99)

The philosophy that supports transformative teaching and learning is founded on the principle that theory and practice are joined to form praxis. Not only must democracy be taught; it must be lived within the classroom, the school, and the community. Lesson designs that spring from this philosophical basis seek to break down the harmful forces of marginalization. This model of lesson design seeks to assure all communities of learners' equity and access to both academic resources and power structures of society.

The transformational activities that I am sharing in this chapter are all meant to be used in the classroom or with families in the community. I encourage you to adapt them to fit the context and the needs of the teachers and learners in your context.

So How Do You Do Critical Pedagogy?

In transformative education, the spirit of inquiry leads the search for meaning. Students need to have classrooms in which they are safe to take risks. In this pedagogical model, teachers shift from control of knowledge to creation of processes whereby students take ownership of their learning and take risks to understand and apply their knowledge. Students and teachers come to realize that their actions can make a difference.

Problem Posing: Jonathan and Wyatt, Examples from the Community

How to do critical pedagogy? Let's reflect together on Jonathan, the student I mentioned in Chapter 1. Why is it that I could learn so much about teaching and learning from him? Was I doing critical pedagogy? Problem posing is central in critical pedagogy; what does problem posing have to do with Jonathan?

Paulo Freire has taught that to teach and learn critically we can follow this straightforward guideline: **to name, to reflect critically, to act.** I have found this to be extremely effective in my own teaching and learning. However, I also have discovered that sometimes educators are doing/living this framework without realizing it. I also have discovered that when we ask teachers and learners to name the problem, they respond, "What?" Sometimes, I suspect that when I ask students to name, they think that I talk funny. When we name a problem or a situation, we are doing nothing more than conceptualizing critically and articulating clearly.

Let's rethink the experiences of Jonathan and Wyatt using this framework as a guide for our own reflection.

- *To name.* In the Jonathan story, to name would be to say that he could not decode and encode; he could not read and write as they have traditionally been defined. In the Wyatt story, he did not start reading at the prescribed time, nor with the "proper" books. Only Pokémon and *Captain Underpants* cracked his reading code.

- *To reflect critically.* What did we do to reflect critically about Jonathan and Wyatt? We listened, watched, talked, read, and thought. In addition, the two sets of parents kept reading with their sons, as they tried not to share their growing concern. What did Jonathan and Wyatt do? They tried and tried, and sometimes they cried.

- *To act.* What did Jonathan's parents do? They enrolled Jonathan in an expensive program, which was very much the opposite of anything that I had recommended. What did Wyatt's parents do? They recognized that Wyatt was learning to decode with reading materials which they found offensive. What did I do? I just kept writing with the hope that others can learn from these experiences.

During all of this time, did I ever think that I was doing critical pedagogy? Never. Not once. Was I doing critical pedagogy? Probably, but I prefer to think that I was simply living my beliefs. I care about Jonathan; I care about Wyatt; I care about children learning to read; I care about teaching and learning. I just had to keep a close eye on all of this. I couldn't stop myself.

However, I suspect that one has constantly and critically to reflect on learning, relearning, and unlearning. This is the hard part.

Here's the point: I believe that many educators are doing the very same thing in their own educational context. Every day with my work with teachers, I observe similar powerful situations. Every night in my graduate classes, I hear incredible stories of teachers and students and families. At the grass roots level, teachers are making a difference in the lives of students. But I suggest that it is helpful to stop thinking of ourselves as just methodologists. We are more than that: Critical pedagogy enables us to understand that we also are professionals and intellectuals who have the power to take part actively in self- and social transformation. Critical pedagogy makes us keep on keeping on.

Problem Posing: Miss Johnson, an Example from Secondary Schools

I have stated that all activities in this chapter are designed to be used in the classroom and/or the community. It is how and why we do activities that make them critical. In the following vignette, we see how Miss Johnson turned her classroom into a community with critical activities. This all took place many years ago, so I am sure that Miss Johnson had never heard of critical pedagogy, but she was doing it.

Sometimes when we try to define problem posing, it can be helpful to reflect on our own teaching and learning. I learned about Miss Johnson from Terry, a teacher and graduate student. Terry discovered the meaning of problem posing by thinking of her own experiences:

> *Problem posing always makes me think of liberation. If the purpose of education truly is human liberation, then why are we always trying to box in ideas? We are always trying to fit powerful ideas into a scope and sequence, a curriculum, a skill continuum, or another district-mandated process. Problem posing cannot be confined to these boxes. When I think of liberated people, I think of Maya Angelou, who flies above all the boxes that others have created.*
>
> *I think of my high school literature teacher, Miss Johnson. In her class, we lived problem posing every day, and we didn't even know it. She opened the world for us; she hated syllabi. Her enthusiasm ignited our journeys of learning. We had tons of books of all kinds in her class, and we had time to read whatever we chose. We read and talked and discussed and wrote. And we created a community in the process.*
>
> *Miss Johnson listened to our hidden voices. She taught us to listen to each other. We learned that any problem could have many solutions.*
>
> *She taught us to name; to reflect critically; and to act. I particularly remember one of the problems we posed.*
>
> ■ To name. *This was during the 1960s, and the girls were not allowed to wear pants to school. We were angry about this. We used to go to her room and talk about*

it. In her class, we knew that we could name anything we wanted. We just didn't know that we were naming!

- To reflect critically. *We spent many lunch periods in her classroom talking about our anger. She would listen to each of us. If it mattered to us, it mattered to her.*

- To act. *After considering several options, we devised a plan that was very radical in those days. We wrote letters and carried them to the student council, the administration, and the school board to ask that girls be allowed to wear pants to school. I remember the boys on the student council, the male administrators, and the men on the school board saying no: Girls had to wear dresses. However, the year after we graduated, pants were allowed for all students.*

Apparently, I have overlooked a significant event in the histories of women of my age. The same week that Terry wrote this reflection, another grad student/teacher handed in a splendid timeline that reflected the educational changes from Comenius to Freire. On this timeline, she had written: "1966—girls finally were allowed to wear pants to school."

Principles of Problem Posing

Teachers and Learners
- Trust each other
- Believe that their involvement will matter
- Understand resistance and institutional barriers to change
- Are aware of their own power and knowledge

If we look back on Terry's experience, we can see that these principles of problem posing were embedded in this process. For example, the students and teacher trusted each other; they believed that they could change the dress code; they knew that the student council members, the administrators, and school board would probably say no initially; and they had a sense that they could make a difference because, after all, the dress code did affect their lives every day. It had very little effect on those who had created the rule. Maybe perseverance should be another principle of problem posing.

The Teacher's Role in Problem Posing

To create a safe place for it to happen

To ask hard questions for the students' musing

To assist students with codification

Miss Johnson opened her classroom during lunch and after school. Terry and her friends knew that they were welcome. As the girls talked, Miss Johnson periodically would ask questions that they had never considered. For example, who made this rule about pants? Miss Johnson had suggested to the girls that they write letters with their concerns; she had led them into the act of codification. As I have written previously, codification is the problem represented in some format. What might this codification look like? It can be captured in clay, in paint, in chalk, in pencil, in music, in any art form. In the process of problem posing, the learners capture their feelings and meanings about a problem.

Problem Posing: Stephanie, an Example from the Primary Grades

Stephanie listened as her students discussed their frustration with never being able to open the containers of applesauce that were served at lunch. The students consistently had to ask a teacher or an aide to open the containers for them. Instead of dismissing this topic as irrelevant because it was outside of the prescribed curriculum, Stephanie recognized the dynamic as one that mattered to students. As the students talked, Stephanie wrote their comments on the chalkboard. Stephanie allowed time for the students to articulate and conceptualize the problem. After the students had clearly named their problem, she asked them what could be done to alleviate this problem. The suggestions began as Stephanie continued to capture all the thoughts and language on the chalkboard. Finally, the group came to a consensus. They decided to write a class letter to the company. With the language on the board, the students were able to write independently to express their concerns. When we last called Stephanie, she reported that the letters had been mailed and they were awaiting a reply.

Doing critical pedagogy is grounded in some form of Freire's legacy of problem posing. In this case, Stephanie and the students recreated their socially generated knowledge to act on one small condition of their own world. The transformative lesson design encourages students to act on their knowledge, and it seeks to create processes whereby students can see that their actions do count. Learning and teaching are integrated for self- and social transformation.

Problem Posing: Codification

Freeman and Freeman (1992, 1998) have clarified problem posing for many teachers whom I know, and they credit Wallerstein (1983) with expanding their understanding. Their codification model is grounded in the work of Freire and is amplified for teachers' ease in implementation. It has been my experience that many teachers are ready to pose problems; however, it is challenging, and they often are confused about codification. Freeman and Freeman (1992) offer the following model of codification:

- The code is a whole story, picture, or film.
- The code is based on the learners' lives.
- Learners identify and solve real-life problems.
- Learners work cooperatively to solve community problems.
- The goal is literacy for the learners.
- The goal is for teachers and students to empower themselves. (p. 112)

Freeman and Freeman (1992) extend their codification processes to their version of problem posing in which they offer six phases. Adapting their model, I offer the following four phases of problem posing:

1. *Begin with the students' own experience.* In schools, we are so focused on doing, on covering, that we don't take time to think, to reflect, to muse. My sense is that we, as teachers, have failed our students by not taking the time to encourage them to reflect quietly on their lived experiences. Yes, learning can take place in noisy, interactive classrooms. Learning can also take place when we silently reflect. I have often heard Yetta Goodman, who teaches at the University of Arizona, say that the only thing teachers hate more than noise is silence. She is right.

2. *Identify, investigate, pose a problem within your own life.* At this point, teachers need to let go of control; student-centered learning is about to begin. Students generate knowledge about the problem; they brainstorm where, when, and how they can learn more about it. Students set out to learn what they want to know. They codify ideas; they interview experts in the community; they find information in the library, through technology, and from any resource that has accessible information. Teachers can facilitate this process by helping students find language to conceptualize and articulate their thoughts. Teachers ask leading questions about resources for more learning and possible connections to students' lives. Teachers stay out of the way.

3. *Solve the problem together.* After conceptualizing, articulating, and researching the problem, learners work together to solve the problem.

4. *Act.* Learners make a plan and act on it. Learners discover that their learning and their involvement really do matter. Learners are empowered by their own learning and action. They realize that their social interaction can lead to self- and social transformation.

Problem posing always ends with action. Once the learners have identified and captured (named) their concern, they take action, find solutions, extend the dialogue of the classroom to the real world. What might this action look like? It can be writing a letter to the editor, governor, legislators, or president; interviewing others; recording oral histories; meeting with policymaking committees; cleaning up a community; or beginning an environmental, social, cultural, or political action group.

Problem Posing: Reggie, an Example from Postsecondary

Reggie, a former dropout and now a college freshman, was enrolled in a writing seminar. Although he was a bright student, every week in the writers' workshop, Reggie sat. He rarely finished more than a paragraph.

■ *To name.* Reggie would not write. Although he had returned to school, he was still angry and refusing to grow and learn and develop. His oppositional behaviors in the writers' workshop were holding back the further development of his own literacy. However, Reggie cared about his own writing and wanted to improve.

The instructor tried many different approaches to get Reggie to write. Nothing seemed to work. Finally, the instructor learned of a method referred to as *voiced writing* at the local university.

■ *To reflect critically.* The instructor tried many different approaches; she discussed Reggie with her colleague and local university professors. The instructor did not give up; she continued to reflect, not only on reasons why Reggie was not writing, but also on how she might get him to want to improve his writing.

Finally, the instructor arranged for a tutor to come to the writers' workshop to work with Reggie by himself. The instructor helped Reggie to understand the work that was necessary to pass the class, because Reggie said that he did want to successfully finish the class. The tutor agreed to learn the method of voiced writing so that he could try it with Reggie.

■ *To act.* The instructor found a tutor and another method, voiced writing, to try with Reggie.

Ultimately, the human relationship between Reggie and the tutor is what brought about the transformation. The tutor discovered that Reggie could not write silently, but he could write if he spoke aloud as he wrote. "Silence him, and he cannot write," the tutor told the instructor. After working with a partner and "talking" his own writing, Reggie discovered that he could indeed write. He simply needed to talk as he wrote.

There are many variations of voiced writing. The process that the instructor followed with Reggie is as follows:

- Reggie was paired with one other student, Lee.
- First, Reggie talked the writing assignment while Lee wrote verbatim every word that Reggie said.
- Second, Reggie read aloud what Lee had written.
- Third, Reggie and Lee exchanged roles. Lee talked the assignment, and Reggie wrote every word that she said.
- Fourth, Lee read aloud what Reggie had written.
- Finally, after Reggie and Lee had done this activity several times, they returned to their own desks and continued to talk quietly and write their own words.

In other words, if you can talk, you can write. Just talk as you write.

As with all methods, how they are used and why they are used are basic to determining whether the process will be effective with students. And as with all methods, there are as many variations as there are needs of students. In what follows, I am sharing two other ways of approaching this activity.

The following activity might work well for students who are preparing for discrete point grammar tests. We teach grammar for twelve years in a row, and students still say, "I don't know grammar," which raises many disturbing questions about meaningful teaching and learning and types of assessment. However, this activity can demonstrate to them that they do know grammar—it's all in their head; they just have to talk it. Repeat the voiced writing activity, but have the pairs of students talk (and record) their oral responses on grammar exercises. Often, students will talk the isolated grammar exercises correctly. It demonstrates to the students that many do have correct grammar in our heads; we hear it on TV, on the radio, and from teachers. Students acquire a lot of correct grammar in this way and don't realize that they know it.

A second variation to use when confronted with students who say that they can't write is to use this same paired activity and focus the talk to a description of the worst teacher they ever had. First, ask them to muse (think of sharp mental images, visualize, feel the memory). Second, the talk student begins to brain dump— just saying all the images and words that are in her head; the writer records every word. Third, the talk student uses these words to talk about that teacher; the writer writes everything. The talk student reads to the writer what has been written, and they exchange roles. This activity of musing, brain dumping, and writing is much more powerful than it looks on paper, but students (of all ages) have to be walked through it the first few times. During the musing phase, the teacher must encourage the students to think in pictures and sense or visualize every aspect. During the brain-dumping phase, students just take the visual images and use words to describe them. During the writing phase, the students use their own language to generate their own cognition. Good problem posing always revolves around concepts that the learners care deeply about or have experienced.

In summary, problem posing takes place when people begin with a spirit of inquiry and questioning of situations that directly affect their own lives. Problem posing ends with actions and transformations in their lives and in their context. Problem posing begins again.

Here is the secret: If you do critical pedagogy, you will be problem posing. To problem pose is to name, to reflect critically, and to act. There you have it: how to do critical pedagogy.

The Essence Is in the Experience

> A primary responsibility of educators is that they not only be aware of the general principle of the shaping of actual experience by environing conditions, but that they also recognize in the concrete what surroundings are conducive to having experiences that lead to growth. Above all, they should know how to utilize the surroundings, physical and social, that exist so as to extract from them all that they have to contribute to building up experiences that are worth while. (Dewey, 1947/1938, p. 35)

In what follows are activities in direct response to the readers of previous editions who asked, "How do you do it?" My final cautionary word on methods: You have to experience them. Dewey was right. Reading about methods is a poor second. Please take these methods and adapt them to your context, to the needs of your students, and to your own unique pedagogical gifts. If you are anything like me, new methods often do not work well the first time. Yes, it takes experience and more experience to understand how to turn methods into critically reflective actions within communities.

The following activities are not new per se. However, one of my most interesting relearning experiences is that many activities can become vehicles for critical reflection and action depending on why and how they are used. I know. I should have known. However, it was yet another relearning experience for me when I wanted to introduce some rigorous ideas to a group of international educators during a fast-paced summer school session. Here is how I now remember what I relearned with this marvelous group of educators.

The more critical the text, the easier the method. I wanted the students to read Pennycook (1994), to understand and internalize the ideas and, ideally, to return to their varied homelands around the world and continue to reflect and perhaps even to act on their learning. I considered many options before deciding how to access the text. Finally, I decided to use activities that were relatively easy and ones I knew well. Walking to class that day, enjoying the beach air of Palma, Mallorca, Spain, I worried that the students might be insulted or demeaned by my selection of easy methods. The exact opposite happened. The easy methods became an effective way of accessing rigorous content.

The students were adults who teach English all over the world; in other words, they were English as International Language (EIL) teachers. Pennycook's objective in *The Cultural Politics of English as an International Language* (1994) is to encourage international teachers to think in new ways about the teaching of English. Pennycook weaves the cultural and political implications of the spread of English throughout the pages of his text. He suggests that EIL teachers are gatekeepers of knowledge even though they might never have critically reflected on their unexamined role in the process. His reference section is complete with the various international scholars who support the idea that teaching English internationally is often not far afield from the sociocultural, political, historical, and economic context. His thesis is a critical challenge to the dominant ways of thought.

Pennycook says that we come from a history that teaches that English is natural, neutral, and beneficial. In contrast to this traditional pattern of thought, he offers a second perspective, as he documents the various ways in which the spread of English has often been quite deliberate. He writes about the worldliness of English. He assumes that a language (English, in this case) is not just "a language," but rather it is an inherent and complex part of cultural perspectives. Language does not exist in a vacuum; it is not neutral. The worldliness of English assumes the plurality of perspectives; it is not monological. Language is in constant change, and meanings are always being created, adapted, and changed. In essence, Pennycook deconstructs the assumptions of many well-intentioned teachers who go abroad to teach English—the very type of teachers I was teaching.[1]

As I assigned Pennycook (1994), I was quite sure that this would be a new idea for this group of teachers. My initial sense was that they had come from a traditional pattern of thought. I was quite sure that there would be resistance, anger, and denial.

As I reviewed the ideas of Pennycook, I considered the various approaches we could use for teaching and learning. I knew the transmission model (me talking and students listening) would never work. I was sure that I had to do something interactive so that the students could play with the ideas. I also wanted something transformative to come from this experience. I was hoping that the students would critically reflect on their own roles in teaching English in an international context when they returned home. However, I am well aware that I cannot control the future. If Pennycook's ideas were to become transformative in the lives of these students/teachers, it was really up to them. If the generative knowledge that we constructed together was ever to be transformative in their various contexts around the world, I suspect that I will never know it. I believe that we can only critically, reflectively, interactively, and actively approach our own pedagogy and hope that students will do the same.

I somewhat nervously approached our six-hour class on the day that we were to discuss Pennycook (1994). With our very tight schedule, I knew that we could devote only a day or two to this text. The students approached class tired and angry, frustrated and fearing that they did not understand the text and/or they understood it only too well. Contradictions are a common experience among critical educators. We began the following easy methods to access difficult text. The results were surprising—in fact, the exact opposite of what I feared happened. This certainly isn't the only time that I have marveled at the contradictions in pedagogy while doing critical pedagogy. As we worked through the ideas of the worldliness of English, I relearned methods, and the students unlearned some of their long-held but previously unexamined assumptions about teaching English internationally. I have since tried this in other contexts with similar results; however, my descriptions of the next four methods will revolve around only this international context.

Popcorn

How to Do It

- Students choose a small section from the text that they liked or didn't like.
- When each student has chosen, one student stands (pops up) and reads her passage. Other students listen. There are no comments or questions until each student has shared individually.
- The first student calls a second student to stand and read. When all are finished with their individual readings, students are encouraged to share with the whole group (or in small groups) their reactions to the readings.

The Experience

First, I can vividly recall the look of relief on their faces as they realized that I was not going to call on them or talk at them. It took this group of twenty adult students about twenty minutes to choose their individual passages. It took the whole group about thirty minutes to slowly read their challenging readings. The ideas were complex, new, and threatening. There were long periods of time when everyone sat and thought about the passage before moving to the next reader. If you had walked by our classroom, it would have looked as though we weren't doing anything. We were reflecting critically; we were thinking deeply. After the individual readings and the subsequent dialogue, Fiona, an adult student who teaches in Palestine, wrote, "It forced us to look deeply at text and decide what hit each of us most. It triggered profound, and often hidden, thoughts about why we felt one way or the other."

Incidentally, I have done the popcorn activity on numerous occasions with the previous editions of this book; it is always lively, fun, and enlightening. I am constantly amazed at how much I have learned with this method.

Pair Share

How to Do It

- Pair students. Each individual within a pair then chooses and explains a specific portion of the text.
- Questions are asked and discussed within pairs.
- After pair sharing, pairs share their discoveries and reflections with the whole group.

The Experience

Again, I remember the relief on their faces when, for the second time, they realized that they would not have to answer questions in front of the whole group and be embarrassed by their lack of understanding or frustration. This text is challenging for many good readers, particularly on the first reading. I could sense the group warming to Pennycook's ideas because they had control of the learning. Fiona wrote, in her ethnography of the class, "We discovered what was meaningful and relevant to each of us. Spontaneously, we began to compare and contrast with our peers' perceptions. Eventually, we created a comparison and contrast chart on the board. Our ideas were so diverse. By the end of this activity, we moved from a personal interpretation to a discussion of why we had our interpretation."

The dialogue deepened in ways that I could never have triggered if I had presented the material in a transmission model of pedagogy. The students began to make meaning of the ideas instead of blaming me for ideas that they found challenging.

Dialogue Journal

How to Do It

- Students choose any portion of the text and read it silently.
- Students write privately in their journals their reactions to the passage.
- Each student shares the passage from the text and her written reflections with another student.

In small group or whole group activities, I believe there has to be an understanding that students can choose not to share. They may simply say, "I pass."

The Experience

Fiona wrote the following in her class ethnography: "We enjoyed the quiet, reflective time to think and write. We discovered that we liked accessing the text on our own terms. And we particularly valued sharing our private reactions with only one other person."

Bloom's Taxonomies

How to Do It

- Choose a specific demanding piece of text before the activity.
- Assign and read it in class silently.
- Divide the whole group into six smaller groups, each representing one of Bloom's levels of taxonomies.
- Assign each small group to relate its assigned level of taxonomy to the reading assignment.

The Experience

First, none of the students could remember all six levels. Can you name them right now? We had a good laugh about this and decided that we needed to shift into a truly generative mode of learning. It was coffee break time, and we assigned ourselves the task of generating the six taxonomies with our colleagues. When we came back to class, each of us was able to recite all six taxonomies: knowledge, comprehension, application, analysis, synthesis, and evaluation. This may have taught more about generative, constructive, interactive teaching and learning than anything I could have done.

Each small taxonomy group shared with the whole group. For example, the knowledge group shared its knowledge; the comprehension group shared its comprehension; the application group explained how one could apply its learning, and so on. It became a process of students realizing that they had grown quite familiar with Pennycook's ideas, which had seemed so abstract, esoteric, and even infuriating only a few hours earlier.

As I reflect on my hesitation to share Pennycook with this group of EIL teachers, I am now aware of how much they were affected by his message and our approach to accessing his message. Although we read several other demanding texts during this summer school session, none hit as close to home as Pennycook. Nothing related more to their lives. These easy methods made the students reflect critically not only on the use of English in the international context, but also on the unexamined role they might be playing in this process.

Teaching and Learning in the Desert

In what follows, I will share other methods that I have used in various places. The stories that follow are all taken from a teaching/learning experience I had with a group of graduate students/teachers in Arizona.

Four Corners

This activity works well in all areas of curriculum: negotiating meaning of text, previewing, reviewing and/or summarizing a body of knowledge. The activity can be used to generate questions from the students or to answer questions that the instructor wants to emphasize. Later, I will demonstrate that it is also effective for bringing in student voices.

How to Do It

- Tape a large piece of butcher paper to the wall at each of the four corners of the room.
- Each piece of paper can be blank for student-generated questions that need to be studied, or the instructor can write a specific question on each of the four pieces of paper.
- Divide the whole group into four smaller groups. Each group needs one colored marker, and each group uses only its own color, which is different from the colors of the other groups.
- After each small group has discussed how to answer each question (or which question the group would like to generate for the whole group), the small groups rotate to each paper, writing their answers (or questions). After the groups have rotated and answered their questions, the whole group can analyze and discuss the answers.

The Experience

We have often heard that we, as teachers, need to bring in student voices (Poplin & Weeres, 1992). But how? This method works well with a little adaptation. Often, we are in a situation in which we know that the students have intense feelings about something that is very meaningful to them. Maybe it is a social event at school or in the community; maybe it is an act of injustice they are feeling; maybe it is confusion about assignments; maybe it is our syllabus—maybe it is our teaching. We all have had these experiences and will again. We come from a tradition that assumes that when these difficult teaching/learning (pedagogical) moments arise, we should take more control: Make the students sit down; make the students be quiet; make the students do a required assignment. Sometimes, we (or, at least, I) have shifted to the old transmission model of teaching to gain control: teachers talk; students listen. I might even have reverted to teaching harder, not better. The next time you want to bring in student voices, I suggest you try this.

> In Arizona, the graduate class was scheduled only on two very long three-day weekends during the semester with various assignments due during the semester. Anyone who has ever taught or learned in class for five hours on Friday night, eight hours on Saturday, and eight hours on Sunday knows that this can be exhausting, particularly because all the students are also full-time teachers, and the vast majority are parents, too. These are people with demanding and complex lives. Without meeting weekly during a semester, it is easy for misunderstandings and confusion to emerge. Therefore, when I returned for the second intense weekend, I wanted to be sure that all students' concerns were taken care of at the beginning of our session. However, because I was so far away geographically from the students, I didn't know what the issues might be. I needed to bring in student voices.

For the first round of the four corners activity, I chose four questions to write on the large pieces of paper:

1. Which assignment is most frustrating at this moment and what should we do about it?
2. What is the most important thing your group learned during our last weekend together?
3. What is the most important thing you have learned since we have been apart?
4. What can I (the professor) do to assist you with your learning, and what can you (the student) do?

When we did this activity in class, the small groups were animated as they discussed the processes of the class, the assignments, and their questions. After each group had answered each of the questions at the four corners, the colored markers made evident to all of us the unique concerns of each small group. I was surprised when the students expressed repeated concern about a particular assignment. It was clear that they did not understand my expectations and that they needed more in-class time working on this major activity. Together, we juggled our schedule for the next eight-hour day to include time for this. Although this activity took an hour of our valuable time together, when student voices were heard and respected, the students were much more ready to hear teacher voice.

The Messenger and the Scribe

How to Do It

- Before the activity, the instructor chooses one piece of text.
- Make copies of the text, and tape them in multiple places on the walls of the classroom.
- Place the students in pairs; one is the messenger, and one is the scribe.
- When the activity begins, all who are messengers run to the wall, read the text, return to the scribe, and repeat the text exactly. The scribe writes exactly what the messenger says.
- Throughout the activity, the instructor can change the roles of the scribes and messengers.
- The instructor needs to stay out of the way. This is lively and fun whether five-year-olds, fifteen-year-olds, or fifty-five-year-olds are doing it.
- When one pair finishes, the activity stops while this pair reads exactly what is written on their paper. If there are any errors, the activity begins again.
- Obviously, this activity works well for listening, for spelling, and for grammar and punctuation.

The Experience

When we did this activity in Arizona, I was not interested in listening, spelling, grammar, or punctuation. I was interested in content. I was interested in an idea. I wanted the group to begin a discussion of parental involvement, so I chose "Models for Parental Involvement" (see Figure 7.3 in Chapter 7). In this case, we placed the copies of text out in the hall, as it was a long Saturday and the building was empty except for us. This made the activity more fun and more challenging. When we finished, the students (adults) discussed ways in which they could adapt this activity to their own context and then slowly began to discuss their various experiences with family involvement in their own community. By the end of the discussion, they were acknowledging the important role they play in improving the quality of parental involvement at their school sites.[2]

Comprehending/Comprehension

I learned this activity from Cecilia, a young woman who teaches in Saudi Arabia. However, there are parts of this activity that remind me of an activity I learned from Roger Farr (Farr & Tone, 1994) several years ago. I suspect that this method has been adapted and adopted several times. I encourage teachers to use their knowledge to shape any method to fit the needs of the students.

Comprehending is a process; *comprehension* is a product. Good readers think about their reading while they are reading; good readers share their thoughts about reading; and good readers write about their reading. Most good readers go through this process of comprehending unconsciously. It is helpful to teach beginning readers some of the comprehending processes, which good readers do automatically. The purpose of this activity is to help readers learn (a) to predict and to share orally their thoughts, (b) to connect new knowledge with prior knowledge as they privately write their thoughts, and (c) to use any context clues in the text or any other thoughts that pop into their head while reading. It is the teacher's responsibility to preread the material and to make decisions about where in the text the readers will be asked to stop reading.

How to Do It

- Students are paired or placed in small groups. Each reader will also need a private journal or blank paper.
- The instructor decides on the three stopping places in the text before the activity.
- First, students read until the first predetermined stopping place in the text. In pairs, the students orally predict with their partner.
- Second, students read until the next stopping place. At this point, each reader connects her new knowledge with prior knowledge as they write privately in their journals. Each reader shares with her partner what she has written—if they choose to do so.
- Third, everyone reads until the last stopping place in the text. At this point, in pairs, the readers share their meaning making from context clues or any other thoughts that popped into their heads.

The Experience

My purpose for doing this with the teachers in Arizona was twofold. First, I wanted them to have an opportunity to experience various methods; second, I wanted to prepare the students for the problem posing that was to follow. Once again, I was using a method simply as a way of accessing text. For this purpose, I chose "Two Ways of Believing and Behaving" (see Figure 7.1 in Chapter 7) because I wanted students to think about their theoretical grounding.

Prediction is the first phase of the activity, and I was hoping that students in small, safe groups would predict some of their future actions on the basis of their individual belief structure.

Writing is the second phase of this activity, and I had chosen The Mess, detailed later in this chapter, because I wanted the students to write (and thus to think) about problem posing. The Mess is simply another way of problem posing (see Figures 6.1 and 6.2 later in this chapter). As the students shared their writing with their colleagues, I knew that they would hear differing perspectives and their understandings would grow.

Talking about context clues or anything else that popped into their heads is the final phase of this activity. As the students talked about other context clues and other things that popped into their heads, I remember them saying that they wanted to enter into problem posing. And so we did.

Problem-Posing Activity: Literacy

The archetypal way of doing critical pedagogy is to experience problem posing: **to name, to reflect critically, to act**—and then begin again. When you have long since lost this book, I hope you will remember one of the greatest legacies of Paulo Freire: problem posing. I have purposely saved this specific example to place here, as a lead-in to the final activity of this chapter, so that you will see that problem posing need not be only a three-step process. If you choose to pose problems in three, five, or even seventeen steps, it doesn't matter as long as naming, reflecting critically, and acting are inherently a part of the transformative process.

How to Do It

- *To name.* Form small groups, and ask each person to name (state) a problem in her school site. After each has named a problem (or contradiction, conundrum, sticky situation, or mess), the small group builds consensus and chooses one problem to name.
- *To reflect critically.* Each small group reflects critically and searches for various approaches to improve the situation.
- *To act.* The small group lists their recommended action to be taken.

The Experience

This experience took place in Arizona with the same group of teachers as in the previous example. You will recall that they had already read about The Mess (see Figures 6.1 and 6.2) as part of their reading assignment for the activity Comprehending and Comprehension. At this point in our relationship, I think that they knew about problem posing; they knew about The Mess. I think they assumed that problem posing had to be only this prescribed three-step process. I wanted them to see that it could be three steps or four or however they organized it. I also wanted them to know that problem posing is cyclical and can be experienced in multiple ways. More than anything, I wanted them to experience problem posing.

To Name

In this context, the problems that were named were the many mandated tests, lack of youth activities, the media, lack of unity and articulation among local school districts, lack of parental involvement, the high social value placed on monolingualism, a lack of local literacy events, and low teacher salaries.

We listed everything on the large blank pieces of paper taped to the wall. Next, the students read the list and reflected privately with their colleagues. Our challenge was to choose one situation as a whole group to continue the activity. We began by eliminating some of the problems that had been posed. After much discussion, the group chose to focus on literacy within the community, including students, families, and educators.

To Reflect Critically

Next, we began the process of reflecting and naming possible approaches to solutions. I encouraged the teachers to think creatively, and they had just read about The Mess, so they knew that there were to be no boundaries on our thinking. We were searching for options to improve literacy and increase literacy events throughout the community.

The following possible approaches were listed on large pieces of paper taped to the wall: support local libraries, buy books for schools, create mentoring processes, reach out to senior citizens to encourage their participation in literacy activities, fund a bookmobile, create reading buddies with older and younger students, and create scholarships. Throughout this process, our codes were as simple as filling in the large blank sheets of papers with the students' thoughts.

To Act

Critical pedagogy calls us to action. Critical pedagogy is good interactive pedagogy that extends to the real world, to the local community. The teachers knew that we were heading for action. Because we had just read about The Mess, we chose to follow that action process and make true individual commitment statements, which were then taped to the wall:

I commit to do the following:
- Get more books for my classes.
- Bring in people to read to my class.
- Allow choice for my students reading.
- Bring more family members into my classroom.
- On my birthday and family members' birthdays, donate books to the local library.
- Take time for reading.
- Bring in scientists to my science classes.
- Clean out my boxes of old comic books and bring them in for the students to read.
- Share my own books with the students in my classes.
- Create fund raising activities.
- Develop an award system in my class to encourage reading.
- Make reading fun in my class.
- Work with the parents of my students on all of the bureaucratic forms they need to know how to complete.
- Provide information for families about what they can do at home with their children to improve their literacy levels.
- Discuss library issues with the staff in my school site.
- Educate myself more about literacy.

What has happened since then? How have those commitment statements become action? As with all transformative actions, it all depends on the teachers and learners who are involved. Just as with the international students who read about Pennycook, I might never know what happens with literacy and the commitment statements in this community in the desert. In the Preface of this book, I likened our work to that of farmers: We plant seeds. How the seeds grow and develop depends on many other factors in the environment. At the time of this writing, I know that these lists of commitments still hang on the walls of this university classroom, the ideas have been sent to a state professional newsletter, and the commitment statements have been published in the local paper for all to see. Freeman and Freeman (1992, 1994, 1998) often write that one of the most effective principles of pedagogy is to have faith in the learners. To be honest, I have complete faith that good things will develop around this group of committed graduate students/teachers.

A Mess

I have saved the best activity for last. I encourage you to adapt this and try it. Make it work for you. There are surprises every time you enter into this type of process.

First, you start with a mess (Figure 6.1). In this case, a mess is any situation within an educational space that needs attention. It is something that is not working for someone.

I adapted this framework from Lieberman (1986) and García (1993). Tove Skutnabb-Kangas also has influenced this model; she immediately thought of the mess as creative chaos. I have been experimenting with various groups with this particular process, and so far, it is has been extremely powerful for all involved. In each case, we needed a minimum of three hours to walk though the process. We worked in small groups at each phase and shared with the whole group after each phase. The commitment statement (the last step, which is really the first) is fundamental to the cyclical process. When you finish, each participant will have made a commitment to change, and each participant will leave with new questions. In all fairness, I must mention that this process does not lead to smaller messes; it leads to more critical questions.

Before beginning the steps of this process, the facilitator and the participants need to generate a list of messes. What are the problems, concerns, or questions? The facilitator captures all the ideas and records them for all to see. The facilitator begins by asking each member of the whole group to reflect privately before joining a smaller group. After this, the facilitator again records more questions from the group. Next, the participants are encouraged to sit in small groups according to messes. Those who are interested in a particular question can pose problems as a small group. Once the participants are in the small group, the facilitator asks that each member individually share her concern with the group. Once this has happened, each small group is given the format in Figure 6.1 to guide their discussion.

At times, I have streamlined the process into the steps shown in Figure 6.2. Depending on the participants and the amount of time available, you might want to use the streamlined format.

FIGURE 6.1   First, you start with a mess

First, You Start with a Mess

Start with a mess (a problem, contradiction, or difficult situation).

- Define it. Name it.

Learn more about it.

- How can we learn more about this?

- Who knows what about this?

- How will we share information with the group?

Alternative approaches.

- List all of the ideas that might work. Think wildly and passionately.

- Dream. Think up utopias.

- Collectively, choose an approach.

Preparation.

- What are the roadblocks? How can we prepare for them?

- What new problems might this approach create? What are possible solutions for these new problems? What could go wrong? What role might others play if we decide to try to change this?

Action plan and evaluation.

- Create a timeline and a plan of action.

- Do it; fix it. Do it; fix it.

Write a commitment statement.

- We commit to . . .

- I commit to . . .

- Members of the group share personal commitment statements and agree to use their own expertise to help fix the mess.

Begin again.

- Redefine and rename the new mess.

This is not a one-shot activity; rather, it is the beginning of more critical teaching and learning with colleagues. The commitment statements that end the activity provide authentic experiences in which teachers and learners discover their own power.

FIGURE 6.2   Find a mess; fix a mess

- Find a mess.
- Learn more about it.
- What could be some alternative approaches?
- Action plan and evaluation.
- Write a commitment statement.
- Name a new mess.

Mayida and the Mess

Mayida tried the shorter version of The Mess when she left her teaching assignment in New York City to become an administrator intern in a K–12 district that served children from thirty-nine different countries. The school is located in Africa. Although she came with rich experiences in critical pedagogy, she was feeling overwhelmed by resistance, fed by a long history of transmission model education. Mayida was committed to collaborative and democratic pedagogy. She decided to use The Mess as a reflective tool to help her find answers with the teachers in her community. She wrote:

> *I found myself in quite a mess. It was difficult to understand what some of the issues were initially, but what I immediately recognized was that teachers lacked support and voice. I knew that the change process would be slow and that I needed to have some understanding of the school's history, culture, and political dynamics before I could entertain the idea of creating change. Teachers were accustomed to being told what to do and how to do it. They had not been given opportunities to apply their professional expertise and creativity in the classroom or within the community outside of the school.*
>
> *First we named: The administration was committed to a hierarchical school model. Next, we reflected on the problems that teachers were facing, and we discussed multiple solutions. The teachers needed immediate and authentic day-to-day support in the classroom from me. In addition, we established connections with teachers and parents who wanted to create change. Together we reflected, shared, processed ideas, and made decisions on relevant and meaningful curricula. Sometimes we accomplished our goals in spite of the resistance, and sometimes we quietly made a difference.*

As I write this, Mayida is preparing to leave this community in Africa. As you read these pages, she will be in the United States pursuing her doctorate in critical pedagogy. She now believes that long after she is gone, many of the veteran teachers and parents who inspired her will have a framework for taking action when they find themselves in a mess.

NCLB Calls Us to the Mess

Teachers, administrators, and families throughout the United States are now struggling to meet the demands of the No Child Left Behind (NCLB) Act. One way for school communities to ask questions and seek answers together is by following the framework of The Mess. The process does not require an outside "expert"; it needs only time for a school community to come together for serious reflection and a willingness to take action on their generated answers. Remember, it is not a one-shot activity. I suggest that time be arranged throughout the academic year for colleagues to work through the framework and implement their own answers.

NCLB is totally changing schools, learning, and teaching. Every person reading this page supports children's learning as much as possible for a future that we cannot even imagine. However, there are those who believe that scientifically based programs will enhance learning; others believe that "scientifically based" is code-speak for federally controlled ideology. There are those who believe that standards are good; there are others who ask "whose standards?" There are those who believe that standardization is the only way to improve learning; there are others who believe that these standards simply direct the money into a specific group of hands. There are those who believe that only standards will guarantee equity; there are others who believe that pedagogy will guarantee equity. There are those who believe that only tests will demonstrate the proof; there are others who believe that one test given on one day proves nothing. There are those who believe that we, in schools, need to be held accountable. I believe that we, in schools, need to speak up and hold accountable those in the federal government and business who benefit from NCLB.

Even among the most ardent defenders of NCLB, there are concessions that it is not perfect. "People like me who support the No Child Left Behind law often say to critics, 'Well, it might not be perfect, but you got any better ideas?'" (Mathews, 2003).

Yes, I do have some ideas, and this chapter is filled with them. In addition, I offer more suggestions from Derek, a high school teacher in a large and very diverse city, who tells the following story of how he raised the test scores of the students in his classroom.

The Proof Is in the Pudding

What works? Engaging kids with great reading materials while embedding and contextualizing the instruction is how Derek finds answers to raising test scores. Derek continues:

> *I teach at a school that has been labeled an underperforming school. In my classroom, I provide access to lots of different reading materials; I provide time for students to engage activity with the text and to negotiate meaning. We generate connections from our reading to the lives of the students, to other books, and to the world. We bathe ourselves in rich conversation. In our class, we have no mindless phonics, phonemic awareness, drill-and-kill fluency. We focus on language, meaning, and life. It's a fight, as our school has adopted a very scripted reading program. If the kids want to read scripts, they can go to Hollywood. At times, I have been ordered to use the mandated text, but the students hate it and immediately tune out.*
>
> *My classes are labeled remedial; the students know poverty, hunger, and despair. Out of curiosity, I compared the students' scores after they had been in my class for one academic year, albeit doing what we are not supposed to be doing: reading good books. Of course, I could not control all variables, but I did have access to the*

standards scores from last year and from this year, when we were required to use a new standardized test; these are the same two standardized tests, which will be used to see whether we are being "accountable"

Out of 125 students, 71 percent (89) grew as readers an average of 15.3 national percentile points. Seventy-five percent of those who increased their scores were speakers of additional languages and in the process of acquiring English (66 of the 89). Thirty-six of the 125 students decreased, but only by an average 5.6 points, which is consistent with research that shows that scores go down the first year of a new standardized test. There were some remarkable jumps: One student went from 27 to 51, a Hmong bilingual student increased from 5 to 47, and a special education male rose from 3 to 38. Another girl, who was already a good reader, increased her scores from 61 to 82. Plus it is clear that nearly all of the students left with at least an appreciation for reading, if not a love. Many have come back this school year wanting to talk about or check out books from my class library.

Yes, we do have better ideas: access to books—lots of good reading materials, a dedicated and knowledgeable teacher who preserves the integrity of the classroom so that students can learn. Not a person reading this page right now would be happy to be mandated to read mindless minutia. Neither are the students in Derek's class.

As research consistently shows, those who read more read better. And those who read more are those who have access to books. In this case, Derek provided the reading materials. In addition, studies show that better school libraries translates into higher reading test scores (Krashen, 2003a, 2003b).

Critical pedagogy is not easy, nor is it easy to speak honestly to power, but that is exactly what critical pedagogy calls us to do. It is where the jargon of critical pedagogy turns into the challenge of today. It where conscientization changes from a big word that is hard to pronounce to a real action.

The Principal: Doing Critical Pedagogy

Principal Parks, a teacher and administrator in elementary and secondary schools for thirty-two years, puts the face on the reality on No Child Left Behind as he speaks honestly to power. Did he think he was doing critical pedagogy? I doubt it; however, he names, he reflect critically, and he acts with the following letter to the editor, which was entitled "No Illusion Left Behind" (Parks, 2003).

It's scary when you feel like you're the only sane person around.

I'm a recently retired Iowa elementary school principal, and I can't figure out why educators all over the United States aren't screaming and yelling about the federal No Child Left Behind law.

It's hard to tell whether this law is more a product of arrogance or ignorance, but either way it's shaping up to be a spectacular train wreck of a collision between bureaucracy and reality.

The main thrust of the bill is that it requires all schoolchildren to be "proficient" in reading, math and science by the year 2014. Hard to argue with that, until you learn that proficiency has been arbitrarily defined as the current 40th percentile of the nation.

In other words, in 2014 every child will score better than 40 percent of the nation today, or roughly 19 million children. We will be essentially trying to get every child in the nation to be "above average," and should probably change our name to something like the United States of Lake Wobegon.

But it gets worse. The law specifically requires that children with serious learning problems (our current special ed population) must also meet this standard. In my medium-sized school district of about 4,800 students, last year's testing found 100 percent of special-ed fourth-graders to be below "proficiency." Surprise? Apparently it is to the Department of Education.

These children currently receive targeted instruction and a specialized curriculum and are often in classes of as few as eight students. They need these intensive services, but even with this extra help they will probably remain well behind the average student.

A second group of targeted students is made up of immigrant children who are just learning English. Is there some educational strategy I've missed that can turn a non-English-speaking third-grader into an average fourth-grade reader in one year? Who writes this stuff?

All schools are supposed to make steady progress toward the outrageous 100 percent success level, and schools that don't keep up face tough penalties.

State departments of education have recently released the lists of those who didn't make it this year. In my neighboring state of Illinois, 627 schools were labeled as failing, and estimates are that number will double.

In Iowa, a preliminary estimate found that up to half our schools could make the failing list, though the final tally for this year was much less. How could half the public schools be failing in a state that has the second highest ACT college testing scores in the nation?

It's obvious to me that when 2014 rolls around and everyone has to hit the 100 percent standard, almost every school in the country will be labeled a "failing school." Is it possible this bill is an elaborate setup, designed by those hoping to usher in an era of vouchers, charter schools and other alternatives to public education? I don't know the answer to that question, but I do know that the draconian provisions of No Child Left Behind will generate increasing amounts of fear, anger and unjust blame as one year's unrealistic goals give way to the next.

What works? We all want to know. I am sure that the answers will vary for each of us. I have tried to summarize what has worked for me in my experiences in schools (Figure 6.3). I recognize fully and painfully that what I suggest is not recommended by the prevailing pedagogical winds; nor does the law of the land, No Child Left Behind, accept it. However, I stand behind my recommendations because of my lived teaching experiences for thirty-five years at all levels of public education, from prekindergarten to the university level. Dialectical learning, critical reflection, and action are never outdated for active engaged teachers and learners. Memorization of discrete facts for a test might make some feel good today, but it will not solve the problems of tomorrow.

Recently, a teacher suddenly raised his hand and told me that you can't really do critical pedagogy; it is more a state of mind. I agree. It calls on us to see and to know in new critical ways. It calls on us to reexamine our own assumptions. We

FIGURE 6.3 What works

Taking time.

Tossing the texts.

Asking, "But why?"

Reflecting.

Conceptualizing and articulating our own philosophical assumptions.

Understanding why and how beliefs change.

Naming the power structures, critically reflecting, and acting on them.

Relearning and unlearning.

Acknowledging the powerful emotions of power, racism, classism, and sexism.

Understanding and being able to articulate the new global realities.

Challenging our long-held assumptions about teaching and learning.

Reading hard books.

Entering into dialogue.

Recognizing the contradictions in our own lives.

Recognizing our own power, expertise, knowledge, and role.

Seeing with new eyes.

Taking time and creating a safe place!

---

don't do critical pedagogy; we live it. We are challenged to live our beliefs. Each of us has a set of beliefs about values and education. These beliefs come to life every day in our behaviors in the classroom. What is it that each of us believes? Why do we believe this? Have our beliefs changed? An examination of our own beliefs and accompanying behaviors can lead each of us to rethink our approach to teaching and learning in our own classrooms.

> *"If you watch a teacher long enough, you will know her beliefs. I call this the Belief Indicator," Gary said to his classmates in the teaching credential program.*
> *"The what?" his classmates said in unison.*
> *"The Belief Indicator," he said. "Just watch your professors; they all have one. What they do every day in class tells you all about their beliefs. It always reminds me of the old adage 'The eyes are the window to the soul.' I think the methods are the windows to a teacher's philosophy."*

Obviously, Gary understands my thesis. Just as Gary told his classmates, our behaviors are a reflection of our beliefs; our practice reflects our theory.

The purpose of transformative education is to create processes whereby students can see that their actions do count. Students are encouraged to take the learning from the classroom and to engage locally and socially. This model of learning and teaching assumes that the generation of knowledge in the classroom leads to the betterment of life for the student or for the community. Knowledge is created to influence their world; it is no longer a passive ingredient designed only for the classroom.

I ask one central question: Why do we do what we do? In the spirit of reflective teaching and learning, in the spirit of attempting to learn how to do critical pedagogy, I challenge you, the readers, to reflect critically on your own philosophy and how it is reflected in your practice. There is no one best way to do critical pedagogy, but all ways involve critical reflection by teachers and learners together.

Practicing Pedagogy Patiently: In the University

Writing a book is a lot of work. However, one of the unexpected joys is that people write to the author and share the most interesting things. It just happens. You get up in the morning, and there in your e-mail is a gift from a stranger, who, of course, soon becomes a respected colleague. This was the case with Evangelina Bustamante Jones from San Diego State University. She read a previous edition of this book and created an activity that worked well with the credential candidates in her classes. We share the process here. Thank you, Evangelina, for the activity and the title you gave it. Thank you to all of you who have shared so much with me. You, too, are writing this book.

One of the most important things I have learned while teaching is that just because I teach something, it does not mean that the students learn it. It has finally become clear that if it doesn't matter to students, it doesn't matter. Therefore, we, as teachers, often loop or cycle back to come at something from a different perspective. The language in the following activity was presented in Chapters 3 and 4.

Talking the Talk of Critical Pedagogy

Objectives of the Activity:
- Create extended understanding of critical pedagogy principles and terms through the accumulated wisdom of peers.
- Model dialectical processes.
- Validate lived experiences of the participants through their visual representations and oral accounts.

Educational Importance:
- Preservice credential candidates must be able to recognize and name societal and school practices that marginalize students, teachers, and community members at their respective student teaching sites.

- Learners need a variety of experience-based and meaning-generating learning activities that access prior knowledge in order to understand and apply ideas, terms, and principles from a body of knowledge that is new to them.

Method:

Before the class does the activity, the instructor writes single terms on individual index cards, that is, one term per card. Next, with a pen or a sticky dot, the instructor places a spot of color on each card. The colored dots indicate terms with similarities or relationships. These colors will later be used as students form small groups. Following is a list of terms associated with the discourse of critical pedagogy:

> codification
> cultural capital
> dialectic
> dialogue
> discourse
> hegemony
> hidden curriculum
> literacies
> praxis
> problem posing
> to groom
> to name
> to marginalize
> to school
> to silence
> to socialize
> voice

In class, the activity proceeds as follows:

1. Each student is given an index card with one term selected from the list.
2. Students are asked to read the meaning of the word in Chapters 3 and 4. Students are asked to think about the definition and to create a pictorial representation, such as a graphic, a cartoon, a flowchart, or a semantic map.
3. Students group themselves according to the colored dot on the card. Then they are asked to present their word, the meaning from the book, and their individual graphic to their group.
4. Each small group is asked to find the relationship of their words. What are the similarities and differences? Students do a comparison and contrast in small groups. Next, each group creates a graphic that represents the larger meaning of the combined words of their small group. Within

the group, students share their personal experience with the word or the example from the book.

5. Small groups present to the whole group. Each participant shares her individual meaning and/or graphic and/or experience with the word. Each small group explains to the whole group how their understandings grew from the collaboration within the group.

Projected Time for the Activity:
At least forty minutes is needed. Activity can last longer, depending on the needs of the class. As a follow-up activity, the process can be repeated with the following sets of words shared with small groups (i.e., one set of words per small group):

> dialectic, dialogue
> hegemony, hidden curriculum, to marginalize
> cultural capital, hegemony, discourse
> praxis, problem posing
> to groom, to school, to socialize, to marginalize
> to name, to voice
> discourse, literacies
> discourse, hegemony

Looking Ahead for Elusive Methods

How do you think you do critical pedagogy?

> [blank response box]

NOTES

1. If you wish to read more about the group of international scholars who deconstruct the idea that the spread of English is natural, neutral, and beneficial, I suggest that you go to the library and explore almost anything published by J. Fishman, R. Phillipson, T. Skutnabb-Kangas, J. Naysmith, D. Pattanayak, or J. Tollefson. This list is not all-inclusive; you will find more to read in the bibliographies of these scholars. For further reading of the power of language on the North American continent, see Crawford (2004).

2. While experiencing "Messenger and the Scribe" with this group of teachers/students, I learned from Natalie Hess, a professor at Northern Arizona University, Yuma, that the inventor of this activity was originally Mario Rinvolucri, who called it "The Messenger Dictation." It is a pleasure to cite him, as he is known to be generous in his acknowledgements of his colleagues. I also thank Natalie Hess, who enriched all of us in this intense class with her knowledge, her pedagogy, her personal library, and her commitment to students and colleagues (November 1998).

7 How in the World Do You Do It with Families?

The purpose of this chapter is to explore ways of living critical pedagogy with families and caregivers in the community. I will share critical family involvement practices that I have experienced. These activities will be theoretically grounded in transformative education. All processes will be linked through reflection and dialogue, which are fundamental in the classroom and in the community. Lawrence-Lightfoot (2003) explores our "essential conversations" and the multiple ways in which parents and teachers can learn from each other. She sees these essential conversations as archetypal examples of dialogue between teachers and families during the ritual of parent–teacher conferences. It is during these moments when we "explore the subterranean dimensions of dialogue" (p. xxix). Lawrence-Lightfoot captures the inherent tensions between the two groups as a time when "parents and teachers negotiate the treacherous and tender terrain—physical, psychological, intellectual, and metaphoric—between them, a terrain that is typically uncharted, where the roles are often complex and overlapping" (p. xxix).

Epstein (2001) posits that the relationships between teachers and families function as overlapping spheres of influence. It is the interaction within these spheres that has the potential to improve students' learning and development while at the same time improving the quality of life within the school and community. Epstein offers six forms of family involvement that result in stronger partnerships between families and schools: parenting, communicating, volunteering, learning at home, decision making, and collaborating.

Ada (2003) wraps her notions of family involvement around the two worlds of each student: the world of school and the world of home. She cautions that if the two worlds do not respect each other, the students are placed in a most difficult predicament. It is through effective home–school interactions that students flourish academically and personally.

> Although teachers can be very effective role models, it is not their place to substitute for the parents, but rather to collaborate with them. It is important to help students see how much they can learn from their families, encouraging them to tap into the parents' or caretakers' life learning experiences or, in those painful cases in which the model at home may contain negative elements, to learn to respect and love their family while knowing that they themselves can choose to be different. (Ada, 2003, p. 11)

Just as there are different approaches to teaching and learning with students in the classroom, so too are there different approaches with families. In this chapter, I will ask you to reflect on family involvement in your own community. All of our classroom and community practices are philosophically grounded, whether we recognize it or not. Previously, we discussed three different philosophical approaches: transmission, generative, and transformative.

Two Perspectives

It is dangerous to reduce pedagogy to three perspectives (transmission, generative, and transformative) as I did previously. It is heresy to reduce it to two. I draw comfort from Jessamyn West, a Quaker writer, who believed that talent was helpful in writing, but guts were absolutely necessary. When we talk about putting the *plural* back in *plurality,* we certainly are not referring to two or three, but something more like seventeen, which Nieto (1996, p. 319) recommends, as it reflects so well the multiple perspectives of complex realities.

There are as many perspectives on pedagogy as there are committed, passionate souls who make their own road by walking (Horton & Freire, 1990). However, most of us have had considerable experience with these stereotypical two and/or three perspectives on pedagogy; therefore, they serve well for reflection and dialogue.

If a teacher or school has a transmission philosophy, the family involvement might look like the column on the left in Figure 7.1. However, if the teacher or school

FIGURE 7.1   Two ways of believing and behaving

Theory	
Transmission Philosophy	Transformational Philosophy
Practice	
Teacher and school own the knowledge.	Families, students, teachers, and school own the knowledge.
Families get knowledge from teacher and school.	Everyone knows something.
Start with school.	Start with families.
Purpose: Teachers teach families.	Purpose: Families and teachers learn together.
Formal schooling has value.	Formal school and lifelong learning have value.
Schools control education.	Community controls schools.

has a more generative and/or transformational approach, the activity with families might look more like the column on the right. It is often helpful to take time to reflect on our own theory and see how it turns into practice in our daily lives.

Tozer, Violas, and Senese (2002) summarize two approaches to teaching and learning with the chart in Figure 7.2. Of course, there are more that two approaches, but as we lay out the two approaches for comparison and contrast, we have an opportunity for reflection. For our purposes here, the point is that we often have a philosophical assumption buried deep within each of us that affects not only the students in the classroom, but also our essential conversations between families and teachers.

FIGURE 7.2   Two models for teaching and learning

	Critical Education	
Description	**Teacher Role**	**Student Role**
Dialogical	Inquires with students	Views knowledge base as the commitment of higher-level thinking
Dialectical	Emphasizes higher-level questions	
Multisourced		Becomes an active generator of own questions:
Grouping variety	Models reading and thinking skills	
Multiple settings	Teaches comprehension	■ Learns and uses metacognitive strategies with teacher modeling
Values student's context	Integrates critical thinking and content	
Heterogeneous ability-grouped		■ Learning is cooperative and focused on the group
Cooperative group focus		

	Banking Education	
Description	**Teacher Role**	**Student Role**
Lecture-oriented	Gives knowledge to students	Masters literal, factual knowledge base
Linear	Overemphasizes literal questions	
Text-oriented		Responds to teacher questions
Large group dominant	Presumes student reading and thinking skills	Acquires thinking and learning strategies by trial and error
Classroom-bound	Tests comprehension	
Ignores student's context	Views critical thinking as a byproduct of content	Learning is competitive and focused on the individual
Homogeneous ability-grouped		
Competitive individual focus		

Source: Tozer, Violas, and Senese (2002), p. 357.

Models of Parental Involvement

Once, during a conversation regarding democratic and transformative family–school interactions, Dawn wanted to know "how to do it." I reminded her of the various family and school activities she had experienced with me while she was growing up. It suddenly occurred to us that we were describing two very different approaches to school-sponsored family involvement. One approach is much more democratic. It seems that even when we do not see our beliefs, they continually tend to turn into visible behaviors that others can see. This happens even when we deny our beliefs. I am sure that both sides of the paradigm in Figure 7.3 think that they are very democratic. However, the actual implementation of theory in practice tells a very different story.

FIGURE 7.3   **Models for parental involvement**

Parental Involvement	
The We-Are-Going-to-Do-This-to-You Model of Parental Involvement	
or	
The We-Are-Going-to-Do-This-with-You Model of Parental Involvement	
Doing It to Them	**Doing It with Them**
Goal	
Change the parents	Change the schools
Objectives	
To melt into the pot	To melt the pot
To discuss building community	To build community
Characteristics of the Meetings	
Teachers talk	Teachers listen
Families listen	Families talk
Families sit still	Families Interact
Everyone leaves immediately afterward	People hang around
People leave space between them	People hug
Kids go to a room with a sitter	Kids work with families
Teachers tell objectives	Families tell stories
Result	
Dysfunctional school	Functional school

Just as theory informs practices and practice informs theory, the two perspectives on pedagogy can take shape in two very different models for parental involvement when schools work with families.

Which side of the chart in Figure 7.3 most accurately reflects your experiences with families?

Family Graph

The family graph activity in Figure 7.4 emerged when the graduate students in a class were creating oral histories. It is designed to demonstrate how much change has taken place in each person's life. It can be done in a class in an hour, or it can be a month's activities of creating and chronicling a family history and making books. I have found that the participants are usually surprised to learn things about their historical roots that they have never known. All you have to do is to ask the participants to fill in the chart in the figure with their own history. After that, just get out of the way. This is student-centered learning.

I initially designed the graph format in Figure 7.4 with graduate students/teachers for use in their own classrooms. Since that time, some of the teachers have been using it with families and teachers also. When Marta first looked at it, she rejected it and immediately sketched her own family's educational background (Figure 7.5). As other family members and teachers talked, some followed Marta and drew other graphs of their families' educational experiences. Others kept on talking and filled in the chart shown in Figure 7.4. The reflection and dialogue led the group to realize that each generation seems to get more education. Dee captured her families' educational history in a different way (Figure 7.6).

As Marta and Dee graphed and charted with the other teachers and families, stories soon began to fill the air. I have been influenced heavily by the critical perspective on teaching and learning of Ada and Campoy (2003), who offer multiple ways of teaching and learning with families. They focus specifically on writing and publishing oral histories as a way of bringing teachers, families, and students together. For example, they offer various ways making student-family ABC books, each letter of the alphabet representing an important word in the life of the family. A second idea is to send home a blank journal book and have the family write a story of their advice for their own children. I am reminded of a story I heard of a woman from Singapore. After she learned that families in the United States tend not to live in intergenerational family groupings, she quietly responded, "But who tells the stories?"

FIGURE 7.4   Family graph activity

My Family

	My Grandparents	*My Parents*	*Me*	*My Kids*
School				
Work Career				
Religion				
Family				
Travel				
Politics				
Beliefs				
Daily Life				

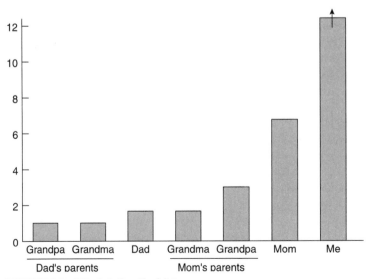

FIGURE 7.5   Marta's family history

FIGURE 7.6 Generational overview: Dee's family and education

	Paternal Grandma	Paternal Grandpa	Mom	Dad	Me
School	Graduated from Sierra High School (in Auberry) in 1945.	Graduated from Easton High School (near Fresno) in 1941. One semester at CSU Fresno.	Graduated from Sierra High School in 1965.	Graduated from Sierra High School in 1965. (Retained in first grade.)	Graduated from Yosemite High School in 1987. Graduated from Humboldt State University in 1991. Teaching credential in 1992. Master's degree expected in 2004!
Work/ Career	Homemaker, school cafeteria cook, wedding cake maker, and Forest Service volunteer.	Joined the Army in 1941 and worked as a mechanic and guard. Then was a carpenter briefly before going to work for the Forest Service as a crew boss and a carpenter.	Various jobs in restaurants and diners early on. Homemaker for 10 years or so. For the last 20 years, she has been the cafeteria manager at my old elementary school.	Various jobs as a mechanic early on. Then a logger for 10 years or so. For the last 20 years, he has worked for the local phone company in my hometown as a heavy equipment operator and mechanic.	Worked my way through high school and college as a cinnamon roll stand girl, a bookkeeper's assistant, a clerk in the English department at HSU, and a jewelry store salesperson. I have been a teacher for the last 10 years.
Religion	Not officially practicing a religion.	Not officially practicing a religion.	Sometimes attends a nondenominational Christian church.	Not officially practicing a religion.	Not officially practicing a religion.
Family	The oldest of two girls. Had three children. Married at the age of 18 for 51 years until her death. Her parents were married 60+ years until they died in their 80s.	The oldest of four kids. Had three children. Married at the age of 22 for 51 years until Grandma died of cancer. His parents divorced when he was in his 20s but remarried for insurance purposes a few years later.	The third child. Had an older half-sister, an older brother, and a younger brother. Her mother died when she was four, then had three stepmothers. Married at the age of 17 for 16 years. Had two daughters. Divorced my father and married twice more. Has two stepsons, four stepgranddaughters and two grandchildren, and one more on the way. (My sister is pregnant with her first child.)	The oldest child of three. Had two younger sisters. Married at the age of 18 for 16 years. Had two daughters. Divorced my mother and married Gail. Has a stepdaughter and a stepson. Has two grandchildren, one on the way, and numerous step-grandchildren.	The oldest of two daughters. Married at the age of 21 for 12 years and counting. Two children: Dylan (6) and Anna (3).

(continued)

FIGURE 7.6   Continued

	Paternal Grandma	Paternal Grandpa	Mom	Dad	Me
Travel	Mostly stayed in California, but occasionally went to Seattle and Hawaii.	Mostly stayed in California, even while in the Army, but occasionally went to Seattle or Northern California.	Mostly stayed in California, but took two trips East: one to Yellowstone and one to Ohio. Has also gone on cruises to Alaska and Mexico and took a trip to Hawaii once.	Mostly stayed in California, but took a trip to Yellowstone, one to Arizona, and one or two trips to Northern California.	Mostly stayed in California, but have visited these places: Yellowstone, Seattle, the Grand Canyon, Mexico, and Hawaii.
Politics	Democrat, I think	Democrat, I think	Republican	Republican	Democrat
Beliefs	Nature is important. Grandchildren are precious. It's better not to meddle or gossip. Be sincere. Visitors are always welcome. Never give up.	Nature is important. The government doesn't know what it's doing. Grandchildren are to be spoiled. You're never too old to learn.	No malingering! Education is important. Independence is important, as long as you still do what your mother says. Kids don't remember the promises adults make.	Educated people are hard to talk to. Daughters are hard to talk to. Cities are dangerous.	Education is important. Nature is important. Family is important. Everyone should have a hobby. Reading is the key to academic success. Promises should be kept. No whining!
Daily Life	Cooked, cleaned, took care of the kids, kept them quiet when Grandpa was home, welcomed visitors, crocheted and wove baskets and beaded necklaces and made wedding cakes when there was time. Also spent a lot of time organizing family photos, negatives, important documents, bills, newsletters, newspaper clippings, letters, etc.	Worked, came home, worked some more in the shop on rebuilding cars or woodworking projects. Took pictures of the kids and grandkids. Read research on forests and trees, trains, and airplanes, corrected errors in books, and spent time playing with the kids and grandkids. Later, spends time building model airplanes in cold weather and in the shop during warmer weather.	Cooked, cleaned, took care of the kids, worked full time, watched TV most evenings, crochets or embroiders occasionally, and makes wedding cakes and birthday cakes as a side business. (She learned how from my dad's mom.)	Works, comes home, feeds the horses and dogs, tinkers with tractors. . . . not sure what else he does!	Works, drops off and picks up kids, goes to lots of meetings, goes to class, spends time with kids while husband cooks dinner, reads to kids after husband gives them a bath, works on homework or schoolwork, watches TV, crochets sometimes, reads about three novels a week. Tries to organize things like Grandma did, but never really has the time. Likes to scrapbook but hasn't done it much lately.

Putting the *Home* Back in *Homework*

Andrea, a fifth grade teacher, is working on her master's thesis and wanted the students in her class to do their homework with their own families. Initially, she prepared homework packets for the most reluctant and resistant readers. Andrea was determined to get the students and families filling out all of the discrete point, fill-in-the-blank dittos; she was sure that this would improve the students' reading ability. From my perspective, her first set of homework packets was very teacher-centered and controlling, and at least for me, they were not meaningful. I tried to envision how much I would not like doing them with my own children, or now my grandchildren. However, I was equally determined to let her learn whatever she needed to learn in the process. She started her pilot study and was very discouraged to learn that her first set of homework packets simply created reluctant and resistant families.

It was at this point that she discovered the work of Ada and Campoy (2003). Andrea philosophically and methodologically jumped across the paradigm divide from transmission to transformative education and created new homework packets (Figures 7.7, 7.8, and 7.9) that were grounded on the lives of the students and their families.[1]

FIGURE 7.7   Packet 1

Homework Packet 1

Please complete three of the following five activities with a parent.

Activities:

- Find an old family photograph you have never seen before and ask your parent about it. Answer who is in the photo, when it was taken, where it was taken, and if it was it taken on a special occasion. Also give any other information about the photo. Please describe what the photo looks like. Use page (1) of this packet to write your answers.

- Ask a parent about their favorite recipe. Write the recipe and draw a picture of what it would look like when the food has been prepared. Use page (2) for this activity.

- Talk with your parent about some of the rules you have at home. Write ten of these rules on page (3). On the same page, tell what the consequences would be if you broke one of these rules.

- Help a parent write a grocery list. Write the list on page (4) of this packet.

- With the help of a parent, write down the agenda of what goes on at home each day. Write this agenda on page (5) of this packet.

I have helped my child complete three of the five above activities.

Parent Signature   **Date**

FIGURE 7.8   Packet 2

<hr>

Homework Packet 2

<hr>

Please complete three of the five following activities with a parent.

Activities:

- Draw and color a comic strip of something funny that happened this week at home to a parent or sibling. Draw the comic strip on page (1) of this packet.

- Ask a parent to tell you about one of their favorite days. What happened this day to make it so special? Write the date and the special events that occurred on this day on page (2) of this packet.

- Find an old family photograph you have never seen before and ask your parent about it. Answer who is in the photo, when it was taken, where it was taken, and if it was it taken on a special occasion. Also give any other information about the photo. Please describe what the photo looks like. Use page (3) of this packet to write your answers.

- Take a walk with your parent around the neighborhood. When you return, draw a map of your neighborhood. Make sure to include street names, parks, schools, and anything else important in your neighborhood. Draw your map on page (4) of this packet.

- Read to your parent for 20 minutes. Have your parent retell what you read. On page (5) of this packet, write down your parents retelling of what you read.

I have helped my child complete three of the five above activities.

_____

Parent Signature   **Date**

<hr>

Reflection to Action

Funwork, as opposed to homework, has been suggested by Enright, McCloskey, and Savignon (1998) and captures the concept that our learning together within family units can be fun, interesting, and pedagogically sound. Ada (2003) extends this idea to say that homework should not be additional schoolwork; rather, it is homework because it requires the interaction of students with their families.

If we think in terms of putting the *home* back in *homework,* we are reminded that homework involves kids and families working together. However, it seems that taking the home out of homework might also offer some options. If we take the home out of homework, the school creates safe times and places where students can informally go for support while they do their homework. Some students come from families that have computers, books, papers, calculators, papers, and pencils and who will encourage homework. However, some students come from homes where less academic support is available. Often, family members are away from home, working long hours. To level the playing field, I suggest districts and schools consider

FIGURE 7.9   Packet 3

Homework Packet 3

Please complete three of the following five activities with a parent.

Activities:

- Draw and color a comic strip of something funny that happened this week at home to a parent or sibling. Draw the comic strip on page (1) of this packet.

- Find an old family photograph you have never seen before and ask your parent about it. Answer who is in the photo, when it was taken, where it was taken, and if it was it taken on a special occasion. Also give any other information about the photo. Please describe what the photo looks like. Use page (2) of this packet to write your answers.

- Ask a parent about their favorite recipe. Write the recipe and draw a picture of what it would look like when the food has been prepared. Use page (3) for this activity.

- Have your parent tell you about the day you were born. How were they feeling? How did it happen? Please write down anything else your parent shares about this special day. Write their responses on page (4) of this packet.

- Read to your parent for 20 minutes. Have your parent retell what you read. On page (5) of this packet, write down your parent's retelling of what you read.

I have helped my child complete three of the five above activities.

_____

Parent Signature   **Date**

safe and friendly locations with music, snacks, and supportive adults working with students on their homework. In these days of limited funds, it seems like heresy to suggest more cost for schools; however, I ask it anyway with the hope that some reader somewhere will take this idea and bring it to fruition for the sake of the chlidren. It seems that tutors, mentors, senior citizens, and/or civic groups might provide some support.

Here I offer five suggestions for putting the home back into homework:

1. Interview a family member and write a short biography. Questions can be generated in class to begin the interview process. Time in class needs to be arranged so that the students read their written biographies of family members. Following are a few examples of interview questions that Dawn has used:

"Tell me about the funniest thing I did as a baby."

"Tell me about the funniest thing that ever happened to you."

"Tell me about my grandparents."

"Tell me about where you grew up."

"Tell me about what you did as a child."

"Tell me about your favorite memory."

"Tell me about how you and Dad/Mom met."

"Tell me about your favorite book and why it is your favorite."

2. Students choose books from the classroom or the school library to take home to read with parents, or students can choose reading materials from their public library or reading materials that are in the home. Arrange for time in class for students to share orally their reading experiences at home. Celebrate the students who are reading with families at home.

3. Students write about projects or experiences they have with their families in the evenings. Students create a book that captures their families. In school, time is arranged to share their individual books.

4. Students write about the various literacy activities at home. Students list all of the contexts of literacy in their life, for example, comic books, magazines, how-to books used at home, grocery lists, computer activities, reading mail at home, and so on. Arrange time in class to chart the home reading activities of all students.

5. Students, with family members at home, write letters to extended family members outside of the home (Wink & Wink, 2004).

School Families

School Families is a concept that costs not a penny to implement and can be adapted in multiple ways. It creates small intergrade School Families of students, who come together in various ways through the school year. Mary, a teacher, explained to me that in their K–8 school, each School Family has one student from each grade; the eighth graders are considered the parents. During the first week of school, the School Families are brought together for an informal and safe time to get to know each other for the first time. The next day, all the School Families eat together, and lunch period is extended. Throughout the year, School Families assemble and sit together for all special events; they are responsible for taking care of each other at special events and during recess. The real family members of the students play the role of grandparents within the School Families. A bulletin board is kept throughout the year with family photos. School Families take part in many intergrade writing projects, with the older students assisting the younger ones. Mary continues with the story of how this works at her school:

> *It is amazing how the School Families bond throughout the year. The eighth graders in my classes tell me that they couldn't wait to become parents in their own School Families. It is interesting to see how many of the older students who are considered behavior problems rise to the challenge of being responsible School Parents. I find it moving to see thirteen-year-old boys and girls kneeling down to talk eye-to-eye with the younger members of their School Families. It is probably one of the best parts of school because they take on responsibility, they are someone's hero, and they see how their behavior sets the tone for the rest of the school. New students feel welcomed into a small group that becomes close, and the children have connections at every grade*

level. The junior high students in our community can tell you who was their School Parent for every year they attended school at our school.

Family involvement with schools takes place in highly diverse ways, but what these varied processes have in common is a philosophical grounding that seeks to increase the academic achievement and well-being of students while at the same time bringing families and teachers together to break down isolating barriers and improve the life of the community. Mary has never met Una, in the next story, and they live vastly different lives, but they both believe in a transformative and democratic theoretical undergirding that guides their actions.

A Library in the Community: Cow Jumped Over the Moon

In a state far, far away and with just a few, few people, one woman is working with families and teachers in a tiny town on the prairies. The population, 350 people, is a mix of white ranch families and Lakota Sioux. The two groups live in the second poorest county in the United States and are in the middle of a devastating drought, which is also drying up the tax dollars to support a library. In this economically deprived community, a long history of isolation exists, separating ranchers from Lakota and teachers from families. The legacy of pain, distrust, and anger runs deep.

Enter Una, a woman who is biologically and historically connected to all the groups—the white ranchers, the Lakota Sioux, the teachers, and the families. Her lived experiences help her to understand and respect each group. In addition, she has lived in other parts of the world and has returned to her local community to open a library, called Cow Jumped over the Moon, in a previously deserted building in the dying business district. She understands only too well that families have to jump over a lot to survive in that community. Her goal is that the library will bring all families together under the safe umbrella of books. Her hidden goal is that families will learn to jump over moons together in order to thrive.

Electronic Communities of Families

Global learning communities around the world hold the potential to include not only the teachers and students, but also the families of students. The concept might appear futuristic; however, drawing on the vision of Freinet, Cummins and Sayers (1995) offers a series of case studies that demonstrate the power of collaborative learning among groups that are vastly separated by time and space. Technology has the potential to grant virtual access to families and students so that all can experience a new world together. Freinet initiated the idea of global learning networks in 1924 in France (Cummins & Sayers, 1995) by creating distance learning partnerships.

Freinet's had three ideas of teaching and learning, all of which are readily adaptable for working with families today. First, the learning walk: In this phase of the learning, students walked through a community to observe and gather information. Second, the learners returned to class to print their new knowledge. Third, once the new knowledge or information was gathered, the students mailed it to other students in other schools.

Galileo: Walking, Observing, Talking, and Recording

Lisa (Westbrook, 2003) shares an example of Freinet's ideas of teaching and learning in an electronic newsletter, which is part of a virtual interactive library being created by families for families and teachers. Galileo, who in 1610 looked at the sky and saw the planet Jupiter, inspired her: He noticed two points of light to the east of Jupiter and one point to the west. His curiosity compelled him to look again the next night and the next and the next. Within a few days he noticed that there was now one point of light to the east and three points to the west of Jupiter. Within 7 days of observation, he gathered enough information to declare that Jupiter had several moons, not just one.

This true story of Galileo's discovery through observation inspired Lisa to take her two young prekindergarten boys out on walks with their journals to record all that they saw. They walked, observed, talked, and recorded. Although they did not discover several new moons around a planet, they soon were fascinated by the nesting habits of the white-winged doves in their neighborhood. This interest in doves led to a trip to the library for the two budding ornithologists. The boys' discoveries are now shared electronically, completing the third phase of Freinet's suggestion for teaching and learning. It is amazing how Galileo and Freinet are linked through Lisa's curiosity and commitment to learning and sharing with others.

Practicing Pedagogy Patiently

Lawrence-Lightfoot (2003) captures the complexities of teacher–family interactions as she explores what is said, what is not said, and what it could mean. Building on the legacy of Dewey, she warns of the dangers of teacher and family communication that becomes nothing more than routine (p. 79), and she offers many suggestions for ways of maintaining the honored ritual of open, honest, and productive communication between teachers and families. Two particular suggestions are heavily grounded in the critical perspective. The very first conference between teacher and parents needs to be a listening conference for the teacher. The teacher is challenged to listen and to hear. A second suggestion, as a way of maintaining a student-centered focus, is for the student to lead the discussion between parents and teachers. I suspect that both of these suggestions will require a very patient pedagogy.

NOTE

1.   As of this date, Andrea Katotakis has completed her master's thesis. The homework packets that I have shared here are entirely her creation. In this chapter, I share three samples; however, more are available at www.JoanWink.com/charts.html.

CHAPTER

8 Why in the World Does It Matter?

Kids matter—that's why. Our future matters—that's why. It is as simple as that. It also is something we all know. This is serious business we are talking about. Students and teachers are hurting. We in education are a mirror of society that is becoming more and more polarized.

But are poles really so bad? Let's relook and rethink poles. Aren't poles just opposite ways of thinking? Yes. Is diversity of thought bad? No. Would it really be so good if we all thought alike? I doubt it. I find it helpful to always think of the continuum that joins poles. Aren't poles just an example of multiple voices and multiple ways of knowing along a continuum of thought? I think so. Are schools big enough for diversity? It's who we are.

We come from a tradition that assumed that differences were bad. Critical pedagogy teaches us to look again and to see again and to know in new ways that are a true reflection of today. Diversity of thought is good for schools and good for society.

Throughout this book, I have tried to show the many contradictions and changes we all are experiencing in our educational spaces. These contradictions and changes often frighten and offend us at first; they feel like polar opposites. We resist, we deny, we object—or, at least I do. Critical pedagogy has helped me to reflect on these contradictions and changes and take action, if necessary, based on my knowledge and experience. The poles no longer tear me apart. The poles are just a part of a larger picture that is our ever-increasing vibrant society.

The world is changing fast, and these societal changes are reflected every day in our schools. Every newspaper that we pick up tells us again and again that what we are doing is not working. Historically, our schools are based on the needs of an agrarian society in which knowledge was controlled and transmitted by the schools; now the No Child Left Behind law is mandating that we transmit knowledge again. It is not only knowledge; it is a certain body of ideologically grounded knowledge. However, at the rate at which new knowledge and information are now being generated, it is impossible for even the very best teacher to be able to transmit it all. Students of the future need to be able to access new knowledge, critically reflect on it, interpret it, and apply it in new ways. The changing world is

dragging us (kicking and screaming, in some instances) into the world of a transformative model of education. Ideologically, some people resist transformation because knowledge cannot be controlled. The purpose of education is to transform
society into a truly democratic environment for all.

> Particularly is it true that a society which not only changes but which has the ideal
> of such change as will improve it, will have different standards and methods of ed-
> ucation from one which aims simply at the perpetuation of its own custom. (Dewey,
> 1944/1916, p. 81)

James Cummins has spoken repeatedly about the changing global realities,
which he calls cultural, linguistic, scientific, technological, and ecological realities. In
the new global realities, diversity of people and diversity of thought are the norm.
This is the foundation for a thriving society; it is only when change ceases that societies begin to die. In a vibrant, dynamic society, diversity of thought enriches us all.
The idea of global realities (Cummins & Sayers, 1995) has been expanded and now
includes the idea of existential realities, which encompasses the sense of fragility we
experience in our relationship with the physical and social environment.

Cummins's idea of the new global realities certainly is affirmed in my own
experiences. I rarely visit a school that is not multicultural, and many are multilingual. It appears to me that the mainstream is very multicultural. These changing
global realities lead us to ask ourselves, "What do students today need to know to
thrive and flourish in the future? What are the needs of students and citizens of the
twenty-first century?"

Students of the Twenty-First Century

We will need bilingual and biliterate students who love to read, can reflect critically, and live their lives with passion and action. We need collaborative, lifelong
learners who are responsible for their own learning and understand that it comes
from their lived experiences. We need students who can generate new knowledge
and apply it in unknown ways. We need students who can write and rewrite their
world from a pluralistic perspective, students who can pose problems and solve
problems with technology that stretches beyond our wildest thoughts. We need
students who know how to access, interpret, and critically use new and emerging
information. Above all, our students will need to be able to work in a multilingual
and multicultural society. The students who will thrive socially and economically
are those who bravely cross borders: cultural, linguistic, classist, sexist, and racial.
We must begin with every teacher and every student and family in every school
today. As a local teacher/graduate student wrote at the end of an essay, "My goal
is to begin today." I think that teacher has something to teach all of us.

I recently asked a group of teachers how they thought we should teach critically and effectively for the students of the twenty-first century. Their answers are
worth sharing:

How to Teach for Students of the Twenty-First Century
- Be passionate about your subject matter.
- Know students and their backgrounds.
- Involve the families as citizens of the classroom.
- Encourage students the freedom to explore and time to sit and think.
- Provide meaningful, practical, and relevant information.
- Show students how to access and generate new information.
- Ask "why?" a lot.
- Make sure students see you reading.

The writing of this book has pushed me along my own unlearning curve. If anyone had told me previously that my study of critical pedagogy would bring me to this point, I never would have believed it. Even a year ago, I would not have believed it. However, by writing my own thoughts, I have discovered some of my own elusive answers. First, I seek my answers in the delicate balance between a caring heart and a critical eye. Second, I follow the path of action that is in that enlightened and precarious place between courage and patience. Third, this all takes time.

The Pedagogy of a Caring Heart and Critical Eyes

It might seem at first that *caring* is poles apart from *critical*. Not for me. They are two parts of a new dynamic pedagogical whole. For me, the critical perspective and the centrality of caring come together under the framework of critical pedagogy, and no one is more surprised than I. I find strength in these seeming opposites. They fit in a new whole picture of schools. A complex picture. A diverse picture. A vibrant picture. And a very exciting and powerful new picture of the potential within all of us. Critical pedagogy has painted this new picture for me.

A Caring Heart

Why should students care if we don't? Caring counts. I would like to see teachers and learners enter into dialogue about some very fundamental human needs that are not being met in our schools. For example, love. It's true, love trumps methods! I really have felt this for a long time, but I had to be patient until I had enough courage to say it (see Wink & Wink, 2004). Critical pedagogy brought me here. I believe this is what McLaren is alluding to when he speaks of "the teachable heart."

I suggest that all of us in education should place our entire discussion of teaching and learning into a larger framework of caring. Nel Noddings has been a consistent voice in raising questions of ethics and values in schools. National educational journals are alive with the importance of caring. But a national teacher of the year said it best when referring to a former teacher who had turned his life around: "He put his hands on my shoulder that first day of class and it burned clear through to my heart" (Hanson, 1994, pp. A1, A11). As we live through these rapid social and demographic changes, I suspect that caring counts. Nowhere are these changes experienced more profoundly than in schools every day.

We come from varying perspectives, experiences, and academic areas, but we all care about teaching and learning. In a safer world, that would be enough. However, in the sociocultural context of education of today, it is not enough. We also must care about ourselves, our colleagues, our students, and our communities. As Elam (1995) comments:

> In a more reasonable society, in a more perfect nation, in a world beyond ugly discriminations of gender, race, and class, our citizens would live in a convivial atmosphere of community. . . . That is why I worry a good deal about the soundness of the national mind and spirit. I worry about public voices that tout intolerance and narrow-mindedness. I worry about the politics of parsimony and isolation. . . . I still take comfort knowing that singular acts of care and compassion take place all the time and I hope for the day when these acts will become the very core of our culture. (p. A11)

Pedagogical caring must be balanced within the dialectic of a critical stance to meet the needs of teaching and learning for the twenty-first century. Critically reflecting on theory and practice and acting on our individual praxis are fundamental to critical pedagogy. A caring heart can be demonstrated in innumerable ways in the classroom and community. But a critically caring heart moves us along a critical path of unlearning.

The caring heart does not mean that we stop listening to the whispering of the juxtaposition: the critically reflective eye. Do not be fooled. Caring teachers and learners continue to look in the mirror, the classroom, and the community to discover their own path of unlearning. The caring heart and the critical eye often bring us to that enlightened and contradictory place where each of us begins to detect elusive answers.

A Critical Eye

Why should students critically reflect if we don't? Teachers often talk about the importance of inquiry, of critical reflection, of active and engaged investigation. However, if we don't do these things, they won't.

The rapidly changing times force us to know in new ways, as Carole, a high school teacher, discovered:

> *A very profound learning experience shaped me as a teacher. When I first began my career, I had high standards for my students. It was to the point of being uncaring. After two years, I decided that love and compassion were more important than strict regulations. Today, the students and their outlook on life are more important than a rule. The irony is that as I begin to focus more on caring about the whole student and less about standards and regulations, the students are learning more. I thought I was exchanging high standards for a little caring. The truth is the opposite: As I care more, the students learn more.*

Carole's experiences demonstrate just how confounding contradictions can be. Carole thought that she used to have high standards. But since she began to critically reflect on her own practice, she has discovered that the students have higher standards for their own learning.

Thirty years ago, a friend told me that teachers can hurt kids. I was shocked and did not (want to) believe it. Kim is a teacher who critically reflects on her own theory and practice. She challenges herself to look again and see again. But even I was surprised when I read her paper. In this story, she emphasizes the importance of a critical perspective, which can often lead us to a caring philosophical stance.

My first-grade teacher was a monster. [Kim wrote this with a black felt-tipped pen and underlined the word <u>monster</u>.] *She was mean. She liked to yell and threaten.*

One day someone turned out the lights while we were walking back to class from music. When we got back to class, she asked, "Who turned off the lights?" I remember how frightened and quiet we were.

"Nobody is leaving this room today until the person that did this confesses," *she yelled at us. The bell rang to go home, and still no one confessed. We sat. We sat for what seemed to be a long time.*

"I did it," I finally said. I was scared because I didn't think the teacher was going to let us go home. The other students were dismissed, and I had to stay in the room alone with the teacher. I remember her cold voice asking me why I had done it.

"I didn't. I just said it so we could go home," I said as I started to cry.

She called me a liar. I remember the shame I felt. I will never forget that day.

My critical reflections of this experience have made me believe in the importance of caring in the classroom.

Pedagogy of Courage and Patience

I have started to notice that my years with students and my reading of all those critical theory books have led me to focus more and more on courage and patience. Once again, you might think that courage and patience are poles apart. Not for me. They are part of that new pedagogical whole: courage sometimes, patience other times. Only reflective action will help you to decide which one when.

Just as teaching and learning make up a dialectical union that propels our professional growth forward, so is the union of courage and patience fundamental to our pedagogy for the future. Daily, I feel the pull of courage and the counterpull of patience. Often, we need to be as courageous as the context will allow. Other times, patience is our greatest ally: patience with ourselves, our colleagues, our context.

I am currently watching a district that is completely divided into two camps. I will call the two teams the White Sox and the Brown Sox. The school is divided, the community is divided, and all are being hurt. In the middle of this great battle is a young, beginning teacher, a member of an ethnic minority, who is being pummeled by the White Sox team. It appears to me that when the dust settles, the Board of Education will offer a contract for another year to the young teacher—a move that will outrage the White Sox and please the Brown Sox. I predict that the young teacher will keep his job unless he leaves in complete discouragement, which probably is the hidden objective of the White Sox players. I watch the young teacher struggle to be courageous and defend himself; I watch him be patient with his adversaries. I can see that the principal is walking a tightrope in her balance between courage and patience. They are in good company: "Paulo Freire lived the dialectic between patience and impatience. He had to be patient, impatiently. It was necessary to be impatient, patiently" (Gadotti, 1994, p. 47).

Candi is a teacher/grad student who works in a very coercive school setting. She understands that the school believes in transmission model education. Candi sees herself as a transformative educator. She has critically reflected and understands the barriers she faces. Candi also knows that her life is in this community and that she must find ways of living, learning, and teaching. She asked whether we could use a class session to pose problems on her struggles with her environment. She shared honestly, as did her colleagues in the graduate class. At the end of this challenging session, they generated a plan based on the dialectical union of courage and patience. They decided Candi would commit to doing the following:

1. Be courageous enough to live her beliefs honestly.
2. Be courageous enough to invite her coteachers and administrators to her room when she would be doing a lesson design based on critical pedagogy.
3. Be patient enough to let her colleagues draw their own conclusions.
4. Be patient enough to listen and be courageous enough to repeat back adversarial comments.
5. Be courageous enough to accept the fact that she can't control others' beliefs; she can only live her own.

One year later, Candi reported that her acceptance of the dialectical union of courage and patience had led her to be a more joyful and rigorous teacher, and she liked her colleagues and school better. Candi recognizes that she herself must be courageous and patient before she asks it of her students.

Time, Time, Time

All of this takes time. For example, the language of critical pedagogy takes time. The thoughts of critical pedagogy take time. Jonathan's literacy took time. A teachable heart takes time. Critically reflective practice takes time. Challenging our own intellect takes time. Reading books on critical pedagogy takes time. Shifting our lesson designs takes time. Shifting our paradigm really takes time.

Time is more important than coverage. The elusive answers that are meaningful for me all seem to be grounded in issues of time. Traditionally, we have been driven by the pedagogy of coverage: We have to cover this now. We have to cover that next. However, coverage is not as important as learning. What good does it do to cover the material in the time allowed if students don't know it? Time traditionally controls teachers; I suggest that it ought to be the other way around. I also think that we, as educators, must continually reflect on coverage and time.

Why should we expect students to take time if we don't? Recently, a former master's graduate called to tell me about a statistics class in her doctoral program. The professor, who was very intimidating, came to every class with fifty problems to cover. The frightened and frustrated students were not learning, but he continued to cover his fifty problems. The students endured for several class periods. They sat quietly and passively and copied every number and every squiggle that he wrote on the board. But in all of this time, no one was learning, they were only covering his prescribed curriculum, fifty problems per class. The students were still too nervous to question him. Finally, in desperation, this former master's student raised her hand to ask for help in class.

> STUDENT: Professor, I did not understand the first problem. Would you please repeat your explanation?
>
> PROFESSOR: No, I have no time to repeat. I have forty-nine more problems to cover.
>
> STUDENT: Yes, but if I don't understand problem one, it really doesn't matter what you do with the remaining forty-nine.

This particular example screams of the dangers of the pedagogy of coverage. This professor thought that he needed to cover fifty problems in the allotted time. Students don't need to cover fifty problems; they need to learn. We, as educators, need to reflect on our perspective of time. We feel controlled by time. However, in our own classes, we need to control the time.

The student had been patient and now was moving to courage. If only the professor had been courageous enough to be patient with his students' learning.

I struggle with coverage and time in every class. I come in with my objectives, my gorgeous transparencies, my planned organization of the three-hour block of time. The students keep interrupting me with meaningful questions. They keep relating their new knowledge from class to their own world. That darned transformative learning! It has even driven me to say, "Stop this learning, I want to teach!"

From Buttercup to Power

Here is the problem with all of these thoughts about a caring heart, a critical eye, and time: It causes us to confront ourselves; it takes away the blame game, and it does it in the most surprising ways for most of us—or, at least, for me. On the surface, the following story might appear to be about a horse. Do not be fooled. Until each of us owns our own power (negotiates our own identity), we cannot be a part of empowerment (negotiating identities with students).

It began so simply. Dawn told me to read Naomi Wolf's *Fire with Fire: The New Female Power and How It Will Change the 21st Century* (1993). Wolf hypothesizes that women's fear of horses is really a disguised fear of power. Her thesis is that preadolescent girls are fearless and courageous and often love horses. As they move through adolescence and seek to be more the way little boys want them to be, girls develop a fear of horses—or fear of power.

When I read that, I slammed the book shut. One of my main myths exploded (Nieto, 1996). This was not a metaphor to me; this was life. I have lived a lot of my life on ranches. I grew up around horses and rode as a child. As a young adolescent, I became afraid of horses. This was also about the same time that I started noticing boys. I remember wishing that they would think that I was "cute." Since that time, I rationalized my fear of horses this way: Horses are bigger than I, stronger than I, faster than I, and certainly smarter than I. I have consistently been in situations in which I had to make excuses about not wanting to go for a ride: "I'm busy," or "I have to cook," or "The kids need me,"—and my personal favorite: "Someone else can use my saddle." Sometimes I didn't succeed in talking my way out of a horse-back ride. Invariably, long hours in a saddle followed as I tried to hide my fear.

It seems that in life we sometimes bump into the right teacher when we are ready to learn. Apparently, I was there, and Wolf was the teacher. I stared out the window and set a new goal for myself: By the end of the summer, I would no longer be afraid of horses. I would be a horse person.

In June, we bought a horse named Cowboy. I immediately changed his name to Buttercup. I was hoping that the change of name would make him gentle and me fearless. My goal was to go for one ride in the country alone by the end of the month. During each day of June, I went for a short, easy ride with my husband, who did not understand my fear but who accepted and respected it. On the last day of the month, Buttercup and I went out for a three-mile ride alone. It was not fun, but I did it.

July brought another goal: Buttercup and I were to race across the prairies with reckless abandon. I succeeded and can even do so with without bouncing in the saddle and without my arms flailing in the wind—a prairie faux pas. Okay, it's true, I shouted with joy as I raced through the pasture.

My goal for August was not just to ride, but also to be good at it. I wanted to actually be helpful when moving cows. I wanted to be able to chase a calf and bring it back to the herd. Goal met. I wanted to be able to move a herd of cows through a gate. Goal met. An angry bull can still bluff Buttercup and me, but this is not a story about angry bulls. This is a story about fear of power.

At rare intervals, the most significant factors in determining the future
occur in infinitesimal quantities on unique occasions.
—*MUMSFORD (1956)*

Teachers Taught Me, Too

Throughout this book, I have written about the many things students taught me to learn and unlearn:

- Teaching is learning.
- If it doesn't matter to students, it doesn't matter.
- Change and contradictions are in every classroom.

In this chapter, I have told you how critical pedagogy has come together for me in new and surprising ways. Critical pedagogy has helped me to understand that it is okay to be critical of processes that we don't philosophically support; it is okay to care a lot. Critical pedagogy has given me courage and taught me lessons of patience, and it is okay if all of this takes time.

> ### *What Teachers Taught Me*

- Caring counts.
  —Alma Flor Ada
- Learning should be rigorous and joyful.
  —Paulo Freire
- Teachers are intellectuals.
  —Henry Giroux
- Coercive relations of power don't work; collaborative relations do.
  —James Cummins
- Meaning matters.
  —Stephen Krashen
- Good teachers and learners start with a teachable heart.
  —Peter McLaren
- A Teams and B Teams are good for the A Team.
  —Tove Skutnabb-Kangas
- It's fun to talk with a friend while we learn.
  —Lev Vygotsky
- It's okay to learn while we teach.
  —The Benson kids

Over thirty years ago when I started teaching, no one could have told me that teaching would bring me to this way of knowing. Education classes didn't teach me these important lessons; students did. We need to listen to and learn more from students. With changes happening so fast in our society today, I cannot imagine what students will teach me in the next ten years. However, I am anxious to learn whatever it will be.

Now a final word about teachers: The truth is that I have been blessed with the best, and I have learned from them.

Now Here Is the Point

Critical pedagogy is about hope. We all want it. Critical pedagogy led me to it. I started years ago reading those difficult, theoretical books. They made sense to me. I will never forget the first time I read McLaren (1989); I remember thinking, "Yes. Yes. Yes." The first time I read Giroux (1988), I remember thinking, "This room is vibrating." These books were like the kids I had been teaching. They were not theoretical pages. They were faces and hearts.

When I first began my study of critical pedagogy, I feared that I would see too much too critically. I feared that I would lose "me" in those infuriating new words and old thoughts. However, the opposite has happened again. I'm not so sure these poles are all bad. Confounding contradictions. Critical pedagogy has given me hope.

Why does critical pedagogy matter? It matters because J. J. matters.

Steve, a friend who is actively involved within his community, told me this story about a young African American teenage boy, J. J. Steve has a special interest in teenage boys who are lost and adrift. J. J. is almost a stereotype of a marginalized and angry young black man. He comes from an economically disadvantaged family; his father abandoned them many years ago. J. J.'s mother works hard, for long hours, with low pay. Gangs, drugs, and fast money were becoming more and more appealing to J. J.

On this particular occasion, J. J. was in trouble (again) at school, and Steve was called in to talk to him. Steve did not talk. He listened.

"You know what you got, and I ain't got? Hope. You got it. I want it," J. J. yelled at Steve.

Steve and J. J. come from worlds that are poles apart. They are breaking those traditional barriers of race and class. They come together in a safe and social environment (the park) every week. This does not cost anyone anything. Steve and J. J. have committed their time, their courage, and their patience. They care about each other. They critically reflect on ways of generating hope in J. J.'s life. Their story is a powerful mandate for what each of us can do. Must do. The kids and the future matter.[1] "And it is through changing the present that we make the future" (Freire as cited in Gadotti, 1994, p. 148).

To Make A Difference

One of the most important lessons that I have ever learned from educators is always to leave them with one final method: something that they can do tomorrow in their own schools and communities. This, then, is my last activity. Critical pedagogy has been assigned many esoteric and abstract meanings, most of which have enriched my life as a teacher and a learner. This critical perspective will continue to drive my own relearning and unlearning.

Most of us went into education to make a difference. For many, this phase soon became just another reason to be cynical. Critical pedagogy has not only taken this cynicism away from me, it has given me hope. It has led me to believe that I really can make a difference. Conscientization. Self- and social transformation. Empowerment. Problem posing. Praxis. Action. They are no longer words to learn; they are no longer things I do; now, they are ideas I strive to live every day.

Bob

Recently, I have been hearing a story about a particular teacher. In fact, I have heard four different versions of the same story. I will tell the story the way I heard it the first time, although I have since discovered what I assume to be the source of the original story (Bridges, 1993). It seems that this teacher decided she would make one small change in her teaching. It would not cost much. She would not have to ask permission from an administrator. It would not take much of her time. She would not have to go to meetings at night, write a document, and seek the school board's permission. It was just one small change. Maybe, just maybe, she could make a difference.

> She went to a local trophy shop and ordered blue ribbons that said "I Make a Difference." When the ribbons arrived, she reflected seriously on each of her thirty students. Each student was special and had made unique contributions to the class and to her life. She knew that she had learned from every one. Reflection. But she had never taken the time to tell the students. Action. She decided to tell the students in front of the class what she felt was their unique contribution to the class and how each had enriched her life.
>
> On the Blue Ribbon Day, she took her time as she expressed her appreciation for each student's distinctive gift to the class and to her life. The students were silent as she spoke and as she pinned a blue ribbon on each shirt right above the heart. She was astounded at the reaction of her students. Some of them had never heard such sincere and honest praise. Many tears and shy smiles expressed their feelings. After the blue ribbon ceremony, she told the class that each of them had to leave with two more ribbons so that they, too, could express their appreciation to someone in their life.
>
> Eventually, one of these blue ribbons made its way to a young junior executive, Bob, at a large company. He agonized over what he should do with his. He was the supervisor for many employees. He went through each name and finally decided that he had to give the blue ribbon to his boss, Paul Long, who had a reputation for being unapproachable, elitist, and grumpy. Everyone, including the junior executives, avoided him.
>
> With butterflies in his stomach, he knocked on the office door of the CEO.
>
> "Come in," Mr. Long grumbled. It was clear to Bob that his boss was distracted, busy, and did not want to be disturbed.
>
> "Mr. Long, I am here to tell you that I appreciate you as the visionary leader of this company. Without your forethought and planning, we would never be able to succeed in this business. You make a difference in my life, and you make a valuable contribution in this community. I would like permission to reach across your desk and pin a blue ribbon on your shirt." Bob pinned the blue "I Make a Difference" ribbon on the pocket of his CEO.
>
> Paul was speechless. He finally managed to mumble his appreciation.
>
> "Mr. Long, here is another blue ribbon. You need to pin it on someone who has made a difference in your life," Bob said as he placed a second blue ribbon on Paul's large desk.

> *Bob left the office with a sense that he had chosen the right person. Paul Long went home to his family. He did not mention what had happened at work that day. His family did not notice his silence because it was his custom to eat dinner and then to talk on the phone in his den. However, tonight Paul was thinking about who should receive his blue ribbon. He finally decided.*
>
> *He walked down the hallway to his son's bedroom. His son, Paul, Jr., was seventeen years old.*
>
> *"Son, I know that I often don't speak honestly with you. I know that I am often too busy. But I want you to know that you make all the difference in my life." As he said this, Paul, Sr. reached over and pinned the blue "I Make a Difference" ribbon on Paul, Jr.*
>
> *His son began to cry and was soon sobbing. His head hung, and his shoulders were heaving up and down with each sob.*
>
> *"Son, what is the matter?" his dad said.*
>
> *"Dad, no one ever told me that I make a difference. I had been planning on committing suicide tomorrow, and now I don't have to do it."*

What good is this story if we don't turn it into action? Critical pedagogy has taught me that my actions can make a difference.

Won't you join us? I will begin to collect all the stories that demonstrate how each of us can make a difference. Without studying critical pedagogy for years, I would never have had the courage to do this or the patience to wait for the stories of power, love, and caring.

Roxanne

Here is one of those stories: Roxanne is an English-dominant teacher and graduate student who is studying bilingual and multilingual education for the first time. After reading Cummins (1989), she shared her feelings with the class. "I cannot solve the whole world's problems, but I can start with myself and the students in my class," she matter-of-factly told her colleagues. "After reading *Empowering Language Minority Students*, I have some thoughts about what I can do."

What I Can Do
- I will not make a judgment about the students based on any test (language or psychological) that is not in the language of the students.
- I will not label. If English is the language of the classroom and the students are not yet able to learn in English, I will find the help. I will not make assumptions about "language difficulties" for bilingual students who are in the process of acquiring English.
- I will encourage all students to speak in their own language.
- I will respect the culture of each student by encouraging students to share and write about their families and traditions.
- I will post assignments in multiple languages all around the classroom.

- I will invite the students' parents to the classroom to read and to share with us.
- I will hang signs around the school in the languages of the students.
- I will encourage all students to speak and to learn in their primary language.
- I will invite community members to my class.
- Most important, I will provide books in the languages of the students.

I have probably read Cummins (1989) more times than I can count. However, I have to thank Roxanne for forcing me to turn theory into practice—an ongoing process for all of us. Roxanne discovered how she can make a difference. She named, she reflected critically, and she acted, which many would say is a good definition of critical pedagogy.

How are you doing critical pedagogy?

Looking Ahead for More Elusive Answers

"Life," said Izzy, "is a series of strange and seemingly pointless stories. Meaning is derived from a relationship of story, storyteller, and listener. By far the hardest task is that of the listener." (Kaminsky, 1991, p. 84, as cited in Vallance, 1995)

You are the listener. Why in the world does critical pedagogy matter to you? This book is filled with my stories, my ideas, my perspective, my experiences, my biases, my voice. However, I think this book would be more valuable if you would read and write *with* me. Reading is one way of acquiring knowledge. Writing is one way of inquiring into your own knowledge. Write your stories, your ideas, your perspective, your experiences, your biases, your voice, and your ways of knowing. Critical pedagogy has taught me to be a listener and a storyteller. I encourage you to listen and tell your stories.

How should I end this book? With a new story, which I think sums up this book. Dayna's story below represents praxis, as it is the union of the theory and practice of that classroom of learners. Dayna transformed a simple writing assignment into a codification (or a picture, in this case) that connected her lived experiences with her vision for the future of education. Dayna named, she reflect critically, and she acted. Her action is a creative graphic of her understandings of critical pedagogy.

Practicing Pedagogy Patiently: Dayna

The Lesson of Dayna: One Size Does Not Fit All

The lesson of Dayna is as important as the gift that she created and presented to me on the last night of class. Dayna is unique, as are all learners. She has her own approach to acquiring, generating, and transforming knowledge. I would even describe Dayna as somewhat of a round peg in a square opening, which has caused her grief throughout her schooling. She comes from a history of school experiences that often mandated that her assignments be done in one way and only one way. The artist in her rebelled.

For the major writing assignment of this particular class, Dayna surprised and delighted the class and me when she turned in the representation of her learning of the three perspectives on pedagogy mentioned previously in this text, shown in Figure 8.1.

FIGURE 8.1   Three perspectives on pedagogy

Source: Printed by permission of Dayna Watland-Hopkins

Enjoy. Dayna's explanation of her art follows in her own words. Thank you, Dayna.

Three Perspectives on Pedagogy: The Artist's Notes

Transmission Model

At the bottom of the picture is a representation of the transmission model, often referred to as the banking model. The teacher is talking in front of the class. You will see that her words are going in one ear and out the other until they get to the student daydreaming in the back of the class. The words just bounce right off of him.

You will notice that the first student has a picture of the subject being taught, but it is not a very realistic picture, as this child does not have the experience to fully understand what the teacher is saying.

The second child has a question, but in this model, many questions are not answered because most of the communication is planned and prescribed, which ignores the needs of the learners within the class. Please note also that the communication flows in only one direction.

The last child represents the students who have difficulty attending to the lesson.

To the right side of the transmission model are the roots and base of a plant, which represents the fact that this model of teaching stresses planting and germinating of knowledge and eventually leads to knowledge sprouting up in the learner. This is the model of education that I experienced when I was a student.

The Generative Model

This is in the middle of the picture. Please notice that in this model of education, the teacher and learners are much closer to each other. Here, the communication flows in several directions, so many more questions are answered for the learner. The child visualizes the flower in a much more realistic way because he or she has been given a more hands-on approach to learning. However, the child can still get an unrealistic visualization, as this method is still limited in that the real world is outside of the window. To the side of this picture are the stem and leaves of the plant representing the generative model's statement that it is not enough just to germinate and sprout, but the learner must show growth as well. This is the model that I learned during my student teaching. It is also the model that I tend to practice as a teacher.

The Transformative Model

This model of education is at the top of the picture. With this model, the learner gets out into the real world and participates in real activities; thus, he or she gains realistic pictures to visualize and to experience. The communication flows freely from learner to learner, and the teacher becomes a partner in the learning process.

One child is wondering, "What if we pollinate this flower to be a different kind of flower?" This represents the idea that transformative model encourages students to create something new with the knowledge they have.

Another child is saying, "We could give some of what we grow to families that need it." This represents the fact that the transformative model involves interaction with the community as a whole.

The last child is thinking, "I could be a botanist or a horticulturist." This represents how the transformative model inspires learners to see what knowledge can do for them in the future.

To the right side of the transformative model are the flower and the butterfly, representing the idea that it is not enough just to germinate and sprout or just to show growth, but the learner should also blossom and go out into the world and reproduce to create something new. This model I am just beginning to understand, and I am aspiring to reach this model whenever possible.

NOTE

1. J.J. is a living example of what Herb Kohl (1998) has found in his four decades of teaching and learning. There is hope for education in the most surprising places and times and with students who have previously had little hope. This is very much what I have learned from students.

BIBLIOGRAPHY

Ada, A. F. (1988a). Creative reading: A relevant methodology for language minority children. In L. M. Malave (Ed.), *NABE '87. Theory, research and application: Selected papers* (pp. 97–111). Buffalo: State University of New York Press.

Ada, A. F. (1988b). The Pájaro Valley experience: Working with Spanish-speaking parents to develop children's reading and writing skills in the home through the use of children's literature. In T. Skutnabb-Kangas & J. Cummins (Eds.), *Minority education: From shame to struggle* (pp. 223–238). Philadelphia, PA: Multilingual Matters.

Ada, A. F. (1991). Creative reading: A relevant methodology for language minority children. In C. Walsh (Ed.), *Literacy as Praxis: Culture, language, and pedagogy.* Norwood, NJ: Ablex.

Ada, A. F. (2003). *A magical encounter: Latino children's literature in the classroom.* Boston, MA: Allyn & Bacon.

Ada, A. F., & Campoy, F. I. (2003). *Authors in the classroom: A transformative education process.* Boston: Allyn & Bacon.

Andzaldúa, G. (1987). *Borderlands/la frontera: The New Mestiza.* San Francisco: Spinsters/ Aunt Lute Book Company.

Apple, M. (1999). *Power, meaning, and identity: Essays in critical educational studies.* New York: Peter Lang.

Artz, L., & Murphy, B. O. (2002). Antonio Gramsci and hegemony in the United States. *The Review of Communication, 2*(4), 383–386.

Auerbach, E. (1995a). Critical issues: Deconstructing the discourse of strengths in family literacy. *JRB: A Journal of Literacy, 27,* 643–661.

Auerbach, E. (1995a). From deficit to strength: Changing perspectives on family literacy. In G. Weinstein-Shr & E. Quintero (Eds.), *Immigrant learners and their families* (pp. 59–62). McHenry, IL: Center for Applied Linguistics an Delta Systems.

August, D., & Hakuta, K. (Eds.). (1997). *Improving schooling for language-minority children: A research agenda* (pp. 17–32). Washington, DC: National Academy Press.

Bancroft, A. (1995, March 28). 20 Years of affirmative action: Still no parity. *The Modesto Bee,* p. A8.

Berger, R. (2003). *An ethic of excellence: Building a culture of craftsmanship with students.* Portsmouth, NH: Heinemann.

Berliner D., & Biddle, B. (1995). *The manufactured crisis: Myths, fraud, and the attack on America's public schools.* New York: Addison Wesley Longman.

Bigelow, G., Christensen, L., Karp, S., Miner, B., & Peterson, B. (1994). *Rethinking our classrooms: Teaching for equity and justice.* Milwaukee, WI: Rethinking Schools, Ltd.

Blanck, G. (1990). Vygotsky: The man and his cause. In L. Moll (Ed.), *Vygotsky and education* (pp. 31–58). New York: Cambridge University Press.

Bowles, S., & Gintis, H. (1976). *Schooling in capitalist America.* New York: Basic Books.

Bridges, H. (1993). Who you are makes a difference. In J. Canfield & M. V. Hanson (Eds.), *Chicken soup for the soul* (pp. 19–21). Deerfield Beach, FL: Health Communications.

Burke, J. (2003). *The English teacher's companion* (2nd ed.). Portsmouth, NH: Heinemann.

Campbell, D. (2004). *Choosing democracy: A practical guide to multicultural education.* Upper Saddle River, NJ: Prentice Hall.

Canfield, J., & Hanson, M. V. (Eds.). (1993). *Chicken soup for the soul.* Deerfield Beach, FL: Health Communications.

Carnes, J. (1995, Spring). Home was a horse stall. *Teaching Tolerance, 50–57*.

Caulkins, L., & Bellino, L. (1997). *Raising lifelong learners: A parent's guide*. Reading, MA: Addison-Wesley.

Clark, S. P., & Brown, C. S. (1990). *Ready from within: A first person narrative*. Trenton, NJ: Africa World Press.

Cooper, A. J. (1892/1988). *A voice from the south*. New York: Oxford University Press.

Cortés, C. (Ed.). (1986). *The education of language minority students: A contextual interaction model*. Los Angeles: Evaluation, Dissemination, and Assessment Center, California State University.

Crawford, J. (2004). Educating English Learners: Language diversity in the classroom. *Bilingual education: History, politics, theory, and practice* (5th ed.). Los Angeles: Bilingual Education Services, Inc.

Cremin, L. (1964). *The transformation of the school*. New York: Vantage Books.

Csikszentmihalyi, M. (1997). *Finding flow: The psychology of engagement in everyday life*. New York: Basic Books.

Cummins, J. (2001). *Negotiating identities: Education for empowerment in a diverse society*. Ontario, CA: California Association for Bilingual Education.

Cummins, J. (1994). The socioacademic achievement model in the context of coercive and collaborative relations of power. In R. DeVillar, C. Faltis, & J. Cummins (Eds.), *Cultural diversity in schools: From rhetoric to practice* (pp. 363–390). Albany: State University of New York Press.

Cummins, J. (1996). *Negotiating identities: Education for empowerment in a diverse society*. Sacramento: California Association of Bilingual Education.

Cummins, J. (1998, March 20). *Honoring the Life and Legacy of Paulo Freire*. Symposium conducted at TESOL '98, Seattle, WA.

Cummins, J., & Sayers, D. (1995). *Brave new schools: Challenging cultural illiteracy*. New York: St. Martin's Press.

Darder, A., Baltodano, M., & Torres, R. (2003). *The critical pedagogy reader*. New York: Routledge Falmer.

DeMarrais, K. B., & LeCompte, M. D. (1999). *The way schools work: A sociological analysis of education*. New York: Addison Wesley Longman.

Dewey, J. (1944/1916). *Democracy and education*. New York: Free Press.

Dewey, J. (1947/1938). *Experience and education*. New York: Macmillan.

Dresser, N. (1996). *Multicultural manners: New rules of etiquette for a changing society*. New York: Wiley.

Du Bois, W. E. B. (1903). *The souls of black folks*. Chicago: A.C. McClurg.

Edelsky, C. (1991). *With literacy and justice for all: Rethinking the social in language and education*. Bristol, PA: Falmer Press.

Elam, R. (1995, March 3). Voices of reason and compassion. *The Modesto Bee*, p. A11.

Elley, W. B. (1992). *How in the world do students read? The IEA study of reading literacy*. The Hague, The Netherlands: International Association for the Evaluation of Educational Achievement.

England, C. M. (2003). *None of our business*. Portsmouth, NH: Heinemann.

Enright, D. S., McCloskey, M. L., & Savignon, S. J. (1988). *Integrating English: Developing English language and literacy in the multilingual classroom*. Reading, MA: Addison-Wesley.

Epstein, J. (2001). *School, family and community partnerships: Preparing educators and improving schools*. Boulder, CO: Westview Press.

Fader, D. N., & McNeil, E. B. (1966). *Hooked on books: Program and proof*. New York: Berkley Medallion Books.

Fadiman, C. (1947). *Party of one: The selected writings of Clifton Fadiman.* Cleveland, OH: The World Publishing Company.

Faltis, C. (1990). Freirian and Vygotskian perspective. *Foreign Language Annals, 23*(2), 117–126.

Faltis, C., & Wolfe, P. (1999). *So much to say: Adolescents, bilingualism and ESL in the secondary school.* New York: Teachers College Press.

Farr, R., & Tone, B. (1994). *Portfolio and Performance Assessment: Helping Students Evaluate Their Progress as Readers and Writers.* Fort Worth, TX: Harcourt Brace College Publishers.

Field, R. (1996). John Dewey. *Internet Encyclopedia of Philosophy.* [on-line]. Available: http://www.wtm.edu/research/iep/d/dewey.htm

Fishman, J. (1991). *Reversing language shift.* Clevedon, England: Multilingual Matters.

Fleischer, C., & Schaafsma, D. (1998). (Eds.). *Literacy and democracy: Teacher research and composition studies in pursuit of habitable spaces.* Urbana, IL: National Council of Teachers of English.

Flood, J., Lapp, D., Tinajero, J., & Hurley, S. (1996/1997). Literacy instruction for students acquiring English: Moving beyond the immersion debate. *The Reading Teacher, 50*(4), 356–358.

Fox, M. (1993). *Radical reflections: Passionate opinions on teaching, learning, and living.* San Diego, CA: Hartcourt Brace & Company.

Freeman, Y., & Freeman, D. (1992). *Whole language for second language learners.* Portsmouth, NH: Heinemann.

Freeman, Y., & Freeman, D. (1994). *Between worlds: Access to second language acquisition.* Portsmouth, NH: Heinemann.

Freeman, Y., & Freeman, D. (1998). *ESL/EFL teaching: Principles for success.* Portsmouth, NH: Heinemann.

Freire, P. (1970). *Pedagogy of the oppressed.* New York: Seabury Press.

Freire, P. (1974). *Pedagogy of the oppressed.* New York: Seabury Press.

Freire, P. (1993, February 4). *Teaching and learning.* Paper presented at the California Association for Bilingual Education, Anaheim, CA.

Freire, P. (1994). *The pedagogy of hope: Reliving pedagogy of the oppressed.* New York: Continuum Publishing Group.

Freire, P. (1996). *Letters to Cristina: Reflections on my life and work.* New York: Routledge.

Freire, P., & Macedo, D. (1987). *Literacy: Reading the word and the world.* South Hadley, MA: Bergin & Garvey.

Gadotti, M. (1994). *Reading Paulo Freire: His life and work.* Albany: State University of New York Press.

Galtung, J. (1980). *The true worlds: A transactional perspective.* New York: The Free Press.

García, H. S. (1993). Shifting the paradigms of education and language policy: Implications for language minority children. *The Journal of Educational Issues of Language Minority Students, 12,* 1–6.

Gee, J. (1992). *The social mind: Language, ideology, and social practice.* New York: Bergin and Garvey.

Gee, J. (1990). *Social linguistics and literacies: Ideology in discourses.* Bristol, PA: Falmer Press.

Giroux, H. (1988). *Teachers as intellectuals: Toward a critical pedagogy of learning.* South Hadley, MA: Bergin & Garvey.

Glass ceiling intact. (1995, March 16). *The Sacramento Bee,* pp. A1, A24.

Goldberg, M. (1995). Portrait of John Goodlad. *Educational Leadership, 52*(6), 82–85.

Gonzalez, N. (2001). *I am my language: Discourses of women and children in the borderlands.* Tucson, AZ: The University of Arizona Press.

Goodman, K. (1998). *In defense of good teaching: What teachers need to know about the "reading wars."* York, ME: Stenhouse Publishers.

Gramsci, A. (1971). *Selections from the prison notebooks.* London: Lawrence & Wishart.

Greene, M. (1973). *Teacher as stranger: Educational philosophy in the modern age.* Belmont, CA: Wadsworth Publishing Company.

Greene, M. (1998, April 17). *Honoring the legacy of Paulo Freire.* American Association of Educational Researchers (AERA), San Diego, CA.

Greene, M. (2003). In search of a critical pedagogy. In A. Darder, M. Baltodano, & R. Torres (Eds.), *The critical pedagogy reader.* New York: Routledge Falmer.

Hanson, D. (1994, August 27). Caring spells career success for teacher. *The Turlock Journal,* pp. A1, A11.

Harris, T., & Hodges, R. (Eds.). (1995). *The literacy dictionary: The vocabulary of reading and writing.* Newark, DE: International Reading Association.

Horton, M., & Freire, P. (1990). *We make the road by walking: Conversations on education and social change.* Philadelphia, PA: Temple University Press.

Jasso, A., & Jasso, R. (1995). Critical pedagogy: Not a method, but a way of life. In J. Frederickson (Ed.), *Reclaiming our voices: Bilingual education, critical pedagogy and praxis* (pp. 253–259). Ontario, CA: California Association for Bilingual Education.

Kaminsky, S. M. (1991). *Opening shots.* Eugene, OR: Pulphouse Publishers.

Kanpol, B. (1994). *Critical pedagogy: An introduction.* Westport, CN: Bergin & Garvey.

Katotakis, A. (2004). Free to a good home: Classroom materials. [on-line]. Retrieved July 17, 2004, from www.JoanWink.com/charts.html.

Kellner, D. (2000). New technologies/new literacies: Reconstructing education for the new millennium. *Teacher Education, 11*(3), 245–265.

Koehler, (2003, January 1). Commentary: Schools need more vigor, less rigor. [on-line]. Retrieved January 1, 2003 from Spokesman-Review.com, http://www.spokesmanreview.com/news-story.asp?date=010103&ID=s1281667&cat=

Kohl, H. (1998). *The discipline of hope: Learning from a lifetime of teaching.* New York: Simon & Schuster.

Kohn, A. (2002). The 500-pound gorilla. *Phi Delta Kappan, 84*(2), 112–119.

Krashen, S. (1993). *The power of reading: Insights from the research.* Englewood, CO: Libraries Unlimited, Inc.

Krashen, S. (1996). *Under attack: The case against bilingual education.* Culver City, CA: Language Education Associates.

Krashen, S. (1997). *Every person a reader: An alternative to the California task force report on reading.* Portsmouth, NH: Heinemann.

Krashen, S. (1998a) Is 180 days enough? *Bilingual Basics, 1*(2), 1–4.

Krashen, S. (1998b, August). Why did California voters pass Prop 227? They thought they were voting for English. *TABE Newsletter, Tucson Association for Bilingual Education,* 3–4.

Krashen, S. (1998c, November/December). Has whole language failed? *ESL Magazine, 1*(6), 8–10.

Krashen, S. (1999a). *Condemned without a trial: Bogus arguments against bilingual education.* Portsmouth, NH: Heinemann.

Krashen, S. (1999b). *Three arguments against whole language and why they are wrong.* Portsmouth, NH: Heinemann.

Krashen, S. (2003a). Navigating the math and reading wars. [on-line]. Retrieved February 13, 2003, from www.csmonitor.com/2003/0212/p10s02-cole.html.

Krashen, S. (2003b). *Explorations in language acquisition and use.* Portsmouth, NH: Heinemann.

Krashen, S., Tse, L., & McQuillan, J. (1998). *Heritage language development.* Culver City, CA: Language Education Associates.

Kuhn, T. (1970). *The structure of scientific revolutions.* Chicago: University of Chicago Press.

Ladson-Billings, G. (1994). *The dream keepers*. San Francisco: Jossey-Bass.

Lamott, A. (1994). *Bird by bird: Instructions on writing and life*. New York: Random House.

Lankshear, C., & McLaren, P. (Eds.). (1993). *Critical literacy: Politics, praxis, and the postmodern*. Albany: State University of New York Press.

Lawrence-Lightfoot, S. (2003). *The essential conversation: What parents and teachers can learn from each other*. New York: Random House.

Leistyna, P., Woodrum, A., & Sherblom, S. (Eds.). (1996). *Breaking free: The transformative power of critical pedagogy*. Cambridge, MA: Harvard Educational Review Press.

Lieberman, A. (1986). Collaborative research: Working with, not working on. *Educational Leadership, 43*(5), 29–31.

Lindfors, J. (1982). Exploring in and through language. In M. A. Clarke & J. Handscombe (Eds.), *On TESOL '82: Pacific perspectives on language learning and teaching*. Washington, DC: Teachers of English to Speakers of other Languages.

Macedo, D. (Ed.). (1994). *Literacies of power*. Boulder, CO: Westview Press.

Mathews, J. (2003, February 11). Class struggle: The ups and downs of No Child Left Behind. [on-line]. Retrieved February 12, 2003, from www.washingtonpost.com/wp-dyn/articles/A56818–2003Feb11.html.

McCaleb, S. P. (1994). *Building communities of learners*. New York: St. Martin's Press.

McLaren, P. (1994). Critical pedagogy: Constructing an arch of social dreaming and a doorway to hope. In L. Erwin & D. MacLennan (Eds.), *Sociology of education in Canada: Critical perspectives on theory, research and practice* (pp. 137–160). Toronto: Copp Clark Longman.

McLaren, P. (1989). *Life in schools: An introduction to critical pedagogy in the foundations of education* (3rd ed.). New York: Longman.

McLaren, P. (1998, Summer). Che: The pedagogy of Che Guevara: Critical pedagogy and globalization thirty years after Che. *Cultural Circles, 3*, 29–103.

McLauren, P. (2003). *Life in schools: An introduction to critical pedagogy in the foundations of education* (4th ed.). Boston, MA: Allyn & Bacon.

McQuillan, J. (1998a). Is 99% failure a "success"?: Orange Unified's English Immersion Program. *The Multilingual Educator, 21*(7), 11. (www.bilingualeducation.org)

McQuillan, J. (1998b). *The literacy crisis: False claims, real solutions*. Portsmouth, NH: Heinemann.

Miramontes, O., Nadeau, A., García, E., & Commins, N. (Eds.). (1997). *Restructuring schools for linguistic diversity: Linking decision making to effective programs*. New York: Teachers College Press.

Moffett, J. (1989). Censorship and spiritual education. *English Education, 21*, 70–87.

Moll, L. (Ed.). (1990). *Vygotsky in education: Instructional implications and applications of sociohistorical psychology*. New York: Cambridge University Press.

Moll, L., & Greenberg, J. (1990). Creating zones of possibilities: Combing social contexts for instruction. In L. C. Moll (Ed.), *Vygotsky and education* (pp. 319–348). New York: Cambridge University Press.

Morrow, L. (Ed.). (1995). *Family literacy: Connections in schools and communities*. Newark, DE: International Reading Association.

Mumsford, L. (1956). *The transformations of man*. New York: Harper.

Nathan, De. (2003, July/August). The new ESL teaches immigrants how to stand up for themselves. *City Limits MONTHLY*. Retrieved December 1, 2003 from: http://www.citylimits.org/content/articles/articleView.cfm?articlenumber=1016

Naysmith, J. (1987). English as imperialism. *Language Issues, 1*(2), 3–5.

Newkirk, T. (1997). *The performance of self in student writing*. Portsmouth, NH: Boynton/Cook.

Newman, J. (1998). *American's teachers: An introduction to education* (3rd ed.). Boston, MA: Allyn & Bacon.

Nieto, S. (1996). *Affirming diversity: The sociopolitical context of multicultural education.* White Plains, New York: Longman.

Norris, K. (1993). *Dakota: A spiritual geography.* New York: Ticknor & Fields.

Oakes, J. (1985). *Keeping track: How schools structure inequality.* New Haven, CT: Yale University Press.

O'Cadiz, M., Lindquist Wong, P., & Torres, C. A. (1998). *Education and Democracy: Paulo Freire, social movements, and educational reform in Sao Paulo.* Boulder, CO: Westview Press.

Ohanian, S. (1999). *One size does not fit all.* Portsmouth, NH: Heinemann.

Oyler, C. (1996). *Making room for students: Sharing teacher authority in Room 104.* New York: Teachers College, Columbia University.

Palincsar, A. (1996). Language-minority students: Instructional issues in school cultures and classroom social systems. *The Elementary School Journal, 96*(3), 221–226.

Palmer, P. (1998). *The courage to teach: Exploring the inner landscape of a teacher's life.* San Francisco: Jossey-Bass.

Parks, J. (2003, September 21). No illusion left behind. Retrieved September 22, 2003 from http://www.washingtonpost.com/wp-dyn/articles/A37561-2003Sep19.html

Pattanayak, D. (1969). *Aspects of applied linguistics.* London: Asia Publishing House.

Patterson, L., Baldwin, S., Gonzales, R., Guadarrama, I., Keith, L., & McArthur, K. (1998). *Claiming our ignorance and making new friends: Case studies in collaborative family inquiry.* Paper presented at the 48th Annual Meeting of the National Reading Conference, Austin, TX.

Pearson, P. David. (2003). The role of professional knowledge in reading reform. *Language Arts, 81*(1), 14–15.

Peller, G. (1987). Reason and the mob: The politics of representation. *Tikkun, 2*(3), 28–95.

Pennycook, A. (1994). *The cultural politics of English as an international language.* New York: Addison Wesley Longman.

Pervil, S. (Ed.). (October). *Primary voices: Democracy in the classroom.* Urbana, IL: National Council of Teachers of English.

Phillipson, R. (1992). *Linguistic imperialism.* Oxford, England: Oxford University Press.

Poplin, M., & Weeres, J. (1992). Voices from the inside: A report on schooling from inside the classroom. Claremont, CA: The Institute for Education in Transformation at the Claremont Graduate School.

Putney, L. G. (1993). *A descriptive study of sheltered social studies for second language learners.* Unpublished thesis, California State University, Stanislaus, Turlock.

Putney, L. G., Green, J. L., Dixon, C. N., Duran, R., & Yeager, B. (1999). Consequential progressions: Exploring collective-individual development in a bilingual classroom. In C. D. Lee & P. Smagorinsky (Eds.), *Constructing meaning through collaborative inquiry: Vygotskian perspectives on literacy research.* New York: Cambridge University Press.

Quindlen. A. (1998). *How reading changed my life.* New York: Ballantine Publishing Group.

Remsen, K. (2003, July 25). No cow left behind. *Burlington Free Press,* p. 11A.

Rinvolucri, M. (1990). *The confidence book.* White Plains, NY: Longman.

Rinvolucri, M. (1995). *Dictation: New methods, new possibilities.* Cambridge, England: Cambridge University Press.

Romo, J., Bradfield-Krelder, P., & Serrano, R. (2004). *Reclaiming democracy: Multicultural educators' journeys towards transformative teaching.* Upper Saddle River, NJ: Prentice Hall.

Rukeyser, M. (1973). *Breaking open.* New York: Random House.

Ryan, M. (2003). *Ask the teacher: A practitioner's guide to teaching and learning in the diverse classroom.* Boston: Allyn and Bacon.

Sacks, C. H., & Mergendoller, J. R. (1997). The relationship between teachers' theoretical orientation toward reading and student outcomes in kindergarten children with different initial reading abilities. *American Educational Research Journal, 34*(4), 721–739.

Scott-Maxwell, F. (1983). *The measure of my days.* New York: Penguin Books.

Searle, C. (1998). *None but our words: Critical literacy in classroom and community.* Philadelphia, PA: Open University Press.

Shin, F. (2004). Should we just tell them to read? The role of direct encouragement in promoting recreational reading. *Knowledge Quest: Journal of the American Association of School Librarians, 33*(3), 49–50.

Skutnabb-Kangas, T. (1993, February 10). *Problem posing within the community.* Symposium for Graduate Students, California State University, Stanislaus, Turlock, CA.

Skutnabb-Kangas, T. (1998, March 20). *The politics of (ESL in) multilingual education: Languages, culture, power, and liberation.* TESOL 1998, Seattle, WA.

Skutnabb-Kangas, T. (2000). *Linguistic genocide in education. Survival of linguistic diversity?* Mahwah, NJ: Lawrence Erlbaum Associates.

Skutnabb-Kangas, T., & Cummins, J. (1988). Concluding remarks: Language for empowerment. In T. Skutnabb-Kangas & J. Cummins (Eds.), *Minority education: From shame to struggle* (pp. 390–394). Philadelphia, PA: Multilingual Matters.

Sleeter, C. E. (1993). How White teachers construct race. In C. McCarthy & W. Crichlow (Eds.), *Race, identity and representation in education,* pp. 157–171. New York: Routledge.

Smith, N. J. (1995). Making the invisible visible: Critical pedagogy as a viable means of educating children. In J. Frederickson (Ed.), *Reclaiming our voices: Bilingual education, critical pedagogy and praxis* (pp. 241–252). Ontario, CA: California Association for Bilingual Education.

Spradley, J. P. (1980). *Participant observation.* Orlando, FL: Harcourt Brace Jovanovich.

Taylor, D. (1998). *Beginning to read and the spin doctors of science: The political campaign to change America's mind about how children learn to read.* IL: National Council of Teachers of English.

Tozer, S., Violas, P., & Senese G. (2002). *School and society* (4th ed.). New York: McGraw-Hill.

Trelease, J. (2001). *The read-aloud handbook* (5th ed.). New York: Penguin Books.

Vallance, E. (1995). The public curriculum of orderly images. *Educational Researcher, 24*(2), 4–13.

Von Sprecken, D., Kim, J., & Krashen, S. (2000). The home run book: Can one positive reading experience create a reader? *California School Library Journal, 23*(2), 8–9.

Vygotsky, L. S. (1962). *Thought and language* (E. Hanfmann & G. Vakar, Trans.). Cambridge, MA: MIT Press.

Vygotsky, L. S. (1986). *Mind in society: The development of higher psychological processes.* Cambridge, MA: Harvard University Press.

Wallas, G. (1926). *The art of thought.* New York: Harcourt, Brace and Company.

Wallerstein, N. (1983). *Language and culture in conflict: Problem-posing in the ESL classroom.* Reading, MA: Addison-Wesley.

Weiler, K. (1988). *Women teaching for change: Gender, class and power.* South Hadley, MA: Bergin & Garvey.

Westbrook, L. (2003, Summer). One day back in 1610. [on-line]. Retrieved January 28, 2004 from www.OneBranch.org1(2), 1–2.

Wheatley, M. (1992). *Leadership and the new science.* San Francisco: Barrett-Kohler.

Wink, J. (2004). Free to a good home. [on-line]. Retrieved January 28, 2004 from www.JoanWink.com/charts.html

Wink, J. (1991). Immersion confusion. *TESOL Matters, 1*(6), 4.

Wink, J., & Putney, L. (2002). *A vision of Vygotsky.* Boston, MA: Allyn & Bacon.

Wink, J., & Swanson, P. (1993). Rethinking lesson designs. *CSU, Stanislaus School of Education Journal, 10*(1), 30–35.

Wink, J., & Wink, D. (2004). *Teaching passionately: What's love got to do with it?* Boston, MA: Allyn & Bacon.

Wink, J., & Wink, D. (2004). In R. Phillipson (Ed.), *Rights to language: Equity, power, and education.* Mahwah, NJ: Lawrence Erlbaum Associates.

Woodson, C. G. (1933/1990). *The mid-education of the Negro.* Trenton, NJ: Africa World Press.

Wolf, N. (1993). *Fire with fire: The new female power and how it will change the 21st century.* New York: Random House.

Woolfolk, A. (2004). *Educational psychology* (9th ed.). Boston: Pearson Education.

INDEX

Credits

Text credits in order of appearance:

p. 85–90, from Paulo Freire speech at the 1993 California Association for Bilingual Education conference. Reprinted with permission of Ana Marie "Nita" Freire.

p. 92, from *Literacy: Reading the Word and the World* (pp. 124–125), by P. Freire and D. Macedo, 1987, South Hadley, MA: Bergin & Garvey. Reprinted with permission of Greenwood Publishing Group, Inc. Westport, CT. Copyright 1987.

p. 96–97, from *Social Linguistics and Literacies: Ideology in Discourses* (p. 31), by J. Gee, 1990, Bristol, PA: Falmer Press. Copyright 1990 by the Falmer Press. Reprinted with permission.

p. 107, from "Portrait of John Goodlad," by M. Goldberg, 1995, *Educational Leadership, 52*, p. 85. Copyright 1995 by the Association for Supervision and Curriculum Development. Reprinted with permission.

p. 114, from *Minority Education: From Shame to Struggle* (p. 390), by T. Skutnabb-Kangas and J. Cummins, 1988, Philadelphia, PA: Multilingual Matters. Copyright 1988 by Multilingual Matters. Reprinted with permission.

p. 120, from *Reading Paulo Freire: His Life and Work* (p. 6), by M. Gadotti (1994), Albany: State University of New York Press. Copyright 1994 by State University of New York Press. Reprinted with permission.

p. 167, from "Caring Spells Career Success for the Teacher," by D. Hanson, August 27, 1994, *The Turlock Journal*, pp. A1–A16. Copyright 1994 by Turlock Journals. Reprinted with permission.

p. 168, from "Voices of Reason and Compassion," by R. Elam, March 3, 1995, *The Modesto Bee*, p. A11. Copyright 1995 by the Modesto Bee. Reprinted with permission.

p. 177, from "The Public Curriculum of Orderly Images," by E. Vallance, 1995, *Educational Researcher, 24* (2), p. 84. Copyright 1995 by the American Educational Research Association. Reprinted with permission.

p. 179–180, from "Three Perspectives on Pedagogy", by Dayna Watland-Hopkins. Reprinted with permission.